reprint 17⁹⁵ (Heather)

(Signed Copy)

IP 97
17.95 hd.

Donated by
Prolepsis Group
to The Heartland Institute
2015

To Virgil A. Harri
With best Compliments of

*[signature]*

May 1, 1961

# CITADEL, MARKET AND ALTAR

## EMERGING SOCIETY

### OUTLINE OF SOCIONOMY

#### THE NEW NATURAL SCIENCE OF SOCIETY

## SPENCER HEATH

THE SCIENCE OF SOCIETY FOUNDATION, INC.

ROADSEND GARDENS, ELKRIDGE

1502 MONTGOMERY ROAD, BALTIMORE, MD.

Copyright 1957
by The Science of Society Foundation, Inc.

Permission to reproduce by quotation or *in extenso* will be granted upon application in writing, provided proper credit is given with full name of author, title and publisher. No permission shall be necessary in the case of brief quotations embodied in critical articles or reviews.

Printed in the U.S.A.

# Foreword

THE AUTHOR of this book is a most refreshing personality. He has been many things in the course of a long and varied life, a lawyer, a businessman, an inventor, and a horticulturist. A believer in the *de novo* approach, he developed basic propeller patents and special machinery for propeller manufacture which were much in demand during World War I. Indeed, some seventy per cent of the propellers used by American planes in that conflict came from Mr. Heath's factory.

*Citadel, Market and Altar,* which Mr. Heath wrote after selling his patents and retiring from business, is a far cry from the world of propellers. But to the job of making a basic study of the organization of human society Mr. Heath has brought his habit of the *de novo* look. This book owes nothing to contemporary sociology, which has been defined by a perceptive Viennese wit as "the use of a jargon invented for that purpose." Mr. Heath is interested in taking a clear, new look at functions and forms. Taking creativity as the deepest need of man, he has sought to discover the forms of human organization which unleash creativity in its widest aspects.

*Citadel, Market and Altar* is filled with new ways of looking at old things. There is Mr. Heath's energy concept of population, for example. When I first heard Mr. Heath expound this, I stopped worrying about the fecundity of the Russians, the Indians and the Chinese. Mr. Heath's idea is that a high-birthrate people with a short average life-span must constitute a low-energy society, whereas a people with a lower birthrate and a greater average life-expectancy utilizes its energies to the maximum.

The idea is obvious enough when you come to think of it—but who ever stops to think of it? A population of a hundred million with an average life-span of thirty years would spend most of its energies in growing up, marrying and reproducing its kind, where a fifty-million population with an average life-span of sixty years would have energy to spare for progress in all the arts and sciences which make life productive as well as reproductive.

Mr. Heath exhumes life out of history. He is not, repeat not, an admirer of the Romans. Although the Romans are generally credited with having invented the arts of free government, Mr. Heath thinks they were predecessors of the totalitarians of today. Mr. Heath's own Utopian past is situated in pre-Norman England, a time and a place in which free men willingly paid rent to their lords without having to render tax homage to politicians. The lords, aside from supplying protection and community service for the rent, left the freemen free to prosper on their own.

From his principles and from his studies in the social organization of Anglo-Saxon England, Mr. Heath goes on to forecast a Model System for the future. He predicts that property owners will some day pool their titles and take over the administration of such community services as water supply, garbage removal, highways, parks, tennis courts and the policing of local areas. Community life thus administered would soon rise to the cleanliness, order and pleasantness associated with a vacation period in a good resort hotel.

I don't know just how far Mr. Heath's ideal system could be pushed—maybe he doesn't allow enough for Original Sin. It seems likely that until men are angels the State must stand ready to pursue a murderer from one privately owned community to another, and to restrain violent madmen in some extra-community institution. Then, too, there is the problem of the jet planes needed to keep the Messrs. Khrushchev and Bulganin at a proper distance. Justice and safety may always require an occasional visit from the tax collector. In Henri Pirenne's *History of Europe* I find a wholly sympathetic description of early feudal times, when freemen voluntarily rendered payment to their lords in exchange for soil, for protection and for community benefits. (This was before feudalism degenerated into a master-serf relationship.) Henri Pirenne sounds very much like Spencer Heath on the England of Alfred the Great. But in Pirenne I also find this sentence: "The magnates themselves needed a king as judge and arbiter." So the State, at least as judge and arbiter of contests arising between free communities, is probably here to stay.

Nevertheless, Mr. Heath's system does not have to be pushed to its logical extreme. Great advantages would undoubtedly accrue to everybody, landlord and renter alike, if a large number of municipal services (now so sloppily and inefficiently rendered) could be brought under the law of the free market.

Beyond Mr. Heath's way of looking at the man-land problem there is the larger issue of freedom in general. Mr. Heath insists on what should be axiomatic to us in the days of Cold War, that ownership is what confers freedom. To be a free man, one must have the right to a home base, something to stand on without asking any politician's permission. But there is more to freedom—and to ownership—than that. One cannot be truly free unless the product of one's energies can be exchanged for other products in an uncoerced relationship. Free exchange depends on contract, and without ownership there can be no contract. Ownership, contract and exchange are thus inseparable links in a chain. Since exchange is the *social* part of economics (as production is personal and physical), ownership and contract are precedents to free social-ization.

Thus Mr. Heath, by the use of a hyphen, redeems a word which has been misappropriated by his Marxist enemies. He proves that true sociality is inextricably bound up with the free enterprise system. When the coercion of the State enters the picture, sociality disappears. One cannot be sociable under compulsion. Socialism, so viewed, becomes a contradiction in terms.

A final mention should be made of the splendid symbolism of the title, *Citadel, Market and Altar*. Mr. Heath envisions the citadel as the protector of the market place. That is its role—and any departure from the role is an unhealthy thing. When the citadel stays within the bounds of its purely protective function, the energies of men rise high—and there is plenty of free play in the human spirit left to devote to the spontaneous side of life, symbolized by the altar. But when the citadel encroaches on the domain of the market, usurping its functions, man falters as a creative entity. There is little left for the altar—the arts fizzle out into sterile repetition, play loses its zest and religion itself becomes a dour and stoical thing.

The reader who comes to *Citadel, Market and Altar* will find a powerful mind freely playing over the whole realm of human activity. He will find in these pages many of those seed-ideas out of which books—and social movements—grow.

JOHN CHAMBERLAIN

# Prefatory Brief

### On Energy in Action

THIS BOOK approaches the subject of society in a wholly new and unprecedented way. From ancient times, men have reasoned and reflected on human life, its meaning and its destiny, motivated chiefly by their hopes and fears. Only in recent centuries have they established units wherewith to reason and numbers wherewith correctly to compare, and thereby gained the kind of knowledge that is creative power. And only in most recent times have men learned how to employ the energy of environment in variant forms to create the things their minds and hearts have dreamed. Despite all crude perversions of this creative power, the time has now come for men, in a like quantitative and thereby rational way, to go forward to new understandings of *human* energy, of the energy that constitutes the lives of men, and, most of all, that portion of it which they raise to the level of *societal* energy through the *contractual* and thereby reciprocal relationships in which they create, in mutual freedom, ever higher order and abundance in their world and so achieve more productive, more creative and ever lengthening lives.

In all knowledge, the basic datum is self-hood, consciousness of self as distinct from environment, and of interaction between self and environment—objective experience. In this interaction, environment exhibits to experience interactions within itself—happenings, events. That which interacts, that which happens and is experienced, is called energy in action.

Energy-in-action, or events, in their various magnitudes or dimensions and in their various qualities or kinds, constitute the subject-matter of all objective experience. But the human capacity for this experience is limited. It is not infinite or absolute. It occupies an ever increasing octave, so to speak, between zero and infinity, between two unattainable and impossible extremes. Because of this, there is a minimum magnitude in which, or in multiples of which and not otherwise, any event can be objectively experienced. This unitary event, this almost infinitesimal fraction of an erg-second, in its physical aspect, is called the *quantum of action*.

Action, or energy-in-action,[1] is composed of three elements or aspects. These are conceived and considered separately, but are experienced only in their three-fold unity or entity as action or event. The elements of events as energy-in-action are separately conceived as (1) mass (2) motion and (3) time, whose units of measurement respectively are gram, centimeter, second; foot, pound, minute; etc. Note that the element of time enters twice, once to establish the *rate* at which energy acts, and again to measure a *quantity* of actual energy, or of energy-in-action, by multiplying its rate by its period, by the number of units of time through which the event continues or extends. Any number of units of mass (or of force inherent in mass) conceived as moving through some number of units of motion (or of length) per each *one* unit of time, is called a *rate* of energy or of energy-in-action. The product of the rate of an event multiplied by its period is called either *energy,* meaning a particular quantity of energy-in-action, or it is called simply so much *action,* using the more technical name.

Energy-in-action, or action, as events, is not only composite, being composed of units of force and of motion in any relative proportions, acting at a rate and through a period of time; it is also to be taken as discontinuous in its *least* organizational units (of mass, of motion and of time) that can enter into the composition of an event,

---

1. *Work* is defined as any force *acting* through any distance. Energy, as usually defined, is the capacity of a body "to do work," such as so many pounds acting through so many feet. Energy thus defined and without action is hypothetical as the *capacity* (of a particle or mass) to act or to do work. When no motion, only position (hence no action), is involved, the hypothetical "capacity to do work" is called "potential energy." When a body has motion at such uniform velocity that, if brought to rest during the passage of one unit of time, it could perform a certain quantity of work (mass or force units times distance units), it is said to have the capacity to do work at that rate during that period of time. This "capacity of a body to do work" is called "kinetic energy." Kinetic energy, as a rate, multiplied by the time during which the body acts at that rate, constitutes energy-in-action or, more simply, *action*.

and in distinct whole multiples of these least units. It thereby exhibits waves, rhythms, cycles, recurring events and specific structures in succession or repetition of form, type or kind. All those actions or events, called quanta of action, which have the least over-all magnitude that can be objectively experienced are thereby, so far as human experience is concerned, objectively equal and indivisible. They are also called "atoms" of action or the "building blocks" of the physical universe. They may be conceived as those actions or events that take place at the border line between what can be objectively experienced, as well as subjectively imagined or conceived, and that which can be only subjectively experienced or conceived—where the physical shades over into the meta-physical realm.

Nature is not only dynamic; she is also *rational*. Therein her creative beauty lies. She makes herself manifest always in units, in specific events and in forms and types of organization that are repetitional, as are waves, each giving succession to others of similar form, type or kind. As visible light is composed of units of energy organized in waves of only three primary colors, so nature exhibits her discontinuous objective actions, or events, always in numerically organized and proportioned three-fold compositions of (a) units of mass or of force per unit of motion (b) units of motion per unit of time (rate of motion or velocity), through (c) definite periods of time. This rationality is the foundation of all objective physical reality. The numerical ratios between masses or forces and their velocities determine the pattern, form or *kind* of the action, organization or event. The time through which it continues and endures—its period of action at the given rate—measures the actuality, the actual *quantity* of action involved, the amount or extent of the *reality* (in the Platonic, the durational, sense of that word) in the organization or event.

At every level of organization, there are basic individual organizational units. For the entire realm of objective physical reality they are the quanta of action—in all their three-fold ratios and compositions as to mass, motion and time.[2] At the level of atomic structure and organization, they are electrons and nucleons. For all chemical organization, they are the individual atoms—during their periods between birth and decay. In all living things, the basic units are the indivisible individual biological cells—between their birth and decay. Likewise, the individuals of the higher plant and animal forms of life have their own periods. And in the integrated organizational groups of living forms, in colonies, schools, flocks, herds, families, clans and tribes, the basic units are the discrete and indivisible unitary forms during the periods of their individual lives.

At every level, all that was fundamental in the lower is included in the higher, and all that is functional in the higher was potential in the lower forms. Even in the simplest of living things, physical, chemical and biological energy are interfused. And as the inorganic is carried over into the organic world, the plant processes into the animal, the physiological into the psychological realm, so there is no real dichotomy between the sciences of his environment, the sciences of himself as an individual and the science of man in his over-all aspect and organization—the authentic science of society.

With all the humbler organizations of life and in all pre-societal groupings, including pre-societal men, the only over-all function performed is that of maintenance, the mere keeping alive of the race or kind. Their only vital technology is adjustment, in a state of dependency; behavior, in the main, is necessitous; subsistence chiefly what the environment primitively and precariously provides. Extinction is warded off mainly by fecundity, by high frequency of replacement through reproduction—all this for want of sufficient productivity to raise the subsistence and thus extend the periods and abundance of better-nourished lives.

---

2. In quanta of action, all having a uniform over-all magnitude, the extremes of these proportions are exhibited when any one of the three components—(1) mass, particle or force (2) rate of motion, or velocity, and (3) period, time or duration—is at its lowest possible magnitude or of least effect. These three extremes of proportion in the quantum composition may represent the same quantity of energy as action under three aspects: (1) least possible particle, hence maximum possible velocity, as in radiation (speed of light) (2) least possible velocity (of particle or mass), hence maximum immobility, as in lowest temperature, and (3) least possible period of time, hence maximum energy rate, as in nuclear explosion.

But when we come to the societal organization of men through their engagement in contractual relationships, voluntary, impersonal and thereby universal among them—distinguished alike from primitive and familial and from political and coercive relationships—we enter into a wholly new realm. Here again the units relate themselves reciprocally and thereby constitute the beginning of a new organic unity, a new entity, the societal life-form. But this new organic unity, so far as it has developed and evolved, is unique above all others. It transforms a portion of the biological energy of its constituent units into *societal* energy. It quantifies—and thus rationalizes—this energy in a system of value units in the exchange of which each member is rationally and reciprocally served by all—and in due proportion as he contributes to all. The non-political, organic society thus liberates, lifts and lengthens the average life of its units and thereby establishes its own energy rhythm and achieves permanent duration in its successive and ever-lengthening generations of liberated lives.

Human life is more than biological—in the ordinary sense. In its societal manifestation, it is a special, a unique kind of organization of energy arising out of the biological. In an interfunctioning population, a societal organization, the least energy-in-action unit is the whole indivisible individual. The period through which this unit acts determines its whole biological energy-in-action—the total energy or action of the individual life, springing from and returning to the environment, and in some manner and degree affecting it with change. In a like manner, the energy or action of a societal population, as a more complex event and form of life, is also discontinuous. But it has no limited life-period, as do its constituent units; it persists indefinitely in successive generations or waves, which similarly, but productively, impinge on the environment. The portion of this energy that acts during a single unit of time is its energy rate. This rate—population per year—multiplied by the period of its rhythm, the average life span of its constituent units, is the total energy, as action stated in life-years, for that generation or wave.

A single individual life is a very complex organization of energy, depending, qualitatively, on the proportions between the forces and the motions in which it consists and of which it is composed and, quantitatively, as action, on its rate or quantity of energy per unit of time, multiplied by its duration or period of time. Thus, the average individual life, taken in connection with its period or span, corresponds to the physical quantum of action. For it is, when taken statistically, treated as a constant quantity and is the least organization of human energy that can function in the societal realm, just as the quantum of action, in all its varieties, is the least objective unit of action in the physical energy realm; and it may be similarly considered and employed.

It is only in the newer civilizations of the Western and predominantly Christian lands that societal and contractual organization—as distinguished from tribal and familial and from governmental and political—has been notably developed, and any considerable portions or proportions of *adult* life-years[3] thereby achieved. With all this Western advance, however, only a portion of the vital energies so liberated and available is as yet transformed into societal energy and thus creatively employed. Yet every extension of the productive, free contractual relationships tends to extend the length of lives and therewith increase the adult energy available to be socially transformed. Upon a further great development of the existing, non-political system of free contractual engagements,[4] and thereby much further transformation of biological energy into societal energy, the future security of the Western and of world civilization necessarily depends.

Human energy is energy yielded up by the environment and transformed into the specifically human type and form. This human energy, like all other merely biological energy, does not raise but tends to degrade, to cause less order for itself in the environment on which it depends. To become creative and thereby secure, this merely

---

3. The energy of pre-adult life-years is not available for societal interfunctioning. It is required in biological maintenance—the necessary replacement of predecessors—hence it cannot function contractually and productively, only reproductively. It is not unique to man.

4. Specifically, the development of real estate administration on the community-wide basis by organizations of community owners providing general services and amenities to their inhabitants, thus creating non-political public revenues and values.

biological energy must be further transformed into social-ized or societal energy. For it is only the energy that flows interfunctionally without conflict or opposition among men that enables them to specialize and coöperate effectively and thereby favorably transform the conditions of their lives. This raising of the merely biological energy into productive and creative power is effected by a psychological process—the free meeting of men's minds—that is called *contract*. This process establishes relationships of exchange that are creative, completely contrary to the political and coercive—not a difference in degree but a wholly new kind of dispensation. And these societal relationships, impersonal and thereby of universal scope, are intrinsically fruitful and harmonious because the energy involved is quantified numerically and thereby *ratio*nally balanced and exchanged. Thus, the primarily biological energy, through becoming quantified and thereby rational, is transformed into societal and creative, and thus into spiritual, power.

The concept of population as an energy flow, and of social-ized energy being freely exchanged, is fundamental to this volume and to the authentic science of society that it attempts, despite its many imperfections, objectively to describe.

The three main divisions of the book are commended respectively to the analytical, to the practical and constructive, and to the esthetic and reflective faculties of the well-rounded mind. The Appendix is, in effect, a recapitulation of the whole.

S. H.

## General Premises

ALL THE SCIENCES are human. But their genesis takes the order of their abstractness—of their remoteness from human values, vices or vicissitudes.

The first is simple number—invariable quantitative and numerical relationships between abstract units and their numbers as magnitudes or dimensions. From this the objective and concrete sciences evolve, in the order of their remoteness from human volition and desires. Counting the seasons by the recurrent positions of sun and stars; then, observation and examination of the earth itself apart from man, astronomy, geography, geology, general physics, chemistry, biology —all have won for mankind fields of dependable knowledge less and less remote.

And the sciences of man himself have in a similar order advanced. For substance and structure he has anatomy, for the interactions of his organs and parts, physiology. For his integrated reactions to the events of his environment, he has psychology. And for the understanding of his social order as a general system of interfunctioning men, he must have socionomy,[1] the objective science of society.

Thus, socionomy is to the evolving system of mankind as astronomy is to the system of the stars. It is the systematic description of the energy manifested in the structure and activity, the mass and motion, of men as organized in the balanced and unforced, the reciprocal relationships of mankind. Just as astronomy describes the grandeur and the glory of the systems of the skies, so must socionomy reveal the peculiar power and glory of society—of the societal system, the cosmic order evolving among all mankind.

This science, newest and nearest to man, thus has its analogy in the oldest and most remote. And the analogy extends even to its name; for, as astronomy, the rational science of the stars, was barred by an earlier pre-emption from taking its most aptly descriptive name, so

---

[1] *Socionomy.* "Theory or formulation of the organic laws exemplified in the organization and development of society."—Webster's *New International Dictionary*.

the science of society also must depart from its earlier and etymologically most appropriate name—and for reasons very similar if not precisely the same.

This volume treats of society as in no wise a "problem" but as a superbly fascinating field of discovery, as a field of beauty and of benefactions, both active and potential, in the system of nature that in no wise excludes mankind. The method employed—that common to all the natural sciences—has won signal success in other fields, and now, being boldly applied, shows splendid results here. Breaking long fallow ground, it discovers basic social processes where least expected, least appreciated or wholly unknown. Themes and theses in numbers are proposed, yet no completeness is claimed; only the broadest outlines are laid down. It is an adventure in discovery, pregnant of new harvests of life, of riches and power.

As in other sciences, the real subject matter of this volume is the functioning of structures—of organizations—as *action,* happenings or events. These are conceived in their threefold aspect as mass, motion and time. The primary conception, the basic abstraction from the whole, is that of substance or mass, having a property called *force,* whereby motion is generated and work or activity, through time, performed. The second abstraction is that of motion as related to time (velocity). The third is that of the time or duration through which the mass-motion activity extends.

The composition of an event, the proportioning of the mass and motion of which its energy is composed, determines not its magnitude but its kind, whatever be its size. And among similar structures —all that form and dissolve—those are dominant and most *real* which have the greatest continuity, the greatest duration of their type or kind.

Among the units of any organization, the *manner* of their motion is qualitative, positively so if they act reciprocally, negatively so if they clash or collide. Only the positively qualitative is functional and endures, and infinite duration is the ultimate qualitative manifestation.

In a population, as elsewhere, motion gives power and vitality to the mass. If there is but little order, much collision, then there is less motion, power is canceled, dissipated, and duration is short. Where there is less collision there is greater order, continuity of function, more power, much duration.

In its political relations, as in its pre-social state, a population is mass with motion but with much collision, therefore with low social functioning, short lived. At the social level, that of voluntary relations, it is mass with motion but without collision, therefore with increasing continuity or duration—a higher qualitative mode of action. In the ultimate social evolvement there can be no collision, therefore no less than indefinite functional continuity, the highest qualitative manifestation.

Such are the broad and general considerations upon which this attempt toward a veritably scientific social analysis proceeds. Let it speak for itself.

S. H.

# Acknowledgments

THIS BOOK owes its being to the author's inveterate desire to know the forward ways of nature, whether of molecules or of men, for the fulfillment that comes with new awakenings of the mind, and for the contemplation of creative power in the knowing application of nature's steadfast laws, whereby the dust is fashioned to the dream and new whole worlds are wrought.

On the personal side, this author owes to Dr. Pyrrha Gladys Grodman grateful acknowledgment of her many inspiring discussions and her unfailing insistence over a long period of time that this somewhat reluctant writer set down his discoveries in permanent and publishable form. The same is due to John Chamberlain for his fine friendship, for his many encouragements and for the generous foreword with which this effort is adorned.

Also, much gratitude to Ian Crawford MacCallum by whose kindness the drawings and diagrams have been redeemed from their original deficiencies and to whose artistic talent all the excellencies of the diagrams and illustrations are due.

And to Spencer Heath MacCallum much appreciation for his fine diligence and skill in preparation of the Index and for his searching criticisms and the quiet energy and perception with which he has helped the author to strengthen and improve the manuscript and shape it to its final form.

Beyond these warmly personal appreciations, a still deeper and a wider debt is due to those searching and devoted few who have sought not blindly to re-order or reform but have been inspired to love and understand the abiding mind of Nature or of God, shown by the myriad lesser organizations of energy in structures and in living forms. For they and they alone have been objective, their method rational, thus universal. They have shown the shining way to a widening wisdom of the evolving social cosmos, the creative organization of mankind—that oft-reviled yet all sustaining, that modern, almost undiscovered wondrous world of man.

# Contents

|  | Page |
|---|---|
| Foreword | v |
| Prefatory Brief | ix |
| General Premises | xvii |

## PART I   THE SCIENCE

*Method*

1. Basic Method and Positive Procedure . . . . . . . 3
2. Delimitation of the Field . . . . . . . . . 6

*Analysis*

3. The Energy Concept of Population . . . . . . 9
4. Qualitative Changes in Population Energy . . . . 16
5. The Energy That Re-creates Environment . . . . 21
6. Freedom the Technique of Eternality . . . . . 26
7. Creative Transformation of Population Energy . . . 30
8. A Century of Lengthening Life . . . . . . . 41
9. The Democracy of the Market . . . . . . . . 44
10. The Energy of Exchange . . . . . . . . . 47
11. Property the Instrument of Freedom . . . . . . 50
12. Citadel, Market and Altar . . . . . . . . . 55
13. The Social-ization of Government . . . . . . . 62
14. Climate and Conquest . . . . . . . . . . 65
15. The Tragedy of Public Works . . . . . . . . 68
16. The Basic Social Pattern . . . . . . . . . . 71
17. The Order of Societal Evolution . . . . . . . 84
18. Public Services by the Community Owners . . . . 98
19. Societal Development Through Extension of the System of Contract and Exchange . . . . . . . . . 104

## PART II   THE APPLICATION

*Introduction*

20. General Observations on Reduction to Practice . . . 111

*The Social Process and Basic Institution*

21. Value and Exchange, A System of Social-ized Energy Flow   114
22. Private Property in Land Explained—
    Its Public Administrative Function . . . . . 122

*Proprietary versus Political Administration of Public Services*

23. The Business of Community Economics . . . . . 141
24. Questions for the Consideration of Land Owners . . 147
25. The Administration of Real Property as
    Community Services . . . . . . . . . . 153

*Forecast of General Results*

26. Towards the Utopian Dream
    A Hypothetical Distribution of National Income
    Under Proprietary Public Administration . . . 175

## PART III   GENERAL SURVEY

*Spiritual and Psychological Implications*

27. The Qualitative Transformation . . . . . . . 193
28. Mind and the Cosmos . . . . . . . . . . 198
29. Society the Crown of Creation . . . . . . . 205
30. The Inspiration of Beauty . . . . . . . . . 216

**Appendix**

On the Meanings of Principal Terms, with Index . . . 227
Bibliographic Note . . . . . . . . . . . . 245
Philosophic Chart . . . . . . . . . . . . 247

General Index . . . . . . . . . . . . . . . 249

PART I

# *The Science*

*I think it probable that Civilization somehow will last as long as I care to look ahead—perhaps with smaller numbers, but perhaps also to greatness and splendor by science. I think it not improbable that man, like the grub that prepares a chamber for the winged thing it never has seen but is to be, that man may have cosmic destinies he does not understand. And so beyond the vision of battling races and an impoverished earth I catch a dreaming glimpse of peace.*

JUSTICE OLIVER WENDELL HOLMES

CHAPTER 1

# Basic Method and Positive Procedure

SCIENCE is the description and measurement of phenomena manifested in events as integrations of mass (substance), motion (space) and duration (time). In whatever field of observation or experience, science describes structures, organizations and their sequences of motion in time as events, in terms of measurement: in terms of their dimensions as to mass, motion and time. In this manner, science discovers uniformities of mode in occurrences; and applied science brings about those concurrences and sequences of events that realize desires.

Science first describes, defines, divides; then it combines, constructs and creates. In the first, the will of man is dispassionate; it accepts humbly the results of its objective analyses. In the second, in its synthesizing, the merely quantitative becomes qualitative, creative; for in this the Creative Will in man is realized and fulfilled.

The analyses and the syntheses of the sciences, their descriptions and constructions, discoveries and applications, depend upon the employment of standardized units of measurement.[1] Science analyses events objectively, appraises them dispassionately; diagrams experience quantitatively, in terms of the invariable ratios of these units within a particular objective context.

These uniformities, discovered by observation, are formulated as scientific principles, natural laws.

Any mode of investigation not employing units of measure or standards of reference derived from or directly referable to the common units of the natural sciences is a mode in which no quantitative analyses are made and therefore no principles or laws disclosed. On such procedures no rational syntheses can be based, no plans or as-

---

[1]. Units of mass, motion, and duration; substance, space and time; such as pounds, feet, minutes; grams, centimeters, seconds; and measures directly derived from or definitely related to these.

pirations of the creative will of man positively and knowingly fulfilled and enduringly achieved. Such are the "social sciences," so called.

The unit or measure of energy employed in a scientific analysis of the societal life-form is the *life-year*. It is the amount of mass and motion manifested in the average life during one year.

This analysis takes no account of the organizations that constitute its units, of the individual lives of which the society is composed; for the societal life-form, as distinguished from its constituent units, exists only in the combinations, associations and relationships among the interfunctioning individuals of which it is composed. The constitution of the individuals themselves belongs to anatomy, physiology and psychology. Socionomy, the science of society, deals with individuals only in respect of their interfunctioning in an organized life-form, only as their common nature expresses itself in the fact of their organization and their interfunctioning therein.

And for the purposes of this science, individuals are considered primarily in none but their statistical effects; for, as in physical phenomena, the social formulations likewise must represent the invariably consistent statistical results of the myriad constituent phenomena. The social functioning, like the physical, is the numerical integration of the individual activities. Its basic unit of measurement or analysis, therefore, is not any individual or particular life, but the *average* life *for one year*.

This unit, the life-year, is constituted of, and corresponds to, the customary units in physical science, such as the erg-second, the horsepower-hour, or the kilowatt-hour. Its combinations and transformations constitute the dynamic subject matter of this new *natural science* of society.

This science, like all its true predecessors, delineates none but its own special field. It does not treat of the nomadic barbarism out of which civilization, meaning society, has so far emerged, nor of the master-and-slave, the ruler and subject relationship upon which its higher functions have so far supervened; nor is it concerned with the present energies of conflict and confusion that still persist and remain to be transformed. It sets forth rather the processes and operations that nature, in her inherently evolving social order, does presently accomplish, has in fact achieved. It is concerned not with evils to be resisted or destroyed, but with the actual and positive, the creative, though far from complete functioning of the societal life-form. It discovers a realm peculiar and exclusive to man, in which man alone and none other can dwell. It fills the eyes with wonders to be seen, beauty with which to be inspired, bounties wherewith to be blest.

CHAPTER 2

# Delimitation of the Field

IN THIS NEW SCIENCE, socionomy, the phenomenon to be examined and analysed is not the "natural" and physical or the environmental world, nor is it primarily any relationship between mankind and the "natural" world. Nor does it sprawl. Not everything that is human, or related to the human, comes within its scope. It has its own special and sharply delimited field.

Atomic physics deals with nucleons and electrons and with energy organized, time- and space-bound, into atoms, but not as yet with the constitution of nucleons and electrons or of quanta themselves. Chemistry deals with molecular organizations of atoms, not with that of the atoms themselves. General biology examines the organization of living cells into the multicellular plant and animal forms. In this general field cytology deals with the arrangements of complex molecules within the organic cells, but not with the specific organization of the molecules themselves. Anatomy and histology deal with the mechanical structures and textures of animals and plants. Physiology is the part of biology that treats of the interfunctioning of cells and of the highly differentiated and specialized cellular structures that constitute the organs of the plant and animal forms. Since psychology treats of the varying reactions or responses of the whole organism to diverse environmental stimuli, it may be regarded as an extension of physiology. The field of socionomy (also an extension of general biology) is the organic relationships and functional processes between and among the individual organisms that thus and thereby constitute the societal life-form. It describes its own special organization or organism. In so doing it has no more occasion to describe the internal organization of its units than physiology has need to take into account the interior constitution of individual cells, or than chemistry has to describe the structure of the atoms of which its molecular organizations are formed.

The new science treats exclusively of men in their practice of the widely general relationship that integrates them into a societal life-form and higher powers. This new life-form is treated as an organization of energy springing from the Universal Cosmos and having capacity to maintain itself by continuous reception and discharge of energy taken from and returned to its immediate environment, and having as a further function the capacity to secure and advance itself by amelioration and re-creation of its environing world. The thing examined or analyzed therefore is first the structure of the society itself and the interfunctioning of its parts, and finally, its self-directed improvement and growth through constant re-creation of the objective world in which it lives and whence it takes its life and powers.

The analysis examines one special, the *societal*, life-form and not any other. Further, it is predominantly positive, the purpose being to ascertain the processes, the uniformities of action, wherein this life-form functions and grows, rather than any attempt to analyze or formulate the absence or opposite or deficiency of such processes. It is analyzed only in terms of its operation, not in terms of its failure to operate; in terms of its functioning and developing, not in terms of its death or decay. Functioning is original and primary; pathology is only secondary and derivative; its only being is in the organism's failure to function; it cannot precede that on which it depends.

This analysis, then, describes the societal structure as it operates and exists, in terms of its mass, motion and duration content, and thus in its actual and functional reality. From this analysis, this certain kind of knowledge, of what has been empirically achieved, desired syntheses will rationally proceed. Quantitative in method, it will be qualitative in its results, for it will flow from the voluntary agreement of individual wills and their integration into a social will —with realizations of both as one. The functioning fundamentals being known, they will be recombined in accordance with aspirations and desires and profitably applied. As in the "natural" world, the inherent laws can be discovered, availed of and enjoyed; but they cannot be concocted and invented or enacted and imposed.

The possibilities of an authentic science of society, founded on the same measurements and analyses, with the same methods of observation and formulation as the natural sciences, are great and high. Its practical applications will consist in the purposeful and profitable development and expansion of present-existing business and social institutions into the kind of community services that will most protect, enlarge and extend the freedom of contract of the inhabitants and thereby unleash their productive powers and build enormous public profits and values in place of deficits and waste. This will bring into being such magnificent community incomes and property values as were never even dreamed before. The field of *contractual* relationships and services will expand into the utmost freedoms and fulfillments at once of the individual and of the social aspiration and will. This master science will, in truth, endow the spirit of man with a higher sovereignty over his social potentialities than he has even now so marvelously attained over his physical and his "natural" world.

CHAPTER 3

# The Energy Concept of Population

## First Step in Social Analysis

MODERN SCIENCE tends more and more to view energy,[1] in all its variant forms and manifestations, as the fundamental reality. All material substances, structures and organizations it tends to regard as particular phases, passing forms, yet relatively stable and complex, into which the energy of environment (radiant heat, etc.) continues to flow and is, in altered form, returned. Non-living organization is the simplest. Here stability is high, duration usually long. There is resistance to and but little if any dependence on external energy. But living structure is far more complex. Its organizations do not resist, but absolutely depend upon the assimilation of environmental energy and its expenditure in altered form. This transformation of energy is functional, vitally essential to the organizational form. Our earth itself springs doubtless from the sun, and all its organic content is a store and stream of solar rays transformed.

Population, as a succession of generations, is a manifestation of that vital stream. But its quantity as living energy is not manifested in its mass and motion alone. The number of its units must be multiplied not only by their mean velocity but also by the duration of their flow.

All living things have mass, motion and duration—structure, movement and length of days. A complex life-form is the integration of the mass, motion and duration of the units of which it is composed. A population, as a social organism, is the structural and functional integration of the units that constitute it. Each unit mani-

[1]. Throughout this work, the term *energy* is not always distinguished from *action*. Unless qualified by the context, it is employed in the customary manner and to denote any unity of the three basic aspects of reality—mass (as force), motion, and time—which, taken together, constitute objective events and experiences.

fests a mass and a rate of mass-movement of itself and of its parts. The average unit has average mass and average velocity—and it has average duration. A population, then, as a society, may be treated as the *organic integration* of a large number of units having average mass and average velocity or potential and having average duration.

The first datum for the measurement of population as a flow of energy is the number of lives. This means the number of basic units of average mass having average velocity. If the census gave also the ponderable mass of the individuals, the average of that would be the mass measurement per unit of the population. If it gave also the average rate of motion (velocity) of the units, as wholes and in their particles and parts, this would give the average rate of energy or action per individual. Further, if it could give the average duration of the lives, then the product of these three average values—mass, motion (as velocity) and duration—would give the average quantity of energy flow per individual; and the integration of this would give the absolute quantity of energy flow, as *action,* in the entire population per generation—per its *period* or average life span.

Now as to average mass there is little precise data, and as to average motion there is even less; but history and anthropology have ascertained that over long periods of time the average mass per individual has not greatly changed. The same is true of the average motion or rate of energy output per individual. We may, therefore, at least provisionally, take the average mass per individual as constant at unity.[2] Similarly, we may take the average rate of energy output per individual also as constant at unity.

But as to the average duration of life much data is available. Duration is well known to be highly variable over relatively short periods of time, even doubling almost within a single century under greatly improving conditions for the maintenance of life. This high variability in the average duration of its members, as contrasted with the virtual constancy of the average mass and velocity factors, is what marks the societal life-form as capable of regression and deterioration and shows its even greater capacity for qualitative advance. For

---

2. Unity is a convenient and proper value to assume for an invariant or constant factor.

the achievement of security and continuity—progressive enhancement of the durational aspect in life and all its attainments—is the cherished ideal of human aspiration.

Since the average mass and velocity factors in the lives constituting a population may, for practical purposes, be taken as unity, their product also is unity. On this basis, the mass-motion aspect or energy rate of an entire population will be represented by the number of its individuals, $N$. But this has no definite significance unless the average duration, $D$, of the individuals is taken into account. Then the expression $ND$ represents the energy flow per generation in terms of life-years. This population energy, being compounded of mass, motion and time, has the same basic characteristics as horse-power-hours or kilowatt-hours in a mechanical or electrical flow and can be similarly measured and transformed.

The unit of measurement for the energy manifested in a population is thus not the highly variant individual life but the *life-year*.[3] One average person living one year constitutes the energy of a single life-year. Ten average persons living an average span of ten years represents the energy of a hundred life-years. A million of population with an average span of twenty-five years is a total energy manifestation of twenty-five million life-years for that generation—or per generation. A half-million population with a span of fifty years represents the same number of life-years. It is clear, then, that a quantity of human life in terms of energy cannot be measured by enumeration alone. The quantity of energy per generation may remain the same throughout great changes in numbers—if the life span inversely change. For a given quantity of life, the number of units and their average duration are *dependent variables*.

From the foregoing it might seem of small consequence how a given quantity of population energy shall manifest itself; whether it be in a numerous population of short lives or in a less numerous one of correspondingly extended lives, so the product be the same. But that is as though we should say that a large stream of small velocity

---

3. Professor Eddington foreshadowed this in his proposal that a population be described in terms of "man-years" as the analogue of erg-seconds or kilowatt-hours. See his *Nature of the Physical World*, Cambridge, 1932, p. 180.

in its many units is no different from a smaller stream of fewer units but with higher velocities, so long as the quantity or rate of flow remain the same; or that a stream of electrons of low voltage and high density would be the same as an equal quantity of flow at higher potential and lower density. The quantity or energy rate can be in any case the same, but the amount of energy of each unit—the energy charge or potential per unit—is less in the former and greater in the latter cases. Each short-lived individual in a large population, each unit of mass moving in the sluggish stream, each electron in the low-voltage flow, possesses less energy capacity than the corresponding unit in the longer-lived population, the swifter stream, or the high potential electric flow.

In a flow of mechanical energy, a mass factor of one pound combined with a velocity factor of 33,000 feet per minute during one minute is a horsepower-minute—being one-sixtieth of a horsepower-hour. A mass or force factor of 33,000 pounds combined with a velocity factor of one foot per minute is also one-sixtieth of a horsepower-hour. The amount of energy or action is the same, but there is a vast difference in its quality—its utility and possible effects.

In these contrasted examples of physical energy flow—each equal in rate and amount for equal periods of time—the mass-motion factors are varied only as to their ratio; as a product or totality they remain unchanged. The only difference between the contrasting modes of flow is in their respective ratios of mass to motion. The product of these two energy factors is constant, as is also the amount of time involved.[4]

But in the contrasted modes of flow of equal amounts of population energy or action as life-years, it is not necessary that the mass-motion ratio be changed. The change is in the ratio between the

---

4. In the case of equal quantities of differentiated physical energy, the constant quantities are: (1) equal mass-motion products (equal *energies,* in the limited and technical sense) and (2) equal quantities of time, the only variables being the unequal factors in the respectively equal mass-motion products. In the case of equal quantities of differentiated population energy, the two variable factors (whose constant products are the equal energies) are: (1) the respectively *unequal* mass-motion products (numbers of individuals) and (2) the respectively *unequal* durational periods (average life spans).

mass-motion *product* and the duration factor as the period of time through which the action at the given rate continues, both of which are variable—dependent variables—their product being a constant number of life-years.

If, for example, the average mass should be taken as 150 pounds and the average velocity of all its movements as the equivalent of ten feet per minute for this mass (meaning this amount of gravitational or similar force), then the power rate would be 1,500 pounds-feet per minute or about .045 horsepower. At this rate the energy per life-year would be about 390 horsepower-hours. Assuming the life span to be twenty-five years, then the energy per individual would be twenty-five life-years or some 10,000 horsepower-hours, and the energy of a generation of a million persons so averaging would be twenty-five million life-years or about ten billion horsepower-hours. If however, this flow of energy can be transformed so that the average life span rises to fifty years, then it will require only a half-million persons to constitute the same amount of energy in an equal twenty-five million life-years. Such a transformation of population energy would give it a vastly higher functional capacity, as will be shown in Chapter 7.

It is, of course, not stated nor is it to be implied that the energy transformations characteristic of any life-form are expressed only in its gross-bodily movements; but, however complex they may be, they must all take some form or forms of energy transfer the total of which would be equivalent to some certain amount of motion of its mass—a certain amount of energy-in-action manifested simply as a given mass, motion and duration. This energy, in whatever complex forms it may be manifested, must have an average value for the individuals of any population. Without necessarily knowing what this average value is, we may take it as holding constant at unity throughout various changes in the one definitely ascertainable variable factor, namely, the average duration of the lives. By such changes the energy may be profoundly transformed without any change necessarily being made in its rate or total amount per generation. The rate of energy manifestation per average individual is taken as constant not only because that must be substantially true, but also in order to examine in isolation the effects due solely to changes in the average life span and not to any other cause or change.

The association of interfunctioning men that constitutes the social organism is being described as an organization of energy. The energy flows into it from its environment and flows back again. As to the members that constitute its structure, it is a discontinuous flow marked by the succession of their individual lives. Its own continuity results from the over-lapping of the periods of the many individual lives. The longer these lives endure, the less frequent their discontinuities, the more they can interfunction without replacement—then the longer the duration of the total organization that they compose.

Each continuity between discontinuities is a span of individual life or of a generation. Each life that comes to maturity is an integration of energy into its completed structure, a return of further energy to environment in functioning upon it, and a final dis-integration of the structure back into the elements of environment whence it came.

Just as the structure of the social organization is an integration of its component parts, so is the functioning of the social organism in the rebuilding of its world the statistical integration of the functional energy that through its individual members flows. This is the creative process and power of mankind that they do not as separate individuals possess, that comes to them only through their incorporation into the social organism and their interfunctioning therein.

Each generation of the population may be treated as an energy wave or a composite train of waves composed of the lesser waves or wave-trains of its individual lives, these having unequal energy but nonetheless having an average magnitude, just as there is an average energy magnitude for the variant wave-train successions of which the sun's radiant energy is composed.

The quantity of energy manifested per average unit in the organized population is its average number of life-years. The amount of energy that a population draws from its environment, transforms and returns to it in the period of each of its successive generations as energy waves, or as organizations of energy waves, is proportionate to its total number of life-years during that period. It may be expressed as the mean number of its units during that period times their mean duration, or $N \times D$. The structural magnitude and the potential (the mass and the motion) of each generation of population as a wave or composition of energy waves, then, is expressed by its number of units $N$; its duration is $D$; and its frequency is, of course, the reciprocal of its duration, $1/D$.

It is thus apparent that a stream of population energy treated as a succession of organized energy waves is susceptible of important transformations through alterations in the period or frequency of its successively generated organizations of waves. And these transformations are not necessarily accompanied by nor do they depend upon any change being made in the total quantity of population energy (as *action*) that constitutes the composite waves. Any change of frequency or of duration is therefore, of necessity, a *qualitative* change—positively or negatively qualitative, depending on whether the change is in the direction of lower or higher frequency of discontinuity—a longer or shorter average life span.

The duration of the individual lives in a population is obviously dependent upon the kind of relationships that the members practice towards one another—upon the changes (improvement or deterioration) in the subsistence and other conditions of living that these relationships create. The interrelations of its members within a society are either free or coercive relationships, either social or contra-social. They are either *creative* exchanges of services in free relationships or they are rude degradations of the social energy through unfree relationships involving duress, coercion or force. Accordingly, their result is either creation or destruction, either an improvement or a degradation of the environmental world. This either extends the duration or raises the frequency of human lives by lengthening or shortening their average span.

It is the possibility of discovering just what are these creative relationships and of rationally extending them, particularly into the public affairs and services of common use and participation, that affords the field for conscious and rational applications of this new natural science of society.

CHAPTER 4

## *Qualitative Changes in Population Energy*

REGARDING population, then, as energy basically one and identical with the universal energy, and having similar modes of transformation, we will examine first some of the more simple and familiar manifestations of energy with respect to the qualitative changes that can take place in them. This may well disclose what kind of transformations in the life-years of a population are to be desired, and thus point towards a basic rational technique for a practical science of society consciously applied.

Radiant energy from the sun, raising vapor from the seas and lands, mantles mountain peaks in crystal splendors that melt away in limpid lakes and racing streams. Through one of these a million cubic feet of water daily flows. When these million feet move in great mass or volume, as through a lake, then each moves with but little power or speed. If they move without succession and in one array, then each will move but a single foot per day. But let their order among themselves be so rearranged that they pass in single file, then each will move with a speed of a million feet a day.

Thus can enormous change take place in the manner, in the *qualitative* power and effect, without any change in the quantity or the rate of flow. The total quantity of flow through any period of time is the product of any volume or mass times its velocity times the duration of the flow, unchanged by any manner or proportion in which the mass and its motion may be combined. So there be no change in the element of time—in the duration factor—the mass and motion factors may be transformed and recombined in any form or ratio, and with highly variant effects and yet the total flow remain in quantity unchanged.

An energy stream of many units having low charge or motion is subdued to its surroundings, controlled by them; an altered flow, in quantity the same, but having fewer units at higher velocity or charge, is adapted to give off energy effectively and thereby impress environment with change. The one is supine to externals, tool or pawn of circumstance; the other impinges on its surroundings and thus, in measure, creates and determines the character of its external world. The low-potential electric charge is balked by resistance, flows only where resistance is low; the high-potential current overcomes resistance and maintains its way. The stream whose units are many, and their potentials low, flows as its surroundings prescribe; its course is determined. The swift stream of few units, but with potentials high, carves its own.

Physical energy, without known organic processes and repetitions, does not have (except in its radiant forms) any ascertained rhythms of integration and disintegration in successive generations, such as the organic or biologic energy of a population does. Hence while it is the object of men to accelerate those changes in environment that are favorable to them, they, at the same time, desire to retard the rhythm of their own reproduction. With respect to environment, they desire to change the mass-motion ratios of the energy, not the duration of its flow. But with respect to the energy that is organized in and flowing through the generations of men, what they desire is not, primarily at least, any change in the average mass-motion ratio but in the durational factor itself.

Men sense their own lives as fleeting. But they have no occasion or desire to extend the durational factor in the processes of their natural and environmental world. So the human objective is not only to transform the energies of environment in ways that maintain and lengthen lives, but to effect these creative changes in the briefest time; maximum achievement within the human life span. Accordingly, all human ratings of efficiency in the transformations of energy are based on equal quantities of time.[1]

Considering the energy stream that manifests itself in the successive generations that constitute a societal life-stream, we find that a mass

[1]. This may account for physicists often regarding work or energy as composed of a constant mass (or force) times a distance, without any reference to time, as in the case of the *pound-foot* or of the *erg* (which is merely a *dyne-centimeter*) without any designation of the time involved and therefore without any objective reality as experience, operation or event—or as *action*.

population of brief and therefore low-energy individual lives must yield and conform to whatever tyrannies are imposed upon it either by nature or by man. However high in activity or potential the individual lives may be, without length of days their creative power is small; their energy is aborted; it does not continue flowing creatively into the environing world. Without dominion over environment, they cannot inherit the earth and must remain themselves supine and subdued.

But the population whose energy manifests itself in longer lives of its individuals has thus far higher possibilities. Though its numbers be far less (and its life-years per generation no more) than those of a short-lived population, it is nonetheless far superior in its power to create—to act and not be acted upon. Without any quantitative superiority in life-years, there is still a qualitative superiority, a fundamentally significant distinction; for the merely quantitative, as such, has no power to create—or to destroy.

In any organization of energy, *quality,* as distinguished from quantity, is the power to create or to destroy, to integrate or disintegrate, organize or disorganize. In its positive aspect, it is facility to *do,* in the Latin sense of *facere,* to make or create. Energy, as an organized stream, is positively qualitative in proportion to its durational content, its length of days. This it gains only from the durational content or time-potential of the energy units that constitute the organization or stream. The longer their lives the more potent the stream. The degree of immortality of a population—infrequency of its deaths and renewals, length of its periodic waves, its members' life span—is the measure of its creative power over its environing world.

In the preceding Chapter, the variability over periods of time of the average life span, the transition of a population from the one to the other form of energy organization—the transformation of the current, so to speak—, was assumed. This is supported by the fact that such transformations have taken place during periods of societal growth and of societal decay. Even in the shorter phases of "bad times" and "good times" the mortality rate rises and falls. A striking example was the extension of life during the nineteenth century in the Western world. A rational technology for this positive transformation of population energy is indicated further on. It is sufficient here to say that the lengthening of the average span follows upon the expansion of free contractual relations—upon the advancement of freedom to produce, and, above all, of freedom to serve by self-sustaining exchange.

The emergence of a high qualitative power in ordinary physical energy, when suitably transformed, and the discovery that there is a corresponding transformation of human and social energy, resolves the problem that through the ages has baffled the imagination and the contemplative mind of man. It reveals the linkage between the physical and the meta-physical, the long-doubted essential unity between natural science and human destiny and hope. Magnitudes and ratios support the intuitions of philosophy and art, and the intellections of science are brought to serve transcendent dreams where mystery and miracle and resort to force alike have failed.

Discovery of this qualitative property, this creative potential in any manifestation of energy, by the mere transformation and higher organization of its own internal structure, independently of any over-all quantitative change, makes clear and firm the long-time shadowy void between the quantitative and the qualitative worlds. In the simple process of transforming population energy by reducing the frequency of its discontinuities and so raising its duration, or time factor, its qualitative, its creative aspect is revealed. In the transformation of energy by rearrangement of its three elementary components, mass, motion and duration, in their merely quantitative interior proportions, but with qualitative exterior *effects,* it becomes the part of purely physical science to disclose, objectively, the qualitative and creative aspects of nature, including man, that religion and philosophy so anciently pre-empted and have so long claimed as exclusively their own. To its grave and reverend elders, physical science proffers rational and practical techniques for effective realizations, in the objective world, of their subjective values and elusive ideals. Its fundamentals are set to serve both saint and singer, sage and seer; its humble modes of seeking and its sure results invite the hearts and minds that under none but *moral* motivation have yet not foregone force nor disdained dependence on the dungeon and the sword.

By this venture into long forbidden land, science widens its own horizons to glimpse the upward way its mighty enginery must lead if they be not self-destroyed. And the votaries of science, as they extend the spectrum of their quantitative world, must find themselves, all unwittingly, children of the same light, seekers, in their practical and precise ways, of the same Beauty that inspires creative art and ideal philosophy and binds the hearts of men to its divine devotion.

CHAPTER 5

# The Energy that Re-creates Environment

ENERGY from the sun organizes the materials of the earth into plants, animals and men. A population is an organization of that cosmic energy into the generations of a complex life-form having the pulsing power of rhythmic succession, and through which cosmic energy continues to flow and to return in altered form.

The return of this population energy to its environment modifies that environment. It transforms it either negatively or positively. If the population is but little or not at all organized into a society, it is unproductive; more than that, it deteriorates its environment, reducing it to a lower level of organization, an inferior degree of organic complexity. The crude population thus shortens its own life. Its destructive effect upon its environment condemns it to a lower state of being and subsistence that shortens its span or wave. Under such circumstances, it can maintain its total energy or life-years and escape degradation to a lower level of life, or even complete extinction into a lower or inorganic state, only by an acceleration of its reproductivity in compensation of its shortened life span.

But when a population has become organized in community relationships, and more fully developed as a general society, then all is reversed. Much of the energy that it takes from its environment is so modified and returned to the environment as to raise and transform it to a higher level of complexity, more suitable to maintain and extend the lives of its members. Such a productive population suffers no shortening of its wave or span. It can maintain its total life-years per generation without increasing its energy of replacement and reproduction. Indeed, by its productivity and creative effect upon its environment, it can so increase its span or wave—the length of days of its generations—that it may suspend its reproductive function in like proportion as it extends its days, without any loss in its total life-years. And not only does its higher organization of itself give it power to transform and re-create its environing world, and thus to lengthen its own lives, but this more highly organized world becomes one in which also new tides of cosmic energy can most freely flow into the organic, the human and the societal life-forms.

All the earth's plant and animal life, all the organic content of its waters and soils, the vast hydrocarbon compounds in its geologic depths, all have come into being through the action of sunlight upon inorganic materials. This process accounts for all the organic matter the world has known since, as a fiery vapor, it was of life wholly void. Oxidation, it is true, does go on, but not with equal pace. Nature constantly creates life. The world literally becomes more alive with every day of sunshine on it.

The creative technique of a population, as a society transforming its world, directs and accelerates this "natural" organization of life. Through its qualitative transformation of itself, it has the power, not only to extend its own lives, but also to make fit the earth for increasing numbers of extended lives. Social and natural processes thus unite to make the earth more and more alive and thus able to sustain more life. And the social transformation is not qualitative alone, at the expense of quantity; it is quantitative as well.

But for the purpose of any qualitative comparison between two populations, or of the same population with itself in its successive generations or waves, as to the extent of its functioning and its state of well-being, it is necessary to keep in view *like quantities* of energy as between the respective populations. This means that for anything beyond merely quantitative comparison, the *product* of $N$ and $D$, numbers and duration, must be constant. This leaves $N$ and $D$ variable, and since, for the purposes of truly qualitative comparison, their product as a quantity must be kept constant, they are, for equal quantities of energy, dependent variables. If equal quantities of population energy as life-years are to be compared, any change in the duration or length of the lives must be considered in connection with a contrary change in their numbers.

By considering the successive generations of men as a propagation of energy waves having a constant average as to their mass and velocity functions but having an average frequency of discontinuity that differs as between different populations or at different times, depending on changes in the average duration of the lives, it becomes possible to employ mathematical investigation in this field. Taking a population as a wave stream, through various changes of wave frequency, or of wave length as the life span, it is possible, by this transformation, to examine what changes other than quantitative ones can take place in the energy flow. These changes are, necessarily, in the interior structure and organization of the energy itself, and are not dependent on there being any change in its quantity or rate of flow. We may regard then, any change in the operations of a society that leads to a change in the wave-length or duration of its lives, as a qualitative transformation—as a higher or lower organic form and functioning of the population energy itself.

Thus the population having a long life-wave, and hence a low frequency of replacement, is a positively qualitative energy flow, in the sense that it is dominant and creative upon its environment, raising itself to higher levels of organization, appropriating and assimilating the re-organized energies of its environment to its own maintenance and growth. In so doing, it re-creates, indirectly, its members themselves and lifts them into a higher and higher order of existence as individuals and as members of an organic society.

When the change in the social organization is in the direction of collision or conflict, contractual relationships are weakened and fewer contracts made, exchange of services and production of wealth decline and individuals deteriorate and live shorter lives. When the change is in the direction of freedom, of contractual, as opposed to coercive, engagements, then exchanges multiply, production increases, environment is improved and the individuals live richer and thereby longer lives. These changes in the social organization are qualitative, positively or negatively so; and they lead to corresponding alterations in the energy stream by shortening or lengthening its waves. For the more the life span is shortened, the more will its energy be repressed and re-formed into frequency of reproduction;[1]

---

[1] "A high death rate among infants, unless brought about by epidemic diseases or other special causes, is normally offset by a higher birth rate." Dr. Victor Heiser, *An American Doctor's Odyssey*, New York, 1936, p. 201.

the more the lives are extended and enlarged—the more creative and productive upon the environment they become—the less reproductive they will be or have need to be.

The potentialities of full-span human lives are greater than those of lives cut short soon after or even before they mature. At the level of human life this qualitative difference between a long-lived and a short-lived population is most extreme, for all the years of infancy are years of dependency on life that has gone before. During his period of growth, the individual incorporates energy into his structure; his social and creative potentiality is accumulating; it is not effective until he matures. Only then can he become a positive agent, a functioning part in the universal process of the cosmic stream.

From the foregoing it is clear that the quality and potentiality of a population, its power to advance and transform itself through the social process in rebuilding its environing world, depends not alone upon the mere number or quantity of its life-years, but rather upon the quantity of its life-years that extends beyond the period of infancy and immaturity of its members; for there can be no productivity or creative power in any system of energy that has no life or power beyond that required for its own maintenance and replacement or reproduction.

This supine condition, however, is characteristic of nearly the entire plant and animal world—the whole realm of life inferior to socially organized mankind. Of the myriad forms of life below the societal life-form, not excepting the biological and consanguineous associations of insects, animals and men, none have any associative technique for the general rebuilding or creation of environment to serve progressively their natures' needs. Primitive men and some of the higher animals do construct temporary habitations to instinctive patterns, but they do not create or multiply their own subsistence. On the contrary, they consume and destroy whatever subsistence their environment affords. If this is abundant, and for a time, easily obtained, even then the increase of their vital energy is not creatively but only reproductively employed. Thus, while numbers increase subsistence declines until few are able to live beyond maturity and only the "fittest" can survive the dearth of subsistence and the predatory practices unfailingly engendered where dearth prevails. With no *social* technique transcending merely biological and consanguineous relationships, the life-form remains, indeed, only a product, a mere *creature* of its environment. It has no power to ameliorate its external world, but must modify and adapt itself to environment or the race not survive.

In all lower life-forms the highest destiny is to achieve maturity, reproduce, struggle and die. Man, *as society,* is the only form of life that can maintain its life and preserve the integrity of its nature against all buffetings. In the social-ized life-form, mankind alone achieves liberation from and creative dominion over the environing world. This command over nature gives the social-ized population power to extend its days and to extend its total life-years per generation, even though its births decline. This power increases in the degree that the society differentiates the activities of its individuals and its institutions and thus amplifies the free interior relationships and processes of consent and exchange upon which its productivity and all advance depends. We shall examine the nature of this interior developmental social change.

CHAPTER 6

# Freedom the Technique of Eternality

IN THE ATOMIC WORLD as in the astronomical, the most perfect organization and greatest continuity of action is observed in those systems in which the units that constitute them move most freely in relation one to another. Where there is collision between the members, unbalanced stress and strain, there is disintegration of these units and a corresponding disorganization of the system that they form.

In atomic structures, where the constituent elements collide, they decompose and as radiant energy fly away. The atomic organization disintegrates, and the structure is radioactive, self-limited as to its duration. Where the elements do not collide the structure is stable and not self-limited, to be dissolved only by assault from without, by invasion of exterior energy or force. Astronomical systems in which the members or parts collide are similarly insecure; but so far as the members move without collision the duration of the system is long, terminable only by very slow retardation or by violence of extraneous power.

In the human and societal realm the like prevails. Here are the same two relationships, that of free action and movement of the units with respect to one another, without collision and consequent disintegration, and that of collision and compulsion which disintegrates the units, inhibits the social functioning and weakens social bonds. The one relationship is harmonious, balanced and free; the other is coercive and destructive. And this is true, whether the violence be criminal and condemned or be sanctioned under governmental procedures and legal forms. The creativeness of free relationships is not affected by selfish aims or lack of conscious altruism in the minds of those who practice them. Nor is the disintegrative effect of coercive relations stayed by any feeling of loyalty or duty with which they may be accepted or of benevolence with which they may be imposed.

The societal organization derives its stability, its enduring powers, from the operational freedom, the full and uninterrupted interfunctioning, of its units and parts. Upon this freedom and consequent productivity with increasing length of days—a lessening frequency of replacement—the societal evolution depends. The lengthening life span and declining reproductive rate that arises out of high contractual freedom and productivity is wholly advantageous. The energy of a high biological turnover and replacement is carried over into the maturer years for societal functioning as creative work upon the environment. Biological reproductivity is thus transformed into social productivity.

Reversely, the higher birth rate of those whose contractual and creative power is repressed or has lapsed into mere biological power, is also advantageous, though indirectly so, under adverse conditions that shorten lives. For it provides a wider numerical field in which favorable variations or mutations may occur among the increasing numbers born. By converting its shortening lives into more numerous ones, the population lays foundation for its possible salvation by the emergence of new members so gifted as to reëstablish the free productive and creative relationships for lack of which their predecessors suffered shortened lives. And the value of a high frequency of births to compensate the shortening of lives, under the coercions of a low or declining state of social organization, can be further seen by considering the consequence if a reverse procedure should take place; for, if the shortened lives were replaced only by less frequent births, the race would move towards extinction at an accelerating rate.

The integration of men into a societal life-form is the only organization of energy that has developed structures and functions beyond those necessary to its mere maintenance and reproduction. It is through these unique and additional powers that the social organization is enabled to make positive and qualitative transformations of its environing world. This creative facility springs from the abundance of life socially conferred upon the individual with his increasing length of days. Man thus has a privilege and a power that no other life-form has. He may suspend his energies of reproduction, in proportion as his days increase, with a qualitative gain and no quantitative loss. Under the conditions of his life thus achieved, social-ized man rises into his higher organic and creative, and therefore spiritual, estate.

In family or tribal relationships, as contrasted with societal organization, man achieves no such transcendent powers. He differs from lower animals by a higher degree of versatility and adaptation to environment that makes every part of the earth his habitat. But, more strikingly, he differs from them in his possession of a creative social potentiality towards an organic societal integration having world-wide scope and range.

All those life-forms that continue must live till they mature and reproduce. They can have no briefer term than this. But during the period of their maturity their reproductive rate is related to their length of days. The greater its hazards and more brief its term, the more prolific an organism becomes. A plant, cut back, multiplies its shoots, and when its days of growth are shortened, rushes into bloom and seed. The animal forms whose lives are most imperiled most rapidly reproduce. Men are most prolific where subsistence and security least exceed the minimum on which they can mature and breed, and where their mature lives thus are brief. Throughout the range of persisting life, fecundity compensates insecurity and brevity of term. It rises with the shortening and falls with the lengthening of the reproductive days.

But men have a societal nature. Beyond the biological, familial and other relationships such as animals have, men tend to form themselves into a wider and a higher organism, in which they have world-creative powers and, thereby, ever-lengthening days. On these, her highest creatures, Nature smiles, and as they gain creative power, she frees them from that quantitative prudence to which her lesser forms of life are bound.

The law of balanced conservation that rules structure and energy in the physical realm extends also to the organic and the social world. Both structures and energies are variously transformed independently of any over-all quantitative change. When a structure of specific size has many units, as they grow larger their number declines; as they grow smaller their number expands. When energy is stated as a specific number of ergs, or of pounds-feet, then, as the force grows larger, the distance grows less. So it is with a specific quantity of energy as life-years. As the lives become extended in respect to time, they grow smaller in respect of numbers; as they are contracted in respect of time, their numbers expand.

Any specific quantity or amount of energy that Nature assigns to and continues to manifest as a population is subject to being variously transformed. It may resolve itself into fewer units or individuals, having a more extended energy content and powers, or it may diffuse itself among many individuals of less enduring powers. Such transformations are not dependent on any total quantitative change. When the transformation is integrative, as the duration of the units is extended and their powers increased, their numbers decline. Under a disintegrative trend, as the individual lives are contracted, their numbers expand. If the stream of life is still to be maintained, then the more frequently its units pass out the faster must they be replaced and renewed.

When energy is integrated into living structures, more enduring and more complex, that is growth; when energy flows through and maintains living structures, that is functioning; when structure ceases to function and disintegrates into energy of simpler form or into less complex structures, that is death and decay. The reality—the energy—does not come into being, nor does it pass; only its forms change. Like all other phenomena, growth and decay, life and death, are but transfers and transformations of and within the Universal Energy. Structure and duration, organization and process, come alike under one law.

CHAPTER 7

## Creative Transformation of Population Energy

A POPULATION, organized as a societal life-form or organism, is resolvable into a succession of energy manifestations in its generations of men. Each generation is composite of its individual lives. The overlapping succession of these lives, and their interfunctioning therein, is what gives life and continuity to the social organization as a form of life.

Taking life-years as energy waves, the succession of individual lives is a discontinuous series of energy waves. The population, as a society, is a multiple system of these discontinuous wave series. Its continuity results from the overlapping of these discontinuities. Taking any generation as a complex of energy waves or as a composite energy wave, the numerical population $N$ represents the mass and motion of the wave, and the average life span $D$ of that generation is the period of its duration—inverse of frequency—the durational length of the wave.

If, therefore, for the purpose of qualitative comparison, a population is to represent, over a number of generations, a *constant* amount of energy or action per generation, there must be no change in the number of individuals under consideration without a contrary change in their duration. When the *given fixed quantity* of energy runs to brevity and frequency of its units, their numbers must increase; when it extends the duration of its units their numbers must decline.

Anthropology gives little evidence of any great variableness in the average rate of vital activity of men—unless over very long periods of time. Thus, the energy rate, the mass-motion or force-velocity component of the average life, may be taken as constant at unity or 1. Therefore, in a whole population as a generation of men, the rate of action for that form of life may be represented simply as $N$, the number of men as statistically observed. This establishes $N$ as the rate of activity for the generation as a whole. This rate must be multiplied by the number of years per generation (average length of lives), $D$, to give the total energy output, $W$. Hence $D \times N = W$. So a given fixed quantity, $W$, of population as life-years may be manifested in various ratios of duration to numbers without any over-all quantitative change. Any generation of men thus has the essential characteristics of an energy wave. The average energy rate of its members being constant, its total rate is a matter only of its numbers, and as in quantum physics, the total energy-in-action of the wave is its energy or action *rate* times the period of time or duration of the wave. Although neither the average mass of the individuals nor their average rate of motion appears to change from generation to generation, the mass of population does change directly with any numerical change that it undergoes. So a given *quantity* of energy as action or work manifested in a population is always the constant product of two variables: of average numbers, $N$, representing the product of mass and velocity, times the average duration, $D$, representing the average length of its lives, the period (inverse of frequency) of the wave.

The preceding paragraph has taken population energy chiefly in its interior quantitative or compositional aspects without reference to such changes as affecting its qualitative or creative capacity and without any over-all quantitative change. Keeping in mind what was said in Chapter 5 concerning the life-years of infancy absorbing energy, only the adult life-years being capable of social functioning upon the environment with creative results, an illustration of exclusively qualitative change will now be made.

Taking the end of infancy and beginning of maturity for the average individual as at the age of twenty years, we will examine the quantity of population energy represented by a generation or wave of twenty-five millions of life-years. We will first consider this energy as manifested in a generation of one million lives, $N$, having an average duration, $D$, of twenty-five years. Then we will compare it with the same quantity of life energy in a population of one-half million lives, $N$, having an average duration, $D$, of fifty years.

In both cases the total energy is, in quantity, exactly the same—

twenty-five millions of life-years. But the million population with a life span of twenty-five years must consume twenty millions of its life-years in the integrating of its structure, leaving only five millions possible for creative functioning upon the environment. This is only one-fourth of its total energy.

Not so with the half-million population living an average of fifty years. This society requires only ten millions of its life-years for its own integration, leaving fifteen millions available for its social functioning in the rebuilding of its world. This is three-fifths of its total energy. The second population, therefore, notwithstanding its great numerical inferiority, has a three times greater potentiality to advance its civilization.

Thus, a society that so transforms the conditions under which it lives as to extend the period of its average adult lives can increase its quality and creative capacity threefold without increasing the number of its life-years or of its lives. In fact, it can, as in this example, increase its powers threefold in the lengthened energies of only one-half its original number of lives.

The comparison just made is between two populations quantitatively equal in life-years, but which, qualitatively and creatively, are as unequal as three is to one. This is a qualitative difference between the two populations, each taken in its entirety, or as a whole. But for the average individual in each case, the disparity is twice as great, for in the numerically larger population he has only five adult years of opportunities and powers, whereas in the second or improved society he has thirty adult years for enjoyment of his life and employment of his powers. The same transformation that raises three-fold the potentialities of the society as a whole raises six-fold the opportunities and possibilities of its individual lives.

The numerical relationships in the foregoing example are given general formulation in figure 1. Here the total work or energy flow, $W$, per generation is derived from $ND$, the number of persons and the duration of their lives. The maximum energy available for creative outflow upon the environment is found by deducting from the total life-years the number of life-years of energy that are required for the mass-integration or growth of the structure of each

## SUGGESTED FORMULA FOR
## QUANTITATIVE MEASUREMENT OF POPULATION
## AS LIFE-ENERGY

AVERAGE RATE OF WORK—Output per individual, taken as unity,      I
    times
AVERAGE DURATION OF WORK—Average Life-Span of Individuals Ascertained over a Sufficient Period, years,     D
    times
AVERAGE NUMBER OF INDIVIDUALS Living During the Time Embraced Within the Average Life-Span,
    equals     N
TOTAL WORK OR ENERGY FLOW Manifested in Those Numbers During that Time, Expressed as Life-Years.     = W

## SUGGESTED FORMULA FOR
## QUALITATIVE MEASUREMENT OF POPULATION
## AS LIFE-ENERGY AVAILABLE FOR SOCIAL GROWTH
## AND FUNCTIONING

HUMAN ENERGY in Total Life-Years, $DN = W$,     W
    minus
LIFE-YEARS OF INFANCY, Required for Mere Physio-Biological Replacement of Predecessors, $20N$,     — 20N
    equals
ADULT LIFE-YEARS—Available for Social Growth and Development—Creative     = $N(D - 20)$

## OPTIMUM QUALITATIVE CONDITIONS

For a *given quantity* of energy manifested in the life-years of a population per generation, $DN = W$, the condition of highest quality, active and creative capacity, is when $D$, average duration, is maximum and $N$, number of individuals, is therefore at minimum.

## COEFFICIENT OF SOCIAL POTENTIALITY—POSSIBLE
## SOCIOLOGICAL EFFICIENCY

$$E = \frac{N(D-20)}{W} = \frac{D-20}{D}.$$

*Figure 1.*

generation, to compensate for the mass-disintegration of the generation passing on. This remaining energy is shown as that potentially available for the positive functioning of the social organism. Thus, for any population its coefficient $E$, of social potentiality, or possible societal efficiency, is found by dividing its total life-years into those that remain after deducting the life-years required for its biological maturation.

In the case of the million population of twenty-five years average span, twenty millions of life-years must be deducted, leaving only five millions to be divided by the total of twenty-five millions. This gives a coefficient of only 0.2. For the half-million with the fifty-year span, we must deduct only ten millions, leaving fifteen millions available. This divided by the same total of twenty-five millions yields a coefficient of 0.6 for the same number of life-years more highly organized and enduringly transformed.

In the above example all life-years, infant and adult, are taken as being of equal magnitude. If it be objected that the available energy of exclusively adult life-years should not be weighed against a total that includes the infant life-years as being of equal magnitude with the adult, this may be adjusted by averaging the infant life-years. Taking the infant life-year as of uniformly increasing magnitude up to twenty years, its average value would then be not twenty, but ten life-years. On this basis, the gross life-years of the generation having the million population would be diminished by ten years, reducing it from twenty-five to fifteen millions of life-years. The adult life-years remaining at five millions as before, the highest possible efficiency becomes 5/15 or .33 instead of .20. But for the longer-lived generation of only a half-million population, the total life-years would be diminished by only five millions, reducing it from twenty-five to twenty millions and raising the limit of efficiency from .6 to .75. In particular applications, still further adjustment of the basic formula might be desired. The period of infancy, for example, might need in a given instance to be taken as less than or more than twenty years, and as beginning with conception instead of at birth, without greatly affecting the general result.

In figure 2, the percentage of total life energy available for

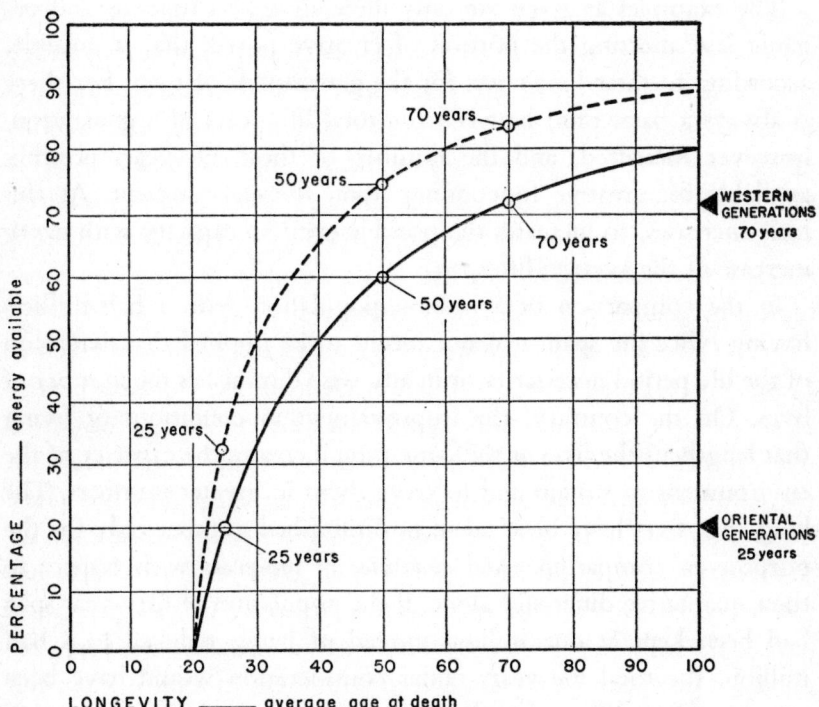

*Figure 2.*

creative functioning as affected by the average longevity is graphically shown. The full-line curve is calculated upon a base that includes all life-years as of equal energy magnitude. The dotted curve shows how these percentages change when calculated on a base in which the infant life-years are treated as having only one-half the energy magnitude of the average adult.

The examples as given are only illustrative of a fundamental organic law affecting the portion of creative power that is possible, according to their longevity, for the generations of men. For there is always a basic ratio between the total life-years of a generation, however measured, and the number of those life-years possibly available for creative functioning upon the environment. As this ratio increases, so increases the possible creative capacity with every increase of the average life span.

In the comparison of a million population with a half-million having twice the span, it is not meant to be implied that extension of the life period necessarily or in any wise diminishes the number of lives. On the contrary, the improvement in conditions of living that lengthens the lives at the same time increases the capacity of the environment to sustain and to serve them in greater numbers. The long-span lives have been taken in diminished number only for the purpose of comparing *equal quantities of life-years* with respect to their qualitative difference alone. If the population of fifty-year span had been kept at one million instead of being reduced to a half million, the total life-years under consideration would have been raised to fifty millions, but the ratio of adult to total life-years would have remained unchanged and the qualitative superiority of the long-span lives thus still the same.

Although for the purpose of qualitative comparisons we must take equal amounts of energy as equal numbers of life-years, it is not likely that any succession of generations in a population is ever stationary, either as to the numbers of the population or as to the number of life-years manifested in the successive generations. The indications are that a degeneration of the societal technique such as repeatedly occurs under the political regulations, oppressions and revolutions, conquests and alliances, that build world-empires, not only shortens the average length of life but, when so long continued or severe that the conditions of living fall below those essential to existence or to reproduction, there is at last an actual decrease in numbers instead of an increase, coincident with the shortening of the span. This condition, however, could never have been worldwide or for a very long time; it would have been the condition of a dying race; and mankind has at least survived. The probabilities are that the average life span throughout the world has never fallen below the number of years necessary for reproductive maturity, for any such shortening of the span would tend to very rapid extinction of the race.

Not under all conditions, therefore, is it possible for numbers to increase in response to a shortening of the average life span. The rule can apply only to a population whose average span is longer than the number of years required to arrive at reproductive maturity. Where good social organization induces a lengthening of the average life span, this diminished mortality causes an accumulation of lives, unless there is an equal decline in the number of births during this change. The population that raises its average life-years has no need to suffer numerical decline. For the improvement of environment that diminishes mortality attracts, doubtless, at the same time a greater flow of cosmic energy to take the organic and the human and the social form. Thus the qualitative improvement is not unfavorable to quantitative increase as well.

Granting that a considerable portion of a population does not reach the reproductive age, then any general lengthening of life must carry this part of the population from a state of sterility right into the most reproductive years at the same time that the maturer lives are being extended into their more productive but less reproductive years. The same general lengthening of lives that carries one part of the population beyond its period of greatest fertility also brings into that period another part that previously had not reached the reproductive age at all. It is the tendency of youth, upon its first physical maturation, to consume and to reproduce; of maturity and age, to produce and conserve. Reproductivity does not depend upon the higher psychologic development that comes with years; creative productivity does so depend. Biologic maturation gives bodily and reproductive power; psychologic development is more productive than reproductive. It leads to greater mental, cultural and creative power.

If a highly reproductive population be divided into two parts, the first containing only those persons whose mean longevity extends well into and beyond middle life, and the second containing those whose average span extends but little into middle life and covers almost exclusively the more reproductive years, the first and smaller group will be found to have the greater accumulation of the means and of capacity for employing these means efficiently, both for general productivity and in the cultural and creative arts. The second group will have accumulated less of the means of production and less capacity for their fruitful administration. Its productivity will be more on the physical plane, and it will discharge a much greater portion of its vital energy in biologic reproduction. A "differential birth rate" in favor of that part of a population whose lives are less extended into psychologic and productive maturity is therefore to be expected in any society that is progressing from a low average life span, with youth and immaturity numerically preponderant, towards a longer average span of maturer and more creative lives.

This higher or increasing birth rate during the early years is not only a normal feature of societal development through creative transformation of population energy; it serves also as protective compensation in those exigencies that threaten to exterminate mankind with the pestilences of war, tyranny and disease.

Through world-wide organization of communications and spontaneous exchange relationships, mankind has become, actually or virtually, equivalent to an enormous organism or super-organism having individual men as its bio-societal cells. Its habitat is the earth and the air that covers it. Its structure consists of myriad individuals and groups united by their interfunctioning in what biologists call "disjunctive symbiosis." It draws its subsistence from the raw materials of the earth. Highly specialized parts of it fabricate these into more assimilable forms. Other parts circulate them by land, sea and air. And a network of electrical and other communications co-

## CREATIVE TRANSFORMATION OF POPULATION ENERGY

ordinates the widely distanced parts into an interfunctioning system of voluntary services and exchange—all within the limitations unhappily imposed by the restrictive regulations of governments in times of peace and of war.

By this hypothesis, when in one part of the world the flow of energy as life-years is balked and ravaged by war or widespread disease shortening the lives, the basic corrective through increase of reproduction takes effect not immediately in the war torn population itself but in more favored parts of the earth where a high average life span, though threatened, has not yet been cut down. Hyperactivity in other and remote parts to counteract a pathology in the one part —a phenomenon quite familiar to physiologists—appears in a similar manner to occur in the social organism. Vital statistics give ample evidence that such compensating changes in the birth frequency do take place. For example, in 1943, while the average life span and the birth rate of the war-torn populations of Europe were diminishing at the same time, a marked upturn of the birth rate in the United States was taking place, without, as yet, any reversal of the long upward trend of the average span.

The general rule of reproductivity being substantially inverse to longevity, if taken without regard to any social advance having been already attained, or, if applied narrowly, without allowance for the effects of critical conditions in distant parts, would require that wherever lives are lengthened reproductivity must decline. But in an organism so closely knit as modern mankind it is quite possible for the reverse of this to occur in one part to compensate the impossibility of birth keeping pace with deaths in another part. This accounts for apparent local deviations from the general rule when critical changes take place in a distant but connected area, and also for temporary deviations under stress of sudden or violent change.

A population can maintain or advance itself only by qualitative transformations of its available adult life-years. The extent to which it social-izes this energy into reciprocal voluntary services is the measure of its exemption from internal conflicts and external wars. The potentiality for this is maximum when, for a given number of life-years per generation, the ratio between the number of lives and their duration is maximum—when the durational factor is in furthest approach towards the infinite. Speculative minds may here discern a scientific parallel to the religious intuitions and aspirations of mortality taking on the immortality of eternal life.

CHAPTER 8

## *A Century of Lengthening Life*

FOR A CENTURY AND MORE, there has been a lengthening of the human life span. In this country, during the National Period, the average span has risen from about thirty to almost seventy years—more than doubled in a century and a half. This has been due, doubtless, to an unexampled freedom during most of this time from governmental or other compulsions and a consequently enormous extension of the area, the complexity and the productivity of free contractual relations. This made possible a continuous rise in the supply of the necessities, and enormous improvements in the physical and other conditions favorable to the extension of life. In addition to this great improvement over Old-World deficiencies, a result has been the extirpation of many pestilences and a marked diminution of disease, especially as affecting the mortality of the younger ages in the population and incapacitation by disease among the middle and older age groups. These favorable conditions, for a population initially endowed with a high biological fertility, made possible a rapid rise in its numbers with the lengthening of its days. And until recent decades, a great influx of virility, and of *property,* from abroad, seeking a field of freer contractual engagements and employment, resulted in a great acceleration of the native increase.

As the general length of living advanced, the population was maintained and increased more by the growing infrequency of death than by its rate or frequency of reproduction, and by the end of the nineteenth century its birth rate had notably declined. This became the basis of much professional prediction that by the year 1960 there would be no further population growth. And this seemed the more likely by reason of drastic political restrictions on the flow of population from abroad. The declining birth rate was publicized, and there was widespread public alarm that through "race suicide" the nation would go into decline. The excitement was aggravated by much public notice that the declining reproductivity was chiefly among those persons and in those regions that had achieved the highest productivity and thereby enjoyed the most ample subsistence and other favorable conditions for the lengthening of their lives, while the birth rate of the less productive elements of the population, and in the least productive areas and occupations, continued to be high. There was thus a double anxiety, on the one hand that population growth would cease and the population decline, and on the other that the continued high reproductivity of the less productive elements of the population would deteriorate the race.

These anxieties, though academically current and widely indulged in before the two world wars, were never justified by events. For population was measured by lives, without regard to their length, instead of in life-years, and the normal inverse relationship between productivity and reproductivity—the conservation of human life in the energies of longer, maturer and more productive lives—was not understood. Little attention, if any, was given to the positive quantitative effect, the increase of numbers, that results from a diminished mortality, and no account at all was taken of the enormous qualitative improvement in the productivity and in the cultural capacity that follows from the lengthening and the thereby prospering lives. On the contrary, there was apprehension lest the "ageing of the population" should take place by extension of its upper age limits alone and thus oppress diminishing numbers of the young and middle-aged under a growing burden of senile dependency in the lives prolonged. And this gave rise to movements and to measures for the benefit of "senior citizens" by public pensions, gifts and doles.

All these anxieties needlessly arose. For statistical data supported the common observation that increased longevity extends almost exclusively the lives of the mature and middle-aged and of the young, but of the very old perhaps not at all; for there are as yet no data pointing strongly towards any general lengthening of lives beyond what has long marked the extremes of old age.[1] Moreover, there is

---

1. Louis I. Dublin and Albert J. Lotka, *Length of Life—A Study of the Life Table*, New York, 1936, p. 32; and various other authorities on longevity and population structure.

not only the well known greater administrative capacity and greater means among persons of or past middle age, but also, in recent times, much evidence of a continuing and improving competency in the generality of persons of advancing years and at the same time a general increase of acute terminations of life rather than through chronic invalidism or long senile decay.

Viewed through the vicissitudes of human welfare and of world affairs, reproductivity seems most to decline in those periods like the late Victorian and in the fatuous "normalcy" that followed almost immediately after World War I, when wars were thought to be out-moded or to have ended and the race felt itself biologically secure. There can be but little doubt, if any, that the current midcentury excitation of the reproductive urge is the biological response intimately connected with the war-time psychology and the deep sense of atomic insecurity that continues to prevail.

CHAPTER 9

# The Democracy of the Market

THE NINETEENTH CENTURY has been called the century of democracy. Doubtless this refers to political democracy—the popular voting of men into office and measures into laws for the exercise of, or for the restraint of, compulsive power. More significantly, it was a century of economic democracy, and to this "democracy of the market" it unquestionably owes the vast extension of the human life span that the century achieved.

The widening of Western geographical horizons—notably in North America—without any corresponding expansion of governmental "regulations" and restraints, but rather with a general reaction against encroachments by governmental power, permitted an unprecedented extension of production and trade. Thus the area of contractual relationships—the proportion of population energy flowing into free and voluntary engagements and productivity—, as compared with that involving compulsion and force, was enormously increased. Production leaped to wide margins above taxation; values of every kind were created and for the most part maintained, affording security to all prudent investment with certainty of fair return upon savings as well as for services currently performed. These were the fruits of the democracy of the market—so far as this fundamental voluntary democracy was permitted to be practiced and performed. Notable was the almost complete freedom of contractual relationships across state lines in the United States, with an unprecedented though always limited freedom of international exchange, especially during the first half of the century.

Under this relatively unlimited yet still far from complete freedom, the technique of social or economic democracy spontaneously expanded and was increasingly carried on. Goods were produced and services rendered and prepared, not for the use of those performing them but for the use of others by way of contract and exchange. The current increasing recompenses or incomes were the current values, and the capitalizations of income from savings and profits—from the administration of capital property—were the growing capital values.

Under the democracy of the market, goods and services prepared for others are voluntarily pooled in public places, whence their owners repair and by bids and offerings vote their wishes and desires as to the measures and terms upon which their common wealth and services, thus commun-ized or social-ized (in the best sense of these words), shall be redistributed among those who have contributed. This voting ascertains the common will and assures its execution forthwith and without any infringement of minority interest or right. This is democracy based on mutual service in mutual freedom —the right to serve in order to be served—the right of voluntary exchange. It is the fundamental democracy to which political democracy has at best a negative value in its partial and transient mitigation of the rigors of those more concentrated forms of government which so sharply impinge upon and finally extinguish the freedom of mutual service by voluntary contracts and exchanges.

In the market we find the social institution by which in a civilized community a substantial portion of the available population energy is social-ized into non-violence and freely transferred and transformed into services and into realizations of the common will and of individual desires. This is not to say that the market is wholly free from restraint or from the perversions so engendered, as restraints on freedom always engender them; but it is to say that the functioning of the market is and gives rise to all the freedom from compulsions that can be practiced or attained. Freedom is not a condition; it exists only in practice—in process. It consists in choosing and practicing the preferred out of various alternatives, all in some degree desirable. An enforced "choice of evils" is slavery.

The process of the market, the making and performing of service contracts, is the mutual choosing from among desirable alternatives and freely acting upon them. This is what gives men their exemption from the compulsions of an uncivilized environment and all the freedom that they have from being compelled—enslaved—by one another. It is the foundation of social freedom and, therefore, of social progress into ampler living throughout increasing length of days.

Any reference to the functioning of the market would be incomplete if it failed to give some account of the time (or change) element as a "fourth-dimensional" technique in the practice of *credit* and of *speculation*.

To escape the narrow limitations of barter by simultaneous exchange, in most transactions the obligations on one side are deferred by a credit which is evidenced by a token or written record. If the credit given was obtained from the general market and may become an immediate charge against the general market, it is called money or cash. If the obligation is that of a particular person or persons only, and deferred to a particular time, it is called simply an obligation or debt. Credit in the first sense, as an obligation against the general market, gives him who holds it wide options as to the time, place, manner, and convenience under which he will exercise it. It gives access to reservoirs of optional satisfactions to consumers, and it brings service power to the hands of those who put their properties to the service of others in the course of production and exchange.

Credit in the second sense—obligations of a particular person or persons deferred to a particular time—enables a consumer to enjoy present benefits without present payment. But what is more significant, it enables producers to prepare services and goods speculatively by anticipation of future market demand. This is a signal social service; by means of it the future needs and desires of a community are anticipated and provided in advance. Speculation, when rightly understood, is found to be the provision through which future needs are met and through which all kinds of new services and commodities are created and supplied. This, of course, refers to speculative *enterprises* and not at all to "pure speculation." In an exchange system severely unbalanced by taxation, speculation may and often does become a further disturbing influence.

CHAPTER 10

# *The Energy of Exchange*

However blind the members of a society may remain as to the integrative and creative effects that grow out of their trafficking to each other of use or possession of services and of commodities into which services have been wrought, however little each may regard the welfare of others or of the whole, still he must give services to others if others shall be either willing or able to return services to him. This symbiotic functioning among the community parts creates and advances the wealth and welfare of both the individual and the group; it catalyzes population energy into creative reaction with environmental energy. It raises both the intensity and the duration of the individual lives and thus the societal integration is effected and maintained. This energy transfer by exchange gives rise to all that fine division of labor and transformation of the materials of the earth that fit it for the habitation and maintenance of mankind. From this comes the emancipation of the individual lives and their fullness of years. And this so far transmutes the environment that increasing quantities of human life may emerge— nature herself being borne increasingly into the human process, form and mould.

The energy that is organized in the bodily structures of men is a biological and not a distinctively social or societal manifestation. Only the energy that flows between and among men can be associative in any sense. At its crudest, this energy that flows among men is dissociative and tends to destroy. At whatever stage of advance, the energy among men that is not balanced mutually in service must expend itself in the impact of compulsions and destruction, conflict and wars. The energy not so transformed cannot be annihilated or blotted out; it remains to be raised to levels of social or societal manifestation. Within the personal and blood-bonded group, the family and the tribe, sufficient is transformed to maintain the bond. At the societal level, a greater portion is transformed. It becomes impersonal, quantitatively reciprocal, contractual and thereby not limited but a service universal among men. Through its advance, conflict recedes, and men realize increasingly their creative, their divine dominion in their world and ever-lengthening days.

The distinctively *societal* process is that of rationally, or numerically balanced, free and reciprocal energy transfers between and among members. This is the basic function or social metabolism whereby the societal life-form grows and is maintained. These energy transfers are mutual. They are carried on by contract and consent and exchange, a purely psychological transformation. This makes it necessary that things be *owned,* for it is not possible to exchange energies or services without the employment of instruments or things. Only those things which are *owned* can be exchanged or used as instruments of service or exchange. This exchange is not transportation; it is the transfer of ownership or title. This is a social and not a physical process. Distribution by contract and exchange, by the voluntary mores of the market, is the only rational (measured and not arbitrary) distribution known to mankind. And this is true whether the subject matter of contract, the thing—property—the ownership of which is being socially distributed, be nature itself—land—or things fabricated therefrom. It is in actuality the social act or service of conveying ownership or title, in whole or in part, by sale or lease, that the democracy of the market reciprocally rewards. The convention of ownership is, therefore, necessary with respect to the things of nature, or land, no less than with respect to the things of artifice and production in order that the social energy which men have for each other may be contractually exchanged and thus take the form of services to the respective recipients and in freedom unite them into an organic whole.

The social organism, like every other complex life-form, is an integration and organization of lesser organisms, an assemblage of constituent and more or less modified and specialized parts. As its body is a mass and motion integration and organization of parts, so its life and continuance is their integration in time or change—the rhythm of change being the signification of time. This time or change relationship, this energy interchange between its units and parts, is the basic process or general function whereby the higher organization grows and maintains itself, and whence arise also all its specific functions and powers. In the social or community organization, this basic metabolism is called trade or exchange, and service is the name for the energy that is interchanged. From this basic, general function, the social organism derives all those specific functions in which it finds its creative dominion and power to transform its world. So far as this reciprocal process is free and unimpaired, the social organism continues to develop and grow into the practice of its powers; when it is unbalanced or constrained, the organic structure is shaken, the functioning of its specialized individuals and parts is impaired, and thus they languish and live shorter lives.

Just as every particular derives from and is still a part of its universal, so every life-form, biological or social, constitutes itself out of its environment. It is created from the whole of which it is still a part, and from the whole it must constantly draw its substance and its strength—all of the energy with which it is endowed. Its capacity to draw this energy depends upon its *self*, upon its interior organization, upon the relations and interactions among its own units and parts. If the organization is not destructive of its own parts, it is efficient; its capacity is high; its life duration is long. Whereas the individual man must adjust himself to his environment, the contractually social-ized man gains the power to adjust environment to him. So far as the interactions among its members rise to the level of freedom and service by consent and exchange, so far as free contractual relations supervene on the primitive and compulsive ones, the social or community life-form achieves its growth and power by its functional integration of its higher and ampler individual lives. Conversely, every encroachment of compulsive power, either anarchical or political and governmental, upon the fields of service that are ruled by voluntary contract, consent and exchange, reduces the life and power of the individuals and thus the vitality and length of days of the society itself. To the extent that this basic metabolism of the society is inhibited or impaired, so must all its life and power as a living organism decline, and its members become less dominant, more abject—subservient to environment.

CHAPTER 11

## Property the Instrument of Freedom

THE SOCIAL ANALYSIS in terms of energy transfers already considered with reference to a society as a whole should be similarly applicable to any of the specific institutions or functional groups of which society is composed—particularly to that primary and basic institution of contract and exchange, namely, property in land.

The social mechanism for extension of the property and contract relationship of service and exchange into public and community affairs is found in the existing institution of property in land and its resources when that institution is examined with respect to the service to society that it now, silently and wholly unrecognized, carries on—and with a view to its great latent potentialities in the public service field.[1]

The first requisite to community life is a social and consensual holding and distribution of its sites and resources. Until this convention of property exists, no other contractual engagements can be entered into or performed; no goods or services can be produced or exchanged. By common consent of all, the society accepts the claims of those in possession. Thenceforth all *new* changes of possession are by a process of peace and consent, by a contractual distribution in place of the former arbitrary one, giving a social security of possession that in no other manner, nor previously thereto, could be obtained. This making of a *social* distribution of sites and resources by the accepted proprietors is the primary and underlying social service by means of which men achieve the possibility of freedom under a community life of contractual relationships instead of either anarchy or tyranny under those of compulsion and force.

The process of transforming primitive human energy into social and consensual forms begins with the adoption of a proprietary and

---

1. See Chapter 22, Private Property in Land Explained.

contractual relationship among and between the individuals as regards the possession of sites and resources. Upon the security of possession and of property so obtained, each creates for others services and commodities. These created things they pool in a common market and there, in turn, make a proprietary or contractual distribution of these artificial things, precisely as they have first made distribution of the things of nature by the practice of property in land. From this process of property and service by exchange, comes all the abundance, the enlargement, the prolongation and elevation of the individual lives that it is the function of the social organization to serve.

The human energy not so transformed remains destructive, antisocial and predatory, as coercion and slavery, tribute and taxation, governmentalism and war. Whether it be by conquest or by consent, when a population goes predominately political, so far as it foregoes contract and exchange, and either submits to or employs increasing force or guile against its socially interfunctioning members, it is in process of disintegration back towards the wholly pre-social state from which it rose. But it must not be inferred that the appropriate proprietary authority cannot properly resort to all necessary force in order to protect and to serve its properties and lands and thereby serve and protect the persons and effects of their inhabitants against force or compulsion, anarchy or tyranny, of any kind.

The legitimate and constructive use of compulsions or restraints is upon those individuals or groups who attempt other than the exchange relationship by which the society lives—upon those who abandon that relationship temporarily or permanently and adopt the reverse. By such conduct they dissolve their membership and become, for the time at least, outlaw to the social body, and must be restrained until they can redeem themselves into the freedom that membership in the social body alone affords. A community in which violence, either private or public, gets out of hand is in process of disorganization, and all values therein, alike to its owners and to its occupants, ultimately are lost.

Apart from the *fundamental* public service—that of making a social and contractual distribution of the community sites and resources and thereby of all the common benefits and advantages attaching to them—that is constantly being performed by the institution of property in land, the energy supply in the whole community-service field under present existing political administration is basically maintained only by coercion and force. There is no other basic method of revenue for a *political* authority, however established and whether chosen or imposed. Political organizations (unlike the societal) draw their revenues in advance of their promised services, taking by *force majeure* within the limits of public tolerance, and indefinitely beyond by the deceptions of debasing the coinage and otherwise adulterating and inflating the medium of exchange, and by creating public debt in the form of promises which it hopes to repay out of future takings but is seldom if ever able finally to do.[2]

The impact of this overpowering practice of direct and of indirect expropriation upon the societal system of contract and voluntary exchange, however well intended or even necessary under the present state of knowledge, nonetheless inhibits the societal process, destroys values, and brings on widespread distress, recurrent wars and social decline.

All general distress, all world-wide wrongs and wars are fruits of the persistence of men in trying blindly and vainly to conduct their public and general affairs on the basis of compulsion, deceit and default instead of by contract, consent and exchange, as men have learned to conduct almost all of their individual and lesser affairs. The last has been in modern times well learned; the other remains to be learned, and the order of nature decrees that the basic technique be the same. The voluntary contractual relationships of ownership of property and of services exchanged thereby on the basis of agreement and consent need only be extended into the field of community property and services. In the degree that this principle is applied in local community affairs and thence upward to the national and the international, the vast available but unsocial-ized human energy can be brought into creative service and only thus cease to

---

2. For a high illumination of this matter of public debt repayment, see H. Scherman, *The Promises Men Live By*, New York, Random House, 1938.

manifest itself in coercive sovereignties, destructive tyrannies and recurrent wars.

Survival and advancement seem to be the prerogatives only of those organizational forms, biological or social, in which the associated members, whether simple cells or highly organized individual units, are best and most served by free energy transformations and exchanges among themselves, and in which the lives of the constituent units are in this manner most advanced and prolonged. This process is the efficient employment by a population of its vital energy, above that requisite for reproduction and replacements. It is the transformation of this surplus energy, by specialization of ownership and services, into service forms freely distributed by voluntary exchange for the automatic elevation of the units of which the population is composed. Quality, value and beauty are selective; they arise from voluntary choosing among various alternatives. They spring from that higher individual power and determination that gives freedom from compulsions and liberty to choose. They are social products and derivatives proceeding from the higher energy endowments and potentialities which the social process of exchanging energy, in free contractual relationships, confers upon the individual lives.

This building up of the life and energy of the unit seems to be the prime function of the social organization. A coincident function appears to be to transform and rebuild, through exchange or cooperative power, the natural world into correspondence with its population's needs and dreams. The ultimate and total function of the societal life-form may well be a progressive and indefinite extension and elaboration of individual life and power in a progressively and indefinitely transformed world.

A society has three basic needs. It continues as a society only so far as it finds creative and non-destructive ways to serve and satisfy these needs. It must have security from violence, that its members may have the services of property by free exchange and the consequent high subsistence and favorable conditions that are necessary to an abundant, a creative and thereby a spiritual life. These three needs, security, property, and spirituality, are supplied through the institutions of politics and government, of commerce and trade, and of religion and the arts. These institutions evolve successively as *Citadel, Market* and *Altar,* the Citadel to maintain freedom from violence, to guard alike against the aggressor from without and the unruly from within, the Market to provide abundance in the necessities of life and the Altar to practice the non-necessitous, the spontaneous and inspirational, the spiritual and esthetic recreations and arts. The first is necessary to the second, the second to the third; but the third, the Altar, is the end-in-itself, the life of creative freedom, above all necessity—the spiritual realm. Upon the free development, differentiation and interaction of these primary institutions, all social advancement depends.

CHAPTER 12

## *Citadel, Market and Altar*

ALL ACTUALITY, all reality that can be experienced, is energy, or *action*. It is composite of mass (as force or inertia), motion, and time. Mass is primordial. Mass generates motion. And out of mass and motion proceeds time, repetition, rhythm, the procession and duration of time. Every organization, every organism, is similarly evolved. From atoms to stars, particles and masses exhibit motion; out of this motion and mass proceeds frequency, periodicity, duration, time.

The individual man is himself similarly organized. He develops a physical and mechanical, a chemical and nutritional and a ratio-volitional system. These three correspond with mass, motion and duration in the less highly organized energy of common experience. The chemical system is an outgrowth of the mechanical; the volitional proceeds from the interaction of the mechanical and chemical. In point of function, the chemical system supplies all energy to the mechanical, and the volitional system coördinates the chemical and the mechanical into functions and ends that for the period of its life satisfy needs and gratify desires. Such is the organization of individual men—of the organism large numbers of which, when organized on the basis of mutual and reciprocal services within the confines of a common environment or community, form the social organism, or society.

This higher organism contains all the structures and parts of its constituent members; and it is itself an organic unit in virtue of its similarly three-fold constitution and its additional functions and powers. Being constituted not only of large numbers of men but of their successive generations as well, the societal life-form indefinitely transcends its individual lives not only in its magnitude and complexity but also in the indefinitely extended duration of its life. Just as the physiological body is entirely renewed by continuous replacement of its myriad short-lived cells, so is the social body renewed and maintained in the succession of its generations of men. And as the lives of men are longer than the lives of their ephemeral cells, so does the duration of a society extend indefinitely through the successive generations of its myriad individual lives. In all its magnitudes—mass, motion and time—the society vastly surpasses the units of which it is composed. But, above all, there is a *qualitative* transcendence as well.

The physiological cell accumulates energy into cellular structure, transforms chemical into physiological energy and disintegrates. The societal "cell" accumulates energy into its structure, transforms physiological energy into social-ized energy by exchange of services, and then disintegrates. The society itself accumulates its "cells" or individuals into the social structure and integrates social-ized or exchange energy into the structure of its environing world. This is the unique, the *transcendent,* function of the social organism: *to re-create* its own world. No other form of life possesses this power. The function of plants, animals and of men (except when organized into this exchange relationship) is to live and to leave progeny, and little or nothing more. But it is the function of a society, through its metabolism of exchange, to create anew its world in ways that raise its individuals' length of lives, the while extending indefinitely its own.

The social organism, like its constituent individuals, also has three great and fundamental institutions, the separate functions of which are *coercion, coöperation* and *consecration*. Their symbols are: *Citadel, Market* and *Altar*—a department of physical force, a department of services measured and exchanged, and a department of the free and spontaneous life of the individuals. These three correspond with what in lower forms of organization are mass, motion and time—substance, power and duration. The Citadel repels assault from without, subversion from within. The Market is an outgrowth of the Citadel; the Altar arises from the interaction of Citadel and Market. In point of function, the Market supplies all service energy to the Citadel. By its ministrations to basic necessities and needs, it releases free and spontaneous energies of men to the practice of the intellectual, the esthetic and creative arts—all those sports and recreations of body and mind towards which they freely incline and aspire.

Like all the creations of nature, man is himself constituted of the energy that for a certain duration is relatively stabilized in his structure and form. This stability is maintained by the reciprocal action of his organized parts in receiving, transferring and transforming, directly and indirectly by absorption and nutrition, the unstructured (unstabilized) energy that into him constantly flows.

The three basic structures of the individual man are: the mechanical, consisting of the skeleton, muscles, tissues, etc., the chemical, including the nutritional, circulatory, reproductive and internal glandular tracts, and the quasi-electrical or neural system of energy transfers, with its necessary structural parts. His biological existence and continuance as an individual depends on a high differentiation of these structural systems. This makes possible the reciprocal relations wherein they have their functional unity. The first transmits and transforms mechanical energy; the second transmits and transforms the energies, chiefly solar, chemically structured in foods, providing all metabolism and cell proliferation, both genetic and somatic; the third employs and transmits those subtle unstructured kinds of energy that are manifested as currents or waves.

The nutritional and nervous systems are dependent on the muscular and mechanical for their ponderable means of operations; the mechanical and neural depend for their subsistence upon the nutritional; and the mechanical and nutritional depend upon the neural for their functional coördination. The successful organism has highly differentiated mechanical, chemical and electrical structures with correspondingly coördinated functions and powers.

There is a resemblance and a like division in the body, the population, of a societal life-form. It has one structure and department that deals primarily with physical, mechanical and compulsive force. This embraces the entire governmental and political organization of which the Citadel is taken as the appropriate symbol.

It has a second great structure or system that maintains the social body in the bonds of service and free exchange. It provides for the physical needs and satisfactions, a high level of subsistence as to material things and all the measurable values of commerce and exchange, resulting in great amelioration and progressive re-creation of the physical world. This is the contractual system of free engagements and accord—the social metabolism under which division of labor and exchange takes place, so far as private or public violence does not prevent or destroy. This social metabolism consists of services reciprocally exchanged—the anabolism of maintenance and production and the catabolism of consumption or of depreciation—, all effectuated by the measured and balanced exchanges of the market. The chosen symbol for this great department of subsistence, nutrition and assimilation is the Market or the Market Place.

The third great structure and system of society has to do with those transfers and transformations of subtler and less ponderable energies without which the social life-form would remain insensible of its own life and incapable of any rational development and growth. This embraces all matters of intellect and imagination, of religion, recreation and the arts—all those manifestations of vital energy that the efficient technology of the Market liberates to the free and optional disposals of the unforced individual will. The accepted symbol here is the Altar, representing all things of the mental, the spiritual, the spontaneous, creative and transcendent life.

These three great and all-inclusive departments of a social organism coexist in, interpenetrate, and actually constitute it at all stages of its formation and growth. They are composed basically of individuals, but also of the sub-organizations or institutions of many kinds into which individuals are functionally grouped and in various of which many individuals act in specialized capacities at the same or at different times. The more differentiation there is among and between the social structures of the *Citadel,* the *Market* and the *Altar,* the more coöperative they may be and the more creative and enduring the society becomes. As in all other organisms, all organizations, unity and continuity depend on the coördination of diverse parts; structural differentiation alone makes possible the functional integration.

Each of these three departments serves the others and thereby the whole, and each in turn is served by the whole. The Citadel, by its services of security and protection, makes the Market possible and is, in turn, maintained by it. The Market, by its material services, nourishes also the Altar. It provides and releases the energy with which the whole world of the intellect and imagination, of science, religion and the esthetic arts, is carried on—the energy with which all aspiration and advance is achieved—and the physical conditions and foundation upon which these rise and depend. Yet the world of the Altar, in its turn, serves both the Market and the Citadel. It brings intellect and creative imagination into the world of production and exchange, improving its efficiency, expanding its scope and elevating its satisfactions. And into the Citadel itself comes the radiance of the Altar, giving promise in the fullness of time to tame crude violence into guardianship and protection, and to turn government itself from rulership and destruction into a vast agency of public service through the extension of proprietary administration into community services and affairs.

Thus government is destined to be assimilated into the voluntary exchange system for the performing of community services, limiting the restraints and compulsions of the Citadel to guardianship and protection of the society against violations of its members or its processes, and to the social rehabilitation of any who may alienate themselves and thus become outcasts, for the time, by their antisocial perpetrations.

Likewise, the Market is destined to be more and more assimilated into the spontaneous technique of the Altar, in which services are performed for spiritual satisfactions and imponderable rewards. The system of measured exchanges governs the production and distribution only of those physical and material things and services that are necessary to sustain life, but which do not of themselves advance it as do the spontaneous and creative, spiritual services of the Altar.

The positive social trend is towards the evolution of rulership into service,—Citadel into Market—and service for measured recompense into service for imponderable satisfactions and rewards,—Market into Altar—and thus towards a complete supremacy of the intellectual, artistic, and spiritual aspect of human life and affairs.

Thus the things that are eternal, that have the utmost duration, take highest rank as the third term in the essential trinity that constitutes society, just as the third term also ranks highest in the triune reality of science—mass, motion and time—and in the Ultimate and Absolute Trinity—*Substance, Power* and *Eternity*. Science can formulate and reduce to principle or law only such processes as continue and repeat. *Eternality* is the third and highest aspect of that Unity and Reality with which theology and science are alike conditioned and concerned.

To these fortunate tendencies and correlations that exist and carry on among the three institutions that together constitute the unity of society, all social advancement is to be referred; but like government, economics, and religion in their separate techniques, these higher relationships between them are as yet only blindly and empirically applied and hence only partially and insufficiently serve men's aspirations and desires. Rational and conscious realization of these high correlations through vision and intellect awaits the science of society. This new child of the Altar is destined to disclose the existing normal processes and potentialities of the social organization, despite the partiality and incompleteness with which they are now realized, and thus open the whole field of social relationships to the possibilities of a rational and practical scientific technique.

Meanwhile, pending full disclosure of the existing positive and creative relationships, the men of the Market, as individuals, still corrupt their operations with a modicum of force and fraud, while special interests and organized groups invoke governmental power and privilege to the detriment of the public prosperity and against the welfare of all. The Altar itself is invaded and preempted by the powers of the Citadel; and the trafficking of the Market is perverted to corrupt, degrade, and enslave the intellectual, artistic and spiritual services that in the institutions of the Altar are born and belong. The rude technique of the Citadel, of government, is physical and mechanical. It is not properly applicable to society itself or to any of its parts any more than the mechanical parts of one's body should strike the other parts down; but only to those persons whose acts are presently inimical to it either from within or by forcible aggression from without. When the Citadel impinges on the Market, it injures the system of production and exchange on which both subsist. Thus an increasing tyranny over the Market destroys the very fountainhead of freedom. Little by little, men are more and more enslaved to the state. As freedom to exchange is progressively infringed, production necessarily declines, until even the Citadel itself at last finds no means of support. Barbarism returns and society must begin anew empirically to evolve.

CHAPTER 13

# The Social-ization of Government

ALL THE SECURITY, all the capacity to permanently endure that a society enjoys comes from the convention of property and the exercise of ownership through the contractual technique of the Market. The Citadel itself doubtless depended for its origin on voluntary relationships such as "commendation" that prevailed prior to the contractual relationship of land lords (land *givers* or *distributors*) and the protected freeholders or users, these last being unforced men having none but reciprocal or exchange obligations towards their lords. This is the fundamental application of the free social relationship that conquest by alien arms or corruption and tyranny of the Citadel have so often perverted and finally destroyed. Any organization consists in the mutual functioning of its parts. Even a successful tyranny depends upon some mutuality of obligation among those who are so organized as to impose it.

Instead of continuing its encroachments upon the free system of the Market, circumscribing the field of freedom and contract, thus undermining the original principle even of its own formation, the Citadel needs to engage itself only with the prevention and punishment of force or equivalent fraud, and to accept the advantages of the *contractual* process in the performance of its public and community services. This social-izing of government itself cannot fail to follow upon discovery of the presently existing operation of property in land and resources as the democratic distributive service through a contractual as opposed to a political and coercive process. This discovery will render obvious the profits and the advantages to all of extending this proprietary public service, contractually performed, into the field of public protection against official and political, as well as against criminal, invasions of personal liberty and property and of the right of the society to exist.

This assumption of responsibility for public protection, and eventually for all community services, on the part of the basic proprietary system, namely, the proprietors of the community territory and lands, adequately organized for unity of policy and concert of action, will introduce a veritable *social* technique and a solvent system of public services in lieu of the prevailing political tyranny—whether this be absolute and unlimited or watered down with popular elections and the ever ephemeral and crumbling barriers of constitutional or other attempted limitations.

When the public community authority rests only upon community ownership and thus has no coercive but only free contractual and therefore mutual service relationships with the community members as recipients of the community services, both protective and positive, the entire available life-years of the population can be freely engaged in the production and mutual exchange of services and goods, and in the free artistries of the creative spirit, the emancipated mind.

The free technique that is peculiar to the market—the freedom to serve and to be served by consent and exchange—as it becomes more universal, will so release the distribution of physical things that their production will rise far above the material needs of mankind. The lengthening life-years of the race need then be devoted only in small part to the physical needs to which they are bound. This efficiency and economy at the physical base emancipates the energies of the population from the compulsions imposed by their material and physical needs and releases them to the unforced and spontaneous expression of creative power. It releases a whole population to do what in the crude and only partly social-ized state is denied to the many and reserved to the few—the practice of creative artistries in all the free adventures of spirit and mind. This is the free realm of spirit rising out of but transcending the compulsions imposed by the physical and necessitous world. The things created here are *real* in the sense that they are abiding; they do not pass away.

These creations of inspiration and joy, these services of the spirit and imagination, transcend the material services of the Market as the free and voluntary engagements of contract in the Market transcend the crude compulsive and destructive techniques of government and all the strongholds of protection and power. But these things of the spirit—children of the Altar, the temple, symposium and school—in their intangible forms cannot be traded or exchanged; nor need they be, for in this realm the givers are enriched in the giving as well as those who receive. Their original and inspired services and creations, their discoveries and formulations, can be performed only once, but they remain the eternal heritage of mankind. As those services are esthetic and spiritual, so is their reward. None other is sought nor even desired.

## CHAPTER 14

## *Climate and Conquest*

THE DEVELOPMENT and practice of the contractual relationship, upon which all societal organization depends, is much influenced by climate and terrain.

Where nature is least bountiful and least accordant to the biologic needs of man, as in polar lands, and where she is most bountiful, as in the warm, moist and fertile lands, human life is either most precarious or most abject. In both conditions life is maintained by what can be appropriated from the environment with but little change. In the one case, the process of appropriation is enormously difficult and even impossible, except through the intimate and immediate co-operation of members of familial groups or tribes. Even thus, the resources are too few and sparse and the conditions too rigorous to admit of either a prosperous or a populous community.

But in warm and fertile lands the ultimate advantage of the better conditions is not great. Here not nature but man himself oppresses man. Even under the most primitive economy, nature's response to the labors of one can afford subsistence for two. Hence the predatory instincts of wandering tribes, carried over into the settled community, determine that one class shall serve while another rules. Thus a high degree of social organization is not found at either environmental extreme.

But under the conditions of moderately high latitude as in the temperate zones, and at moderately high altitudes in the tropics, the predatory relationship is too inefficient to prevail. Here the contractual relations of division of labor and exchange, industry and trade, most tend to spring up. Where the physical conditions are highly diverse, changeable and relatively sparse, only the freer and more efficient social relationships can prevail. Moreover, there is stimulation to the development of intelligence, versatility and personal competency and power, in contrast to the enervation of masters and the degradation of slaves in the constant and more bounteous climes. This seems to account for the historic conquests of the ages coming always from the higher latitudes and altitudes and impinging on the warm, flat and fertile lands, wherein the victors accept, adopt and maintain the compulsive technique of the vanquished, with its attendant personal degradations and deteriorations, and are in turn themselves enervated and overwhelmed.

As trade relations geographically and in other ways expand, specialization develops and all productivity is raised. The enslavement of persons gradually gives way to depredations on trade. The personal enslavement of individuals gives way to the less palpable but more remunerative mass enslavement of populations by official depredations on their property, production and trade by the imposition of taxes at home and the exaction of tribute abroad. This gives rise to colonial systems in which power follows conquest, still proceeding from the colder and dominating the warmer parts of the earth. Personal absolutism gives way to political tyranny, chattel slavery to political sovereignty.

Thus two great systems have developed, the system of property, service and production with distribution by *contract* under mutual desire, consent and exchange, and the system of depredation by coercion and force under some form of political organization, domestic or foreign, drastic or mild. Thus is the House of Man divided against itself. Mild governments practice a degree of warfare upon the productivity of freedom under contractual relations; drastic ones make war in greater degree against the productive *processes* that they live upon and destroy, alike during their periods of armed peace and in the convulsions of their international wars. These wars consolidate cities into states, states into super-states and colonial empires. Empire expands, on the one hand, by conquest and annexation; on the other, by the defensive alliances in federations in which the stronger ally always dominates the league or some central power subjugates the federated whole. Each conquering imperial power, in its turn, either annexes its rivals by conquest or by new alliance, and the last federation is itself absorbed. The cycle of political history is the story of centralization and decentralization, the consolidation and collapse of sovereign, war-making powers; it is a swing from many petty sovereignties through the anarchy of wars to the world-wide tyranny of a *Pax Romana* and the swing back again. Such is the long rhythm in the world history of political power.

The wars of the current century are an imperial strife for compulsive dominance over the Atlantic world. They are but a mammoth modern replica of the ancient struggles that consummated in Roman dominance over the Mediterranean world. But whatever Atlantic power at last prevails will reckon with Oriental empire under some Asiatic banner in contest for supremacy over the Pacific and, thereby, a destructive dominance over all the world.[1]

This self-liquidating technique of the political powers leading to final "survival of the fittest" in the world of empire is but a global exemplification of the Darwinian process of struggle and survival that seems universal to every realm of conflict, compulsion and force, and which none but the social order, the creative power of contractual relationships, can finally transcend.

From the socio-biologic and natural-science point of view, the current struggle for world supremacy, like all its predecessor conflicts, is a re-arrangement of the mass, motion and duration factors or components, a degradation of human or population energy to a lower order of relationship and organization.

This descent through political strife into a more acutely anti-social relationship among the nations of men is only the crude manifestation of erstwhile social energy that has been de-social-ized by the impairment and abrogation of contractual relationships. Until service and not force becomes the instrument of government, while war continues to be the only consummation of governmental power, a population must lose at last even in victories all that it ever feared to lose in defeat.

1. This paragraph was written before December, 1942.

CHAPTER 15

## *The Tragedy of Public Works*

EXTENSIONS of governmental power, long continued, are always followed by social decline. Periods of transition between social growth and social decline are marked by great proliferations of political pageantries in state-supported arts and architecture and public works. These are the flowers that spring from social decay. They garnish dying dynasties with temples and tombs, pyramids and hanging gardens; they clothe moribund democracies in Periclean beauty, and preside with Augustan grandeur where republics are enslaved. Even when they are not produced by the forced labor of captives and slaves, great public works nonetheless rest upon the depredations of coercive governments invading the freedom and ending the bounty of the contractual world.

The supposed services of government, though often praised, are seldom weighed against their tragic cost. The destructive effect upon civilization is often obscured by the obvious near-term (but ultimately self-defeating) advantages to special individuals and classes who are the recipients of its special and insidious favors.

This more comprehensive view discloses the universal trend of all compulsive relationships towards a shortening of the average life span. Life becomes less abundant as it becomes more enslaved. The wages of social wrongdoing is not abundant life and length of days either for the individual or for his race. Failure to utilize constructively in contractual ways and service forms the vital energy with which men are endowed, leaves it untamed to degrade them in peace and destroy them in war. In periods of active warfare, the casualties of battle and of disease are but the shortening of lives, and a more than temporary population decline is averted only by the increased biologic reproductiveness that appears always to be stimulated by wars.

Thus the technique of government by force, compulsion and war, is so opposed to the technique of service by contract and exchange that it brings about an opposite change in the organization of energy that constitutes a population into a societal life-form. The *durational* element, the quality by which it endures and abides, is diminished with a qualitative loss, and the gross quantity of the energy is conserved only by the higher reproductivity of the shortened lives at a lower qualitative level of organization and life. These seem to be the steps by which civilizations lapse back through organized tyrannies into unorganized barbarisms, in which subsistence falls so low that large numbers of lives cannot be maintained; for, even though rapidly born, they must quickly languish and die.

Does fate then set iron bounds against the achievement of an enduring social organization and abundance of life? The answer is found in the potencies of freedom as manifested in the voluntarism of exchanging services and goods under contractual engagements as to their distribution and flow. When the practicableness of this technique in the field of public and community services and affairs has become well disclosed, it is as certain to be profitably applied as were the underlying principles of physical phenomena profitably applied in the technical arts as they came to be known.

The desire for profit or recompense for services seems to have been the prime individual motivation underlying all the advances of civilization that have been brought about through reduction of scientific discoveries to practice and the merchandising of them as products or services to the generality of mankind.

Similar results under similar motivation and for similar rewards cannot fail to follow upon similar scientific disclosures—in terms of the objective standards employed by all the natural sciences—concerning the phenomenon of society as an energy flow. This may occur either soon or late; all things must await their day. Meanwhile, political governments can only repress, inhibit and disorder the societies they are assumed to serve. Such governments, practicing force, are restrained by oppositions, and the successful opposition is in turn opposed until the society, on which they all-unconsciously prey, becomes too weak of will to oppose or resist and through a long tyranny expires.

But the emergence of new orders and relationships in nature, when they come, come quickly. This is true, in general, of all evolutionary advance. There is a long, long darkness but the full light comes suddenly once it dawns. And there are "signs and portents" that may be the heralds of a social dawn. Modern science had its ancient precursors, but its dawn is yet young. Its slanting rays have opened many erstwhile mysteries of the natural world so that great and wide services to mankind could be profitably performed. We need not doubt the potency of its rising rays to dissolve the mists that shroud mystic beauties and potentialities in the social order, far transcending those of the natural and material world.

CHAPTER 16

## *The Basic Social Pattern*

ORDER is said to be Heaven's first law. It is that into which the dynamic cosmic energy ever increasingly tends to evolve. For in all organization of energy, from the humblest to the highest, a single basic pattern ever prevails. Whatever be the structure, be it inorganic or organic, the non-living or the living form, it is a composition or organization of lesser units in interrelationships of reciprocal freedom whereby a higher unity is created. This higher unity is the product of the order and harmony that prevails among the lesser units of which it is composed. This functioning of the higher unit depends on the orderly interfunctioning of its component units and parts, and the more harmonious and perfect this interfunctioning the longer will be the functioning period, the living duration of the higher unit that thus they compose. And the functioning periods of the lesser units themselves, through their creative interrelations one with another and with the whole, are lengthened and prolonged. The cosmic energy evolves into ever more enduring manifestations and forms, and the more orderly the pattern, the more perfect and enduring the form. Thus do the more orderly and harmonious organizational forms increasingly and of necessity prevail.

A society, like an individual, depends for its duration upon the orderly and non-collisional interfunctioning of the organic units of which it is composed. Like the individual, it must be born into a specific organic pattern and, like the individual, it can normally develop and mature only into the basic pattern in which it was born.

Men do have associative relationships prior to society, but like those of insects and animals, all these relationships are biological and particular, not appertaining to any general society but only to limited consanguineous groups, tribes or clans. For these pre-societal relationships can obtain only among individuals who are in direct and conscious contact and communication in the manner of packs, herds, flocks or swarms in which there is no organic unity extending beyond the particular blood-bonded group. Inter-group antagonisms of necessity tend to prevail, for these biological associations have no general and impersonal system of service and exchange and therefore but little if any productive power over their environment. They consume without replacing whatever environment affords and thus tend to make it less habitable for themselves. Conflict or armed neutrality is as natural for them as is war among the sovereign political organizations that consume and destroy but do not produce or create. For among political powers, as among biological and tribal exclusional groups, survival arises upon gains that involve losses to others and not upon the mutual welfare that springs from creation by voluntary coöperation and exchange. Not the tribal and instinctive nor yet the political and coercive, but only the *societal* organization creates the means to great abundance and through this a higher quality and duration of life.

Emergence of this higher and wider, this more general and inclusive relationship, marks the birth of the truly societal life form. Within the society, familial and biological relationships still subsist, but they do not distinguish it. For they involve dominance and submission or, in their higher forms, responsibility and loyalty and love. But these fine amenities are restricted. They do not extend beyond the conscious awareness of personal and biological bonds. What does distinguish the societal organization is its system of *measured* and thereby *rational* exchanges. This practice of *impersonal,* contractual relations, wherein men come not into collision but into *rational* accord, lifts the level of their lives by creative transformations, each for others, of the environment in which they live.

Employment of the contractual process instead of the political or coercive for the holding and transfer of sites and resources establishes the institution of property in land and thereby brings into being a community occupied by the societal life-form. For with this basic social-ization[1] of the things of nature that no man creates, it becomes possible for individuals, or corporate bodies of them, to hold possession by title instead of by force as the authority for all possession and exchanges of things both natural and artificial. This authority to make contracts with respect to any property is what constitutes its ownership and accounts for its being property, in the societal sense.

The birth of a society, properly as such, occurs when erstwhile nomads or other merely blood-bonded groups cease their dependence on mere animal instincts as to their occupancy of territory and possession of natural things. It begins with their gradual adoption of private ownership and thereby of the contractual process for the rational distribution and the secure individual possession of these natural things. For any large numbers to unite in community as distinguished from family life, the first essential is a rational instead of an arbitrary or coercive mode in the distribution of sites and lands. The granting of social authority to make contracts with respect to sites and resources is what constitutes social and individual instead of tribal and collective property in land. Thereafter, the land is held and distributed not arbitrarily, but under a moral (*per mores*) sanction and title, an accepted social authority to make valid contracts concerning its possession, transfer or use. Thus ownership is more than mere possession. Savages, even animals may have that. There may be possession without title and there may be title without possession, but only under a socially sanctioned title can valid contracts—capable of being performed—be made. The making and performing of such contracts is not a political privilege, not the exclusion but the inclusion of others. It is a vital social function performed under

---

1. The word *socialization* is used in its scientific signification, not in the popular sense, which is precisely the reverse. In the objective science of society, things are *socialized* when they are brought under proprietary administration by their owners for the use, benefit or service to others through free contractual relationships of administration and distribution. All real and personal property or its products that is held by its owners for the use or service of others as purchasers is thereby *socialized* property. All property that is under owner-administration as *capital* is *socialized* property.

social authority and rewarded by an automatic social recompense. The recompense for this distributive public service is called *ground rent,* often miscalled *unearned* income or increment.

Any dense populations must have lived first in warm, flat and fertile regions of the earth. In these more clement lands, communities were formed and civilizations began. Here the earth was so fruitful not all needed to work; slavery could be practiced and the population yet live. In dealing with his community inhabitants, the patriarch or proprietor could depart from the voluntary mode based on kinship or contract, and tax or enslave them. In their condition of ease, the original authorities either lapsed from their protective to the political and predatory relationship or themselves fell victim to other men who seized their places and usurped their powers. In proprietary communities, voluntary rent or rent service became perverted into forced labor. Thus freeholders became serfs or slaves, and the yoke of tribute and taxation fell on all those who were not directly and personally enslaved. Whether by default or by defeat of patriarchs or proprietors, it was through lapses of the village authority that the predatory political sovereignties anciently arose and the political institution of slavery, maintained by the power of the state, continued throughout all ancient times. And with the modern passing of crude chattel slavery, it is by extension of their tax-taking and other compulsive powers that the political sovereignties of modern times have made their world-wide rule supreme.

The early deterioration of free communities by their transformation into political sovereignties took place chiefly in those lush regions where slavery and taxation could be practiced and the inhabitants yet live, and where the marching and marshalling of armies, the recapture of slaves and the rigors of government could be easily applied. But in lands of high latitude or high altitude and of rugged terrain, the sparseness of natural subsistence forbade the inefficiencies of a servile state. Nor would such terrain favor military operations, other than defensive, or the capture and recapture of slaves. In such lands, men must practice the free relationships of mutual service in order to survive. They alone have limited their sovereignties. Their kings and councils have been heroes and leaders, the lords (Anglo-Saxon: *givers*) and exemplars, and not the drivers and rulers of men. Through the ages, and from such sparse origins, came the great warriors who conquered the political slave states of the lusher lands, adopted their enervating ways and were in their turn by virile conquerors deposed. The grasslands and the hills have ever bred the power to win—and lose—dominion of the olive and the palm.

When free barbarians took the lands no longer ruled by Rome, they left their wandering ways and adopted the settled community mode of life. But they did not at once form political cities or any slave states. They brought with them a strong native tendency towards the uncorrupted proprietary or free feudal type of community organization, the basic social pattern, in which tribal wanderers and instinctive village groups seem first always to emerge. But on the Continent, such free institutions were corrupted at their birth. Only the formal pattern, without its substance of liberty, prevailed. Influenced by the political philosophy and the legendary glories of once imperial Rome, the free barbarian leaders became corrupted by the spirit of their new surroundings into despotic princes and kings. Hence the new social beginnings, though they took the proprietary *form,* were wholly perverted by grafting on that form the arbitrary and compulsive methods of a political sovereignty or state. The free contractual relationship between the public authority and the inhabitants, between land lord and free men, did not develop. Compulsory levies supported by force were instituted in place of voluntary rent induced by the services recompensed by it. Proprietors became tax masters instead of land lords. In consequence, there could be no free holders, hence no free men. The result was not the original free feudal or proprietary system but a political and military feudalism of despotic rulers over serfs and slaves.

This political method of public administration impoverished the communities and incited them to the alliances and wars that brought on their consolidation into petty kingdoms and eventually into nationalistic states. And these, by further conquests, expanded into colonial powers, rivals for empire as the Mediterranean slave powers once struggled for dominion over the world.

But in the remoteness of ancient Britain, after the Roman prestige and power was gone, the Anglo-Saxon invaders emerged out of mere tribal solidarity into proprietary communities untouched by the traditions and the politics of Rome. In this remoteness, the Anglo-Saxon system of proprietary administration by land lords for free men evolved, and through almost five centuries became the rude but free society that flowered in the "Golden Age of Alfred" until it was destroyed by the Norman power and its liberties submerged under a political and essentially totalitarian rule.

Social origins are necessarily obscure, yet history and anthropology unite in evidence that as men develop their sense of personality, of having individuality apart from the family or the tribe, then, circumstances permitting, they pass beyond their merely instinctive and familial groupings, and the authentic society based on individual property and the free contractual relationship begins to emerge. In lands widely remote, as in early Mexico and ancient Japan, there is evidence of merely tribal groupings having given way to property and contractual good faith in respect to security in the individual occupancy of land. And in Saxon England, owing doubtless to its isolation, the continuance was long. In a people who had come not as roving tribes on land but organized for migration by sea, functional individuality could the more easily supersede mere familial unity, and the reciprocal obligations of contract supersede the merely consanguineous bonds. As this new relationship developed on land, the parties to it were the *de facto* accepted public authority on the one hand and the several free holders or free men, usually heads of families, who, together with the subordinate aides or employees of the accepted ownership and authority, constituted the general population. The prime subject matter of this contractual relationship was necessarily sites and resources—the separately and exclusively occupied portions of the community lands. For it was only through their occupancy of particular sites that the free holders could receive or in any way avail themselves of the common or community services appurtenant thereto or make any use of the common and public, the unenclosed portions of the land. And it was only from the hand of a public authority acting as *owner* of the community, and not as ruler over the persons and properties of its inhabitants, that these community services could be obtained by voluntary contract and for market value received. The first "essential public service," essential to the very existence of any truly free community, was not to tax or otherwise rule the inhabitants but to safeguard the whole community—as a public service to the common-wealth—against violence, whether from without or from within.

For the services to free men of *contractually* distributing among them the sites or lands so safeguarded and protected, a socially limited amount of ground rent or of rent service was rendered. Thus the consideration on both sides was services—the service of giving a societal, non-political distribution of the sites, including the common protection and all other advantages appertaining to them, on the one hand, and, on the other hand, the services rendered up voluntarily by free men as rent, the market equivalent of the public services so received.

Under this basic contractual relationship, imposing neither forced labor nor forced payments as taxation upon the thereby free men, the community became a safe and secure, a well served place for the production, ownership and the like contractual distribution of other forms of property, or of their products or services, as *capital* properties. Thus, under a customary covenant of "quiet possession" in exchange for an amount of rent limited by the custom or agreements of the market, it was possible for "free enterprise" to begin.[2]

The transition from pure nomadism to the proprietary system was not always, if ever, immediate and direct. In Eastern Europe and also among the more advanced aboriginal North Americans, there is much record of village communities in which tribes or clans dwelt for long periods in a state of folk organization intermediate between the nomadic and the truly societal. In this form of organization, the individual is but little differentiated from the group. Pride

---

2. Free enterprise is properly so called because none of the parties is under domination by any other. All the parties to it, as such, are equal in authority over their respective persons and properties.

in tribal membership and acceptance seems the chief cohesive bond. Subsistence is consumed immediately from the environment, whether by fishing and hunting, as on the American Northwest Coast, or, most generally, by a primitive agriculture. There is no general system of contractual or measured exchange; only crude and occasional barter, and that only with more or less alien clans or tribes. There is systematic allocation of fishing waters, hunting grounds or plots for cultivation, usually outside of the community itself, under tribal custom and regulation that many writers have regarded as a kind of free communism in land. These village communities are essentially biological and instinctive rather than rational, for without separate jurisdiction over property, the individual is merged in the mass, and there is no basis for any quantified and thereby rational system of free contract and exchange. For lack of any public authority, proprietary or political, such communities are poorly organized either for aggression or for defense. Throughout much ancient time, even into recent centuries, such weakly organized, instinctive village units have either developed beyond patriarchy toward the free feudal and then, through corruption or conquest, become political and predacious, or—more frequently—they have been broken up by political sovereignties extending their realm and rule.

It was the proprietary form of organization, where it developed, that held promise for the future. It is not to be supposed that, in the early making and performing of contracts with respect to quiet possession and enjoyment of community lands by free men under protection of proprietary authority, there was any conscious knowledge or understanding of the societal implications. So far as these are concerned, there is no reason to suppose that, then as now, any plan or intention beyond a blind empiricism prevailed. The strong man in his stronghold and the free man in his freehold were alike unaware of the basic pattern, of the social foundations, for an eventually free world that they laid. Yet it was thus that the transition from barbaric nomadism and village community to the modern civilized community form of organization in all probability was made. The ownership of and the observance of title to property, however much it may be politically infringed, is still the ancient foundation for all the creative relationships of contract and exchange that distinguish the social and civilized from the merely familial and tribal or the completely political and totalitarian mode of life.

Nowhere has this transition from tribalism and mere folk organization into the free community pattern been better exemplified than in the social foundations that were laid in England by the Saxon migrants from beyond the German Sea.[3] The basic English community pattern is diagrammatically set out in figure 3. Here the nucleus of the societal organism is the strong man in his stronghold, like the captain of his ship and crew. Clustered around him are his paid retainers, through whom he defends his community against outside aggression and maintains internal liberty and peace in fulfillment of his covenant of quiet possession in exchange for the rent that maintains him and the services he provides. Thus, under a common defense—a com-*munito*—the truly societal form of life begins. Its structure is analogous to the physical atom and to the biological cell. For in each there is a central nucleus of great stability to which are gathered peripheral elements in non-collisional, reciprocal relations to it and to one another. And just as the physical or the biological structure disintegrates when these free relations are greatly impaired or destroyed, so must any societal organization cease to function and thus cease to exist when its free and reciprocal processes can no longer be performed.

The Western world has been so long indoctrinated with the Norman and the Classical traditions of political rulership over servile-minded and tribute-burdened populations that any suggestion of moulding public institutions to the basic pattern of the proprie-

---

3. Of all tribal peoples, those having the background experience of successful migration by sea are thought to have been thereby best prepared and most free—since ships' crews are recruited across kinship lines—to effect community organization on the societal basis of a rational coöperation by property and contract in lieu of total dependence on kinship and emotional or biological bonds. Hence their basically free, proprietary communities—in high contrast with the tax- and tribute-bonded city sovereignties and slave-bound nationalist states of ancient times. See A. Toynbee, *A Study of History*, London, 1934, Volume II, p. 97.

tary or free feudal communities is almost sure to be decried as a return to slavery and to barbarism itself. Yet history affords the one striking example, already referred to, of proprietary government as contractual services springing up spontaneously out of the merely blood-bonded condition and growing through a half-millennium into a state of freedom and of cultural achievement in sharp contrast to the darkness and degradation that prevailed in its contemporary European world. The Anglo-Saxon community organization culminated in the Alfredian Renaissance. It had its seeds in the Roman evacuation, five hundred years before, to strengthen the hard-pressed legions on the frontier of the Rhine. Into this void came the seaborne Barbarians to build anew in the genius of "men who never would be slaves." For half the dark millennium, the aftermath of Rome, in almost secret isolation, they built their communities on the basis of free men receiving services from and giving services in return to land lords. Once the land was possessed, there was no more offensive war, for there was no public revenue but rent; taxation, like slavery, *as an institution,* was unknown. After Alfred, the Danish invaders laid taxes for eleven years which were continued until the English Edward, coming to the throne, denounced and abolished them as contrary to Anglo-Saxon custom and law. But Norman ideas and example were having their effects in the discord and divisions that laid England open to the Norman arms and victim to the Roman mode of political administration, based on the seizure of property under which Rome herself at last went down.

Rude as were the ages and harsh the times, the Saxon development of proprietary public service was a magnificent example of a society, unperverted by any ideology of public force or of imperial domination, rising through only five centuries to the premier cultural position of its time through development of the proprietary pattern in which it was born.

The Classical precedent and practice of public administration by force is almost universally accepted. In its milder forms, it is exalted as "democratic" and "free." Where it is more drastic and complete, it is accepted as absolute and ineluctable. Even the possibility of an alternative and opposite mode of administration is widely ignored.

# THE BASIC FREE COMMUNITY

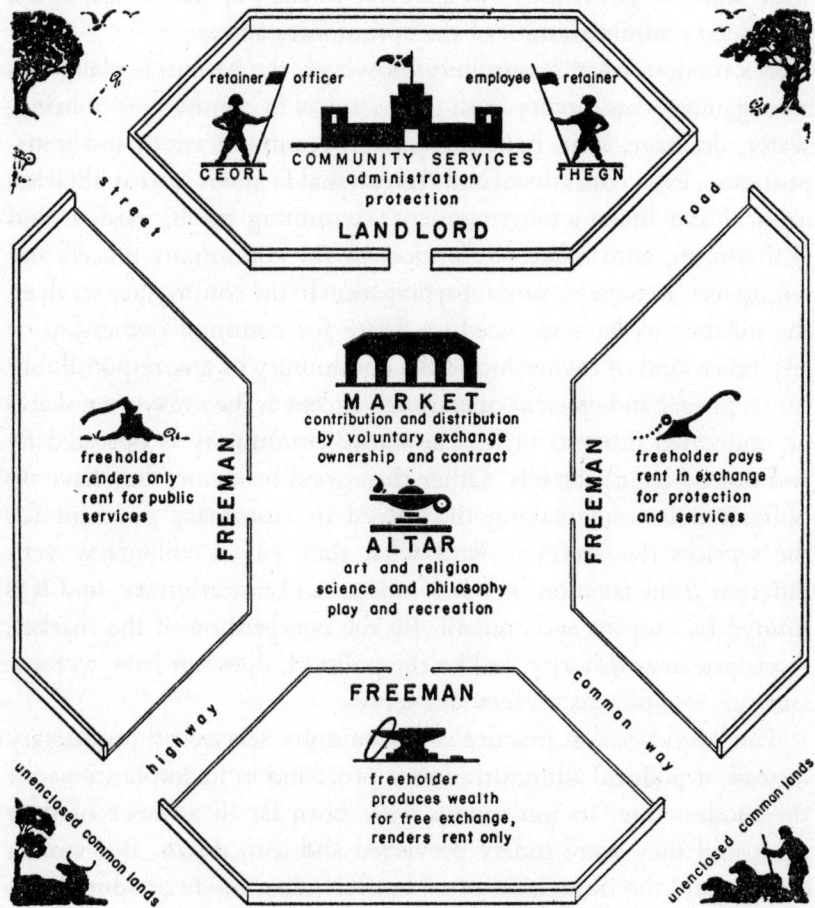

**DIAGRAM ILLUSTRATING IN PRINCIPLE**
- THE ANGLO-SAXON TYPE OF SOCIAL ORGANIZATION
- THE BASIC FREE COMMUNITY
- EMERGENCE OUT OF FAMILIAL ORGANIZATION

*Figure 3.*

And, beyond the basic public service that land owners everywhere unknowingly perform in their *contractual* distribution of sites and resources and lands, there is no present-day example, on a nation-wide scale, of government as a service to the population through a proprietary administration of the community affairs.

In a modern hotel community, however, the pattern is plain. It is an organized community with such services in common as policing, water, drainage, heat, light and power, communications and transportation, even educational and recreational facilities such as libraries, musical and literary entertainment, swimming pools, gardens and golf courses, with courteous services by the community officers and employees. In their common participation in the community services, the inhabitants have no need or desire for common ownership or any other kind of ownership of the community or any responsibility for its proper and efficient operation—except as they may own shares or undivided interests in it. The entire community is operated *for* and not by its inhabitants. Other than good behavior, they have no obligation beyond making the agreed or customary payment for the services they receive. And what they pay is voluntary, very different from taxation. For it is *rational* and not arbitrary, and it is limited by custom and consent, by the competition of the market. A proprietary authority, unlike the political, does not have to force and rule in order to protect and serve.

The Anglo–Saxon practice of community service by proprietary instead of political administration is profound in its implications for the modern age. Its institutions were born far in advance of their time, and they were rudely perverted and torn down. But violent capture and the imposition of an entirely alien mode of administration no more disproves the essential soundness of the free feudal form than the improper or destructive use of a finely specialized machine discredits the sound principle of its operation.

The need to discover and practice sound principles in public affairs has been long and widely proclaimed; yet its fulfillment need not be despaired. For the principle of freedom, of security, stability and growth through free and reciprocal relationships, extending from the atomic to the cosmic in the physical realm, is operative also in the evolving societal organization. Optimists may rejoice and pessimists may take heart to understand, for this leaves no doubt of the providence of nature for the eventual, if not the immediate application of this free principle in the conduct of local, national and even world-wide community affairs.

CHAPTER 17

## The Order of Societal Evolution

*Everything ideal has a natural basis, and everything natural has an ideal development.* —SANTAYANA.

THE ORDER of development of the public authority in a community, from the tribal or familial through various forms of consensual and of political organization towards the fully developed societal organization and mode of operation—by extension of the *contract* process and relationship, based on individual ownership and voluntary exchange, into the field of public and community services as well as private services—seems, in the main, to be:

1. TRIBAL AND FAMILIAL GROUPS

—without settled communities—which gradually cease wandering and become

2. PRIMITIVE VILLAGE COMMUNITIES

—strongly blood-bonded and custom-bound communities, instinctive, like insect colonies, with but little sense of individual personality or separate property—tending to develop out of patriarchy into

3. EARLY VOLUNTARY FEUDALISM

—mutual obligations of land lords and free men, protection and services by proprietors without serfdom or servitude—that, through forced labor, especially in warm, flat and fertile lands, lapses into

4. PREDATORY SLAVE STATES

—military despotisms under monarchy, aristocracy or a democratic elite—or, in more rugged lands, gives way to

5. SERVILE FEUDALISM

—monarchy with local community autonomy by barons over serfs or slaves—which, by political and despotic power, the taxing authority, passing from kings and political land owners to transiently elected authorities without the responsibility of community ownership, gives way, in the Western world, to the modern

### 6. PREDATORY POLITICAL STATES

—nationalistic organizations exercising a supposedly limited taxing power and thereby increasingly assuming unlimited powers—destined always to fall, until they are redeemed from their political character and become

### 7. PROPRIETARY COMMUNITY-SERVICE AUTHORITIES

—community services by the community owners organized as such, with no taxation or other coercion beyond necessary policing against offenders—creating community value and community income offered in return for occupancy and enjoyment of community facilities and services, including, primarily, security against compulsions, either public or private, and finally associating in a

### 8. WORLD ASSOCIATION OF PROPRIETARY COMMUNITY-SERVICE AUTHORITIES

—inaugurating and executing international projects and agreements of mutual and world-wide interest and utility and creating and maintaining common, world facilities in aid of unrestricted freedom of intercourse and exchange.

Organization is always numerical. It is an assemblage of whole units or integral parts so acting with respect to one another that a new organic unit is created, a higher synthesis effected, a new type or species evolved. When the units or parts are most similar and least differentiated, that is when the newly integrated unit is at the least development of its potential powers.

The most primitive association of men is based, doubtless, on likeness rather than unlikeness. Kinship, likeness of blood and birth, is the earliest bond. Mutual amenities and satisfactions spring from like behavior instinctively within the blood-bonded group. There is little if any feeling of self as separate, independent or unique. Custom and conformity is automatic in ways that, by and large, favor survival of the group. Lacking productive arts or crafts, subsistence is by appropriation. Hence, tribal nomadism marks the earliest associative groups. Its units are custom bound and but little differentiated, behavior is uniform, solidarity strong and conflict seldom among the members of the group.

Merely familial and tribal associations are, in principle, the same as those of the animal and the insect world. They subsist on the spontaneous gifts of nature alone, and these they do not create but only consume and destroy. When nature is generous and her rigors mild, they live longer lives and their numbers increase; but when numbers outrun subsistence, the condition is reversed. Their need makes them inimical to all outside their own familial bonds. Conflict and harsh conditions shorten their lives, and they are preserved only by flight to greener pastures or by the greater reproductivity that their higher mortality entails.

Instinctively, headship in the primitive association appears early if not immediately as an element of organization, the first step of differentiation within the group whereby to coördinate the activities of food gathering and the like and the performing of ceremonials deemed essential to the tribal welfare. There is a second activity, protective and defensive, which includes the combative. As scarcity prompts wandering, so it inspires jealousies and fears among mutually alien groups. This different kind of feeling directs a different kind of behavior towards alien members and groups, all the more hostile because of the intense solidarity of each with his own. Thus arises a need for temporary war leaders or chiefs. And out of the general need for headship comes gradually a permanent patriarchal authority in the group. The higher security brought about by this differentiation of authority is accompanied by improvement in the arts and crafts, and the crude productivity thus achieved gives in many places more permanent abode. Agricultural *village communities* arise widespread in many regions, extending with but little change over long periods of time.

In the village community the bond is kinship, the organization sedentary, land and most possessions are the common property of the group and a non-aggressive patriarchy tends to prevail. This earliest and widespread form of community life has an extensive literature.[1] Its chief feature concerns the manner of allocating the use of the community land, no part of which can be alienated from the group by any member. Distribution is made according to common consent in the village *moot* presided over by a patriarch or elder to whom the distributive function is allowed and by whose authority allocations and re-allocations are confirmed under the force or sanction of custom or common law. The patriarch presides over community affairs much as a modern trustee, or as a chairman, under the custom of parliamentary law, determines and carries out the will of the group.

The most primitive village community unit lacks the organizational structure essential for effective or sustained defense. Increasing need of protection prompts its members to accept the authority of him who is foremost and ablest to protect and defend their respective occupancies. The community authority, primarily patriarchal, comes to be relied upon not only to allocate the land according to the spontaneous will of the group but also to defend the allocations so made. The security of what the old deeds guarantee as "quiet possession" to particular occupants as tenants or freeholders is thus assured. And in recompense for such security, allegiance is given and rent service paid. The relationship of the patriarch to the members of his own community tends to become proprietary and thereby contractual, instead of political and thereby coercive—even though he be defensive or even hostile towards the members of other tribes or groups. The early proprietor carries out the determinations of the public *moot* just as the free market is the land owner's monitor today. He receives his administrative revenues from the inhabitants by the custom of contract, according to their freehold allotments over which he presides. In this manner, the blood-bond allegiance to the tribal patriarch or chief is gradually transformed into the *societal* bond. Contract supersedes consanguinity, and at its foundation distinguishes the societal community from all preceding forms. Thus

---

1. See the general writings of Sir Henry S. Main; also P. Kropotkin, *Mutual Aid*.

out of tribal and village life, *early voluntary feudalism,* as the authentic social advance, begins.

The patriarchal proprietors of communities occupied by kindred tribal groups unite in counsel and agreement as common needs arise. When wandering or invading tribes menace the security of their communities, they concentrate their protective function in one of themselves as war leader, *koenig* or primitive king—much as King Alfred's fellow proprietors united their defensive function in him to resist the Danes. A like regional expansion of the ceremonial function doubtless takes place, as represented in later times by priestly hierarchs and oracles, leaving only the local protective, distributive and ceremonial functions to the proprietary authorities in the village groups.

The tendency in the primitive village community is towards contract; towards evolving early *proprietary* communities. But seldom in the record of history has this development of free community administration shown more than its earliest beginnings. Except in Saxon England, where it took firm hold, early voluntary feudalism may be only a short-lived intermediary between the primitive village community and the predatory slave state that in ancient times reached its political culmination in the world dominion of Imperial Rome.

The contractual association of men is *the basic free community pattern,* impersonal and thereby capable of becoming universal, transcending the narrow bonds of common kinship or descent.

Nowhere in ancient times did the normal development of society pass beyond the stage of the primitive free community. Invariably was it arrested, overwhelmed by a contrary mode of organization based upon force and itself invariably doomed to defeat. This was not due to any vice inherent in the normal pattern. Normality does not beget abnormality. The primitive free communities either fell to conquest or were themselves corrupted under stress of unfavorable pressures and influences alien to them.

Lacking the structure for effective or sustained defense, the primitive village fell easy prey to the depredations of those tribal groups who continued their nomadic ways. In easy-living lands, where the rigors of a political administration over the primitive productivity can best be survived, aggression by raiding became conquest and the permanent subjugation of populations. The *predatory slave state* was born. Authority tended to center in war leaders who became conquerors and kings. These were neither patriarchs nor were they proprietors; they were predators. Their administration was political, maintained by force, not sanctioned by native custom, contract or consent. They were the first progenitors of the ancient predatory slave states and of all the political sovereignties, whether autocratic or popular, of the modern world.

These political states, organized systems of force, became a greater menace to the early settled communities than the maraudings of nomad tribes. Village communities are primitive but self-sustaining and sound. Yet through whole ages of history nomad armies and predatory slave states despoiled and destroyed them, even into modern times, where the barbarian's love of freedom still survived. The political history of all ancient times is but little else than the clashing and consolidation of rival slave states and their encroachments on barbarian freedom to extend their domains and build mighty empires until barbarian conquerors from freer lands brought their insolent glory low.

All political institutions are founded on force. They flourished widely in the "Fertile Crescent" and other ancient easy-living lands. It was here alone that the *slave*-based military sovereignties characteristic of nearly all ancient times arose; for it was here alone that their worst rigors could be withstood and the population yet survive. In rugged or remote and less fertile lands where movement and migration, especially migration by sea, had occasioned more efficient relationships than kinship alone affords, the political submergence was delayed and of necessity less complete. It was here that the non-coercive authority of proprietorship, growing out of patriarchy, tended furthest to evolve and the political domination, when it followed, took less drastic forms. Free relationships gave way to *servile feudalism*, and this, in turn, to *tax*-based sovereignties imposing direct and personal servitude only in case of special circumstances or offense.

When the primitive voluntarism of many ancient settled lands gave way to sovereignty over slaves, greater rulers made war against the lesser, and those conquered but not destroyed became satraps or viceroys under kings. Not the proprietary but the sovereign power grew. Slave states and powers alone prevailed. These despotisms ran through long dynasties of the Near and Middle East, the valley of the Nile and Mediterranean shores. They turned the "Fertile Crescent" into starveling lands, set the pattern for absolute government for all later time and, in the slave-founded democracies of the Greeks and the slave-based republicanism of Rome, established the Classical tradition for the founding of modern "free governments" when both servile feudalism and the kingly power declined.

In rugged lands the primal bounty of the earth would not yield subsistence to both masters and slaves. Only to free men could the earth sufficiently respond. It was here that free feudal communities best evolved and neither absolute sovereignty nor absolute slavery was known. Not in the alluvial lands nor in the great grass plains but among the mountains and in the wooded lands, the ancient seeds of liberty were sown. Great tribal princes from the treeless plains could scourge the empires of the East, but they could build no empires of their own. Subsistence on their great grasslands was seasonal; it kept them too much on the move to form communities, either slave or free. As deserts encroached upon their grassy plains, men of like breed drove westward to the Golden Horn and took dominion far and wide but brought no breath of freedom there. It was the barbarians of the wooded west, and not from the east, who attempted to set up free institutions where their arms prevailed.

When the imperial power of Rome went down upon the ruin it had wrought, the barbarians took dominion and free communities, far and wide, again were formed. They were always predial—based on the tenure of land—and thus tended to become proprietary instead of political. Far into the dark aftermath of Rome, the more peace-loving possessors of land conveyed their allodial or other holdings to stronger lords on pledge of protection against violence and took freehold or leasehold titles, with obligation of rent or rent service, in exchange. These medieval beginnings of voluntary feudal-

## THE ORDER OF SOCIETAL EVOLUTION

ism were, on the Continent at least, overwhelmed by the Roman ideology and tradition of political domination and power. Feudalism, in its free proprietary and non-political operation, was perverted by Roman politics into the servile feudalism that kept Continental Europe in darkness for a thousand years. But in Saxon England, the fall of freedom was long delayed and she came into a glory all her own before her subversion was complete and Roman institutions were imposed by force of Norman arms.

Nothing in history is more certain than that the Teutonic tribes generally had none of the Roman concept of an absolute mystical or transcendental sovereign state. They had no multi-millennial tradition of slave subservience or of abject loyalty to an abstraction under cover of which priest and potentate alike claimed sanction for naked force and conquest of arms. Their suffrages went to leadership and service, to personal worth and not to investiture of office and arbitrary power. They *"stamped out the Roman State"* and organized *"according to the immemorial fashion of their own politics, on the basis of freehold tenure of the land and local administration."* But on the Continent, *"government gradually worked its way out from the individualism inherent in the habits of the German races back into an absolutism not unlike that of the Roman Empire."*[2]

The new barbarian beginnings were profoundly affected by the Roman traditions of absolute power and the mystical ideology of the Roman State. As one writer describes it,

> When the German settled down as master amongst the Romanized populations of western and southern Europe, his thought was led captive by the conceptions of Roman law, as all subsequent thought that has known it has been, and his habits were much modified by those of his new subjects; but his strong element of individualism was not destroyed by the contact.[3]

Prompted by the same instinct towards societal instead of political organization as their Anglo-Saxon kindred overseas, the northern

---

2. Woodrow Wilson, *The State*, Boston, 1909, pp. 167, 169; and various other authorities.
3. Woodrow Wilson, *op. cit.*, p. 584.

tribes that broke through the Roman barriers at the Rhine established in their new possessions not political but *proprietary* public institutions based on the ownership of land for authority and on voluntary rent for public revenue. But they came among people who had never been accustomed to anything but political domination and who continued to idealize the iron authority and the austere codes and institutes, the administrative law and supposedly protective power of once imperial Rome. These imperial traditions beguiled the barbarian mind even as they ruled the Classical and still so much mislead the modern learned mind. Thus again in the emergence from tribalism to freedom, the nascent institutions of free society were compromised at their new beginnings. As in Saxon England, the basic *form* was that of voluntary feudalism, the free proprietary; but the spirit became that of politics and war. For the revenues for community needs came not to be paid by free men to land lords by contract and consent, according to the value each received, but by perversion of rent into taxation and of public proprietorship into the essential tyranny of tribute-taking sovereignties in the manner of decadent Rome. Thus arose the servile feudalism that darkened Europe for a thousand years—a repetition, only measurably humanized, of the predatory slave states of ancient times. The submergence of Anglo-Saxon England by the Norman Duke completed the destruction of free community development in medieval times.

Nonetheless, rising out of barbarian freedom and fostered by the Church, a new spirit was rising in the hearts of common men. They began to feel themselves as individuals distinct from their fellow men and from the whole, that each should own himself and thereby own other things and thus be able to make free engagements—contracts—with respect to himself, his services and his property according to the consensus of all present and the particular agreement of those with whom he dealt. Rival barons amid their local wars had not consolidated into kings, and there were no great sovereignties over land or seas. Hence, out of the break-up of servile feudalism, men found a measure of liberty to prosper one another through contractual engagements and not to be wholly tax-despoiled. Guilds were formed and market towns and fairs. New communities and free towns, "oases in the feudal forest," were established, wresting their freedom from feudal lords. Pirates became merchants and their coastal cities rose to wealth and power. By the eleventh century, servile feudalism was beginning to decay, and men found freedom, even riches, in the industries and trading of the cities and towns. The "Twelfth-Century Renaissance" promised a new era.

But in mutual wars, the power of landed dukes and barons slowly fell to central kings, and the free communities, towns and leagues, in their rivalries and wars, likewise lost their independence and their liberties to sovereign central powers. Then popular governments arose to abolish serfdom, the power and privilege of the landed lords, and to curb the taxing power of kings by transferring to periodically elected persons and to a permanent establishment set up by them the general power to tax and rule—all under constitutional limitations which these governments themselves, and they alone, had authority to interpret and apply. Thus developed nationalistic central sovereignties—the modern *predatory political states*—raised on the productiveness that grew out of new freedom when the inefficiencies of servile feudalism forbade continuance to its rigid forms.

Born out of revolutionary violence, holding no property administratively as proprietors, employing no wealth productively as capital, these present-day political states have no natural or unforced revenue. Hence they must depend upon widely organized systems of collection and coercion that are not self-limiting, as is community rent, but tend constantly to expand. Thus they grow increasingly inimical to the continuance of civilized society. Such systems of revenue by compulsion in place of contract, however much accepted or resisted, are the bane of free society today as were serfdom and slavery in medieval and in ancient times.

Yet a benign and beneficent, a creative alternative is in the making and, in the degree that it is discovered, will the more increasingly prevail. The current deficiency of robust research in this field is what exposes many to the harsh logic of absolutism, with its siren seductions of government *in toto* and society *nil*.

There are rich traditions from the past and endless examples today

—too long neglected in scholarly research as in current thought—of community administration that employs no coercion yet yields to their administrators a natural income gauged to the value of such portion of the common services as each tenant separately enjoys and for which he willingly pays. This is the *proprietary* method of administration. It is characteristic of all free enterprise and is expressly exemplified historically in the Anglo-Saxon free community, in modern corporate hotel communities and in all other community properties whose occupants, permanent or temporary, are well and justly served and in no wise taxed, ruled or enslaved.

Evidence of free communities and of early voluntary feudalism are found in ancient Mexico and Japan and in many lands, but nowhere so definitely or for so long a period as in Medieval England before the Normans came.

The Anglo-Saxon tribes were the least and the last to be affected by absolute and imperial conceptions. The free proprietary pattern of responsible public services through contractual engagements between proprietary authorities and free men had, in England, respite of a half-millennium to grow and come to flower with Alfred in his Golden Age. When the sea-borne Anglo-Saxons invaded Britain, they were no more confronted with Roman institutions than they were with Roman power. Here, out of rude barbarism, in virtual isolation from imperial traditions, a basic system of proprietary public administration through centuries of tribal conquest and confusion slowly and imperfectly evolved. It resisted but also set example for later kindred invaders from overseas and, in a peace without victory over the kindred Danes, it blossomed under Alfred, the "Servant of Servants," in the midst of Europe's darkest gloom. The public authority, beginning with the local community affairs, was not maintained by the exercise of force upon the inhabitants. Not taxes but rent or rent service was the public revenue. And it was not arbitrary; for it was determined by contract or common custom of the market, thereby gauged to the value of the public administration, and assessed by automatic consent of the free-holders themselves. This development was necessarily gradual and uneven. Doubtless there were at all times communities in various states. But all public authority was based on the ownership of land and maintained wholly by the dues or revenues, in service, coin or products, that the public servicing of the lands brought forth. Slavery was not unknown, but for lack of any *political* system to support it, slavery as an institution could not be maintained. The Anglo-Saxon kings were primarily land owners. As war leaders and kings, they were chosen from among their fellow proprietors only by election or in emergency. During the heptarchy there was a tendency towards the Roman type of kingship, but this came into its full and final effect only in the polity of force imposed by the might of the Norman arms—a Roman type of absolute state whose compulsive processes and powers have passed since then with but little change from kings to predatory lords and then to commons and cabinets elected or supported by popular vote.

Of high historic significance for the modern growth of free community has been an important though little remarked development of the last two hundred years. Just as the ancient Classical democracies and Republican Rome rose in rebellion against monarchical excesses and decay, so in our own times have their modern imitations, our predatory political states—democratic in theory yet essentially predacious, internally at least—again risen in rebellion against the kingly power, *and landed barons* along with sovereign kings lost all their former power to tax and rule. Thus, the institution of property in land is transformed in modern times from a political and coercive authority into a most essential non-political department of society for the social, that is, the *free contractual* distribution of sites and lands, and for the vastly further public functions that it is destined, as it evolves, freely and with enormous profit to perform.

The next great step in free community development, rooted deeply in the simple freedoms of the past, still waits the future. Early historical research, the great Anglo-Saxon precedent and the modern owner-administration of hotel and similar properties that supply community services to their inhabitants, all give warrant to predict the formation of *proprietary community-service authorities* at the general community level, by the basic realty owners pooling their separate titles and holding equivalent undivided ownership interests in the whole. Political administration being what it is, community owners will not long fail to unite once the many advantages are seen. United as a business and organized to serve, they will give not mere occupancy alone, but positive and protective public services as well, for sake of the new rents and higher values that will accrue to their properties and to their organization—a community revenue and value created by their community services and not extorted by force. In this clear and far-sighted business opportunity, there is promise of public authorities qualified to give governmental services without resort to government as force, creating their own revenues and thereby solvent, exempt from the historic cycle of rise, decline and fall.

Proprietary community-service authorities will be formed, small perhaps at first, but, because of the prosperity of the populations served and protected by them, growing in number, size and scope. Such authorities will develop interrelationships respecting joint and reciprocal projects and services that will constitute them eventually into that world-wide integration of public service and protection for which the hearts of men so deeply yearn and as yet so vainly dream. These public authorities will administer enormous properties and earn such abundant profits that virtually the entire highly prospered general public will seek proud investment in their securities and shares. Thus, authentic community democracies will naturally evolve. In this there are enormous implications too extensive and ideal to be expanded here. But the intelligent imagination can foresee proprietary community-service authorities, organized as local community proprietors over extensive areas, comprising many communities and establishing associative relationships among themselves in order to provide wider services on a regional, a national and eventually on an international and world-wide scale.

THE ORDER OF SOCIETAL EVOLUTION 97

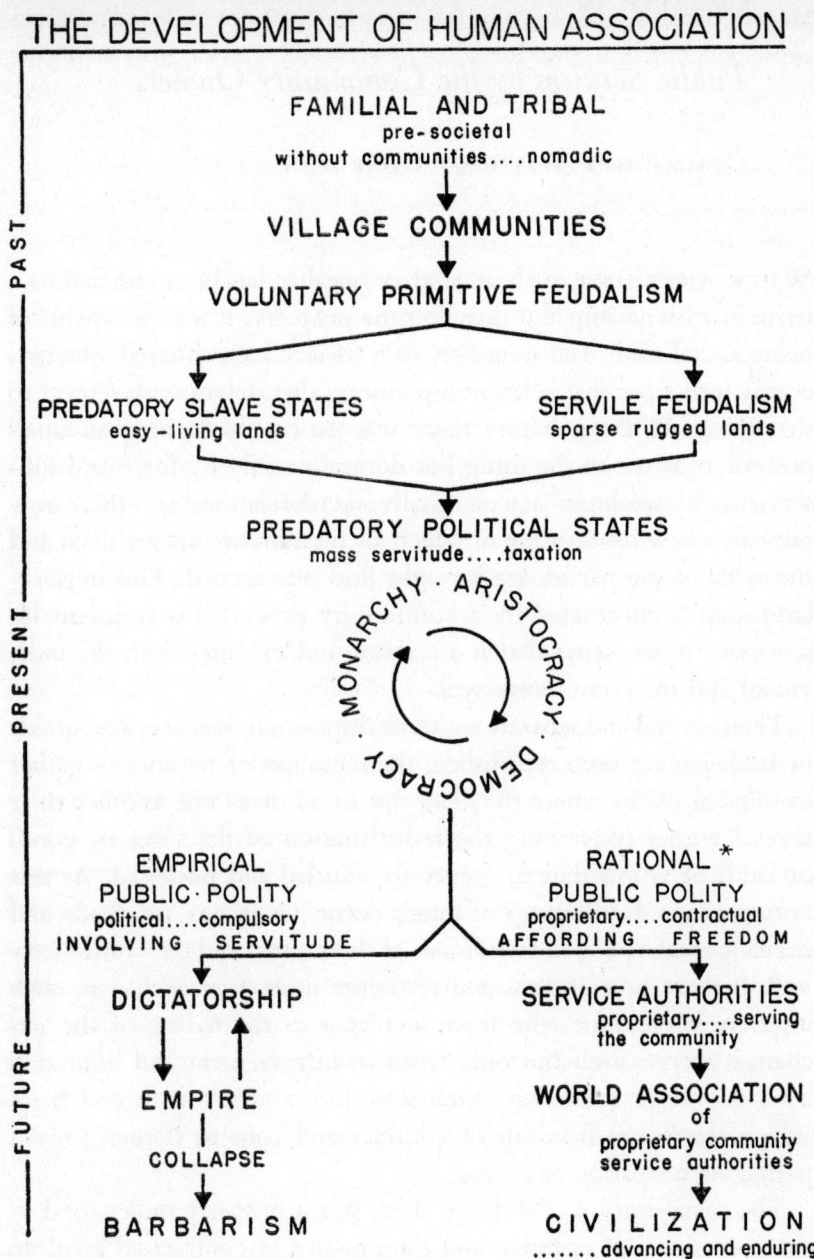

Figure 4.

CHAPTER 18

# Public Services by the Community Owners

## COMMUNITY WITHOUT COERCION

WHEN ANYTHING, such as land or wealth, has been reduced to a particular ownership and thus become property, it is then capable of being social-ized. The members of a society have entered spontaneously into a peculiar relationship among themselves with respect to that thing. Whereas before there was no rule governing anyone's possession or use of the thing but dominion only by force and subservience by weakness—an essentially slavish relationship—there now prevails a new relationship in which all antagonisms are resolved and the wills of the parties are brought into one accord. This new relationship is effectuated by a community process that is essentially *democratic* in the sense that it ascertains and executes both the individual and the community will.

Their several and separate rights of disposition over services, goods or lands having been established, the members of the society gather in suitable places where they call out to all or to one another their several wishes concerning the redistribution of the services, goods or lands of which they are severally entitled and possessed. As this voting proceeds, meetings of minds occur. Contracts are made and exchanges take place in fulfillment of the mutual and the community will. If there be coercions and restraints upon free exchange, such interferences cannot arise from anything in the nature of the exchange process itself but only from its infringement and limitation by a power or condition extraneous and contrary to it and from which this social freedom of contract and consent is then only a partial emancipation or escape.

The social-ization of a thing, then, when properly understood, is the abrogation of coercive and the practice of contractual relations between and among men with regard to its disposition and use. Ownership is, therefore, a condition precedent to social-ization, for men can dispose or use by contract, exchange and mutual consent only such things as an individual (or corporate entity) can *own,* and then only to the extent that the ownership remains free and not infringed by taxation or other limitation forcibly imposed.

In a social-ized community, lands, improvements and other capital goods let out or otherwise used for the purposes of production and trade are owned not exclusively but *in*-clusively of others, the others being included in the use and benefit of them by the social process of mutual service by contract and exchange.

At the very foundation of this *social* system, this using of property for the serving of others, lies the institution of property in land.

Until the day when, by a social convention, specific persons are recognized and accepted as owners of the land and thereby invested with community authority to hold it or distribute it by a *contractual* process, the land remains *un*-social-ized and there is no security of possession or possibility of productive use. Upon it no society can exist. But as soon as it can be contractually held, distributed and disposed, then it may be peaceably and productively used, and then, but not until then, can wealth be produced and exchanged and the societal process and function thus be performed.

It is important to distinguish between production and exchange. Production is primarily physical. When, and only when, it is conducted in anticipation of or in connection with exchange, does it have any societal significance. Exchange, however, is wholly social, denoting a change in human relationships; it is beyond all physical processes, a matter of title and jurisdiction over physical things. Title does not depend upon production; it determines only the authority and the mode of distribution—that property may be distributed socially by purchase, sale or lease instead of by political or coercive administration, by the free Market instead of by the Citadel or state. And where production and distribution are separately considered, as is the case with those persons who purchase for resale, the legitimacy of high recompense for distributive services is seldom, if ever, questioned. Such distributors create, peaceably and democratically through the market, a new relationship between the members with respect to ownership of, or jurisdiction over, the thing sold.

The principle is in all respects identical in the case of property in land. Land owners do not physically produce land, any more than the separate distributors of merchandise, or of its use, produce the property of which they distribute the ownership or use. Their land titles represent the authority conferred upon them to distribute land without having produced it precisely as the owners of merchandise distribute property that they have not produced—and for such similar recompense as the open market in both cases awards.

Land owners thus do create the value of land—that is, the value that the market awards to them for the service of distributing it by the societal process in lieu of primitive force or of governmental decree. If a land owner fails to perform such service, then he forfeits all recompense for it. He may, indeed, become a land *user,* but he can obtain no recompense or value for any distribution not performed by him.

In periods of expanding contractual freedom with consequent rising productivity, there is a growing social need and effective demand for this contractual distribution of land. Such services, becoming increasingly important, are increasingly recompensed by the rising rents and values of land. During these periods of increasing productivity, land of all kinds is more intensively used and more land is drawn into use; hence there is greater need and higher recompense for distributing it.

In the contrasting periods of more restricted and therefore less profitable productivity, such land as is being used is used less intensively. There is less social need and demand for its distribution; the recompense to land owners declines, and much land loses value and passes out of use. During such times, the owners of unused lands can perform only potential or stand-by services with respect to distributing them—such services as are performed with respect to distributing many other kinds of properties or essential services by persons who keep them available for long periods against the day or infrequent occasion when they shall come into active, perhaps urgent, demand.

These periods of diminishing contractual freedom are periods of rising disemployment and idleness of capital, hence of labor and, consequently, also of land and of its owners and their agents and employees who would otherwise be engaged in its contractual distribution. In such periods, many owners of lands are compelled to relinquish them to the arbitrary administration of political authorities, the owners' alternative, if any, being to suffer continued confiscation of their wealth or property of other kinds by way of taxation based on and penalizing them for their ownership of land. Such political liquidation of land ownership, if not reversed, will of course result in the land being distributed by political persons who impose compulsive taxation and all its derivative tyrannies. Land administration would again fall back into the former ill repute from which it even now suffers as heritage from the historic past when it was undifferentiated from political power. The former political perversion of land administration by the tyranny of political lords over their tax-ridden land users still prejudices many otherwise competent minds against present-day land ownership, despite the complete divorcement of this modern institution from all political authority or other destructive power.

The modern differentiation of land ownership out of the Citadel and into the contractual or service technique of the Market has been probably the one fundamental, although least remarked, social advance following upon the violent political revolutions that marked the latter part of the eighteenth century.

The present twentieth-century reversal—this current tendency toward a complete "totalitarian" dominance of Citadel over both Market and Altar, ever encroaching on the freedom to own and to serve by exchange, imposing a compulsive and therefore destructive administration of property by persons who do not own it—is a dark menace to the future of society and its free civilization. It is a certain guarantee of continuing world wars, lower levels of subsistence and a diminishing duration of life. This grave de-social-ization of men out of society by the increasing pressure of government upon contractual freedom can lead to nothing but poverty, slavery and war. The sword of tyranny must tomorrow make new and deeper wounds than those of yesterday and today.

But in utter contrast to vain political expedients, all civilized communities do now receive their fundamental public service through the institution of property in land. This institution is all that stands between them and anarchy on the one hand or tyranny on the other in the distribution of land: the administration of nature's gifts to mankind. Its services are *societal,* not political. All its processes are contractual. It is wholly of the Market. It claims no sovereignty, makes no conquests for loot, levies no tribute on society. Instead, it receives a voluntary revenue in the exact proportion that it serves. Once the nature of property in land is perceived and its potentialities realized, it will automatically and without substantial opposition extend its proprietary administration ever more widely into the community services and needs and will receive its voluntary, its just and honorable rewards.

The public services that the public owners now perform—namely, their non-violent and non-discriminatory distribution of the community advantages, sites and lands—need only be extended to the full administration of the common properties, the public ways and lands and their capital improvements and the community services supplied thereby, to transform government from an essential tyranny into a prosperous agency of highly recompensed public service. Such community authority, being proprietary instead of political, will establish its own community services, both positive and productive, and lease out its sites and resources to the most efficient and productive occupiers under guarantee of quiet and unmolested possession. In the interest of its own income and values, it will neither impose nor permit the imposition of taxation or other violence. For the unforced revenues coming to such owner-administrators, not alone from their merely distributive services, as at present, but from the sale also of community services in general—peace and protection against violence, whether public or private, as adjunct to possession —will render taxation and the like compulsions profitless and vain.

The value of any property lies in its administration. When it is administered by being sold, the value is the price received; when it is administered by being let out, its value is the rent received. The value of a community, of a city or of a state, is the value received by its owners for whatever community services they give or perform.

Let those services so protect and aid and convenience the inhabitants that their productivity can be high, then the community income and the community values will be high. Such is the natural automatism of public service and reward—to the full extent that the public services are performed by the public owners, both now and in the time to come. Automatic *social* revenue to the community owners, suitably organized to take over increasingly the public services, is the grand creative alternative to the tax and deficit practices, to the essential bankruptcy and habitual failure of all political administration and political power.

CHAPTER 19

## Societal Development through Extension of the System of Contract and Exchange

IF SOCIETY were a mere collection of lifeless materials, a structure might be designed and built from them to specification and plan, the energy being applied from without. But society is a living organization of energy, an organism constituted of living parts interfunctioning among themselves; the impulse and guidance of its higher transformation is not to be externally applied; it must arise from within. The process of the transformation, therefore, cannot be imposed, but it may with high probability be forecast—extrapolated out of the present and the past.

Written history is largely an account of the injuries, of the wars and enslavements, that have been suffered and imposed. But civilization has grown and exists only because of the *services* that have been performed and mutually exchanged. The story of the advance of civilization is not the story of its opposite—of the conflicts and wars that have impeded it; it is the story of the widening reciprocation of services under the golden rule of exchange, in which civilization finds its life and on which all its glories depend. A civilized society is distinguished from the uncivilized by the system of services and exchange by which its parts interfunction to give it organic unity and life. The historic development of this interfunctioning has been manifesting itself in the growing quantity and variety, quality and beauty of the services and goods that have been performed and exchanged, the services being specialized and in large part, but not exclusively, incorporated in properties and goods prior to exchange. Such incorporation of services for others is commonly called "production." It transforms the environment and thereby raises the quality of human life and extends its term.

When the services performed do not change any physical things but do change the relationships of men towards one another as owners with respect to physical things, then these services are called "distribution."

The social recompense for one property or service is the property or service that is obtained for it by exchange. Each of these is the *value* of the other. Value is not intrinsic but *social* and, therefore, extrinsic to the thing given, for it consists, for each giver, not in what he does or gives nor in anyone's thoughts concerning it, but in the actuality of what he receives. The value or valuation of anything with reference to future or possible exchange should be thought of as conditional or in the future, since it looks forward and is speculative. Nothing, however *useful,* has any such property as value *in itself,* but only in *exchange.* Value, in the present tense, refers to that which is actual as service or physical as wealth and which possesses also the social attribute of equivalence in exchange arising out of an actual exchange process.

Since all services and goods that have social significance are pooled or social-ized in open or public markets and thence redistributed by contract and accord of the individual and of the social will, it is not necessary that exchanges be carried out simultaneously or "in kind." A system of money and credit provides intermediate tokens or records as representing obligations, future charges, against either the general market or against the resources of particular persons as debtors. The immediate (or future) liquidation of these tokens, or the future liquidation of these charges into tokens and thence into services or goods out of the market, completes in actuality what was theretofore only a formal or symbolic completion of the exchange. These intermediate symbols are often referred to as values, because they measure the future recompense or value to be received but not yet actually received.

In the making of contracts to exchange, and in the symbolic future completion of them, the tokens of future values are taken numerically and by fractional subdivision, and the corresponding actual and concrete values are in future ascertained and measured by these. So far as the Citadel does not by force interfere, the Market establishes its own tokens, giving preference to those it finds most serviceable in facilitating exchanges and finally abandoning those found less serviceable or unjust.

The whole development of the "law merchant" in medieval times was an admirable instance of efficient symbolic tokens or instruments of exchange being developed and successively employed under natural or customary law without any of the compulsions of political enactments or decrees. Although these token instruments had no value but the value of the commodity specified in them, they were nonetheless valid and highly adequate and efficient instruments of exchange.[1] The generally prevailing domination and dilution of the token system by the compulsive political authority is an important example of the many impediments to social growth due to lack of sufficient differentiation between the Citadel and the Market, insufficient social-ization of government.

The service and exchange system, according to its degree of freedom and growth, has operated throughout history always to raise the duration and the quality of life. In one period or part of the world, it flourishes like the green bay tree and is then with much pomp and magnificence despoiled by government and war. At times it has gone into eclipse, but has always emerged out of the darkness and in time attained a higher growth and wider expanion than before. This essentially democratic system of service and exchange is within itself highly differentiated as between its own manifold departments and parts, and from the system of government and force, the state, and also from the system of religion and arts, the church, both of which systems it supports. It claims no authority of either force or belief and denies all legitimacy to force or fraud in any of its operations. It has turned raiders into traders, pirates into merchants, robber barons and landed aristocrats into harmless and useful merchandisers and distributors of locations and lands. It has taken land ownership out of government and turned it into a service of the market, purged of all political power or coercive authority. Blindly and without conscious understanding or plan, these social

---

1. Any token of exchange not issued by the market as the evidence and value-measure of a contribution thereto yet commanding some distribution therefrom is of necessity a false token, essentially an instrument of tyranny or theft.

advances have been slowly and impersonally made. Nor will they cease.

But a *rational* technique is near at hand. The phenomenon of society, of men associated organically in a relationship of mutual service by contract and exchange, submits to the same kind of examination that the natural sciences have made of the organization and processes of the natural world. The nascent science of society is now at the point of discovering to the intelligence of mankind the full proprietary relationship that the institution of property in land bears to the administration of public capital and community services. This knowledge may be publicized rapidly or it may remain hidden for a time, but when it breaks forth and is clearly seen it cannot fail to draw the present-day land and site owning interests, and their more enlightened and better organized successors, into effective working organizations for the rationally ordered public services, both positive and protective, that their communities greatly need. This will bring to them rents and values, highest profits and the richest of rewards as true and worthy servants of all.[2]

The higher order among men cannot burst full grown. It stirs in the yearnings of their hearts from time of old, a dream of freedom, of self-fulfillment for all and none to be afraid. The heart dreams the attainment, the end, before the mind perceives the means, the creative rationale, whereby to play its part in the never-ending, the eternal cosmic bloom.

---

2. The principles of this matter are more fully set out and their practice indicated in Chapters 20, 24 and 25.

PART II

*The Application*

*We may say that the movement of the progressive societies hitherto has been a movement* from Status to Contract.

SIR HENRY S. MAINE

CHAPTER 20

# General Observations on Reduction to Practice

IN KNOWLEDGE there are always horizons beyond. Every true science is but an incomplete, a finite description of finite and particular reality in terms of phenomena as events and as experience. Science examines the three aspects of reality as manifested in specific experiences and measures them by reference to and by repetitions of its standard units, to which these aspects are objectively and quantitatively referred. It thus describes the particular existent reality by analyzing it into the particular magnitudes of its fundamental aspects. By a reverse process, applied science re-synthesizes the threefold manifestation of reality—mass, motion, duration—into objects and events that are desired and aspired to, planned and dreamed. Thus, science, while wholly quantitative in its descriptive or analytic technique, is also qualitative, positively or negatively so, throughout all its applications, in its effects and results, whether for good or for ill. Science describes things and events in terms of their magnitudes and ratios or relationships. It is thus an abstraction from but still a part of the cosmic reality. It differs from ordinary knowledge in that it is generalized over a wide range. Scientific knowledge is thus realizable forward; it can be projected into particular objects and experiences in ways that realize desired ends and dreams.

The science of society is no exception. Its discoveries, its descriptions, are motivated by intimations and apprehensions of the beauty it reveals; its application resolves beauty into use and, where the application is high, creates beauty anew.

In Chapter 21 immediately following, the purpose is to bring the social-ized service energy of free contract and exchange distinctly under the same generalizations that reduce to one conception all those variant forms of energy which the natural sciences have brought so far into the technological service of mankind. This basic identification of social energy with energy in other forms and the delineation of its modes of measurement and flow in the transactions of contract and exchange, is to make clear the relevancy of the energy concept in the ensuing chapters, especially in Chapters 24 and 25, dealing with property in land and real estate administration. For in these chapters the language of practical business is employed, at some sacrifice of technical precision, for the sake of a greater practical appeal.

Chapter 23, on community economics, re-emphasizes the dynamic and functional character of community organization and particularly of its basic institution, property in land. Here the energy concept is clearly implicit, although its specific terms are not directly employed.

Chapters 24 and 25, on real estate administration, are very specifically addressed to the interest of land owners and others concerned with the administration of real estate. Its vital importance to the whole of society justifies the extended treatment given to real estate administration, with special reference to and emphasis upon the need and opportunity for responsible administration of the *lateral* improvements to the private holdings that lie adjacent to, between and around them and constitute the *public capital* of the community.

Chapter 26, the final chapter, on the hypothetical distribution of national income under proprietary administration, is a forecast of the more or less ideal and Utopian form into which the now existing system of voluntary service exchanges will certainly grow as it becomes liberated from governmental obstructions and restraints through the public capital being responsibly administered for profit and public services thus coming to be socially and non-coercively performed.

The immediate prescription, the one clear path to freedom and profit, plenty and peace, is that the owners of communities unite in corporate or similar form for relief and protection of their populations in exchange for the *new* ground rent sure to arise out of the mighty productivity such public services will of a certainty release. The responsible owners of a community are thus to extend the service technique of the Market into the field now dominated by the Citadel at so great cost and loss. Though on behalf of all, the appeal is still frankly to the same "profit motive" that has actuated all great and widely applied transformations of human energy into the service, without servitude, of civilized mankind. At the same time, it shows the utter dependence of profit upon *Service;* how great new services may with safety be performed; and how their recompense and values, and yet more their honors, are certain to be high. In the realm of free business, of mutual service by exchange, the basic and justifiable desire is still profit or gain. But successful practice dictates a high regard for *giving;* hence this motivation may in time take the lead. So obvious and high are the intellectual and the artistic and spiritual implications of its free technique, no apology is required for the profit motive as the practical and profitable, the purely business basis of social advance.

CHAPTER 21

## *Value and Exchange, A System of Social-ized Energy Flow*

EARLIER PAGES have disclosed that the social organization, like any other organic integration, is a particular manifestation of the cosmic and universal energy. We have considered this energy as manifesting itself at the social level in a mode that, while basically identical with that operating at all levels and in all other things, has a peculiar and specific kind, a higher analogue, in the living structures, the social integrations of mankind. We have to deal with living energy in a new form, with a metabolism, not between biological cells, but between those complex integrations of biological cells, the individuals, who are in their turn the basic units of the social structure.

We cannot measure the social metabolism by the amount of carbon oxidized or its dioxide respired. To attempt it would be like trying to employ a mechanical dynamometer to measure thermal, chemical or electrical energy, or a yardstick to measure temperature. The several modes of energy have their separate unit-standards and appropriate instruments for their measurement—dynamometer, calorimeter, electrometer, etc., and while some of these forms of energy are known to have quantitative inter-equivalences, the separate employment of them within their respective fields is not at all dependent on this.

Similarly, in the observation and discovery of how social energy is measured and the equivalence of its exchanges maintained, it is not necessary to take into account what quantitative equivalences it may and doubtless does have with measured energy in other forms. We do know that in each field a quantitative balance is maintained throughout all its energy exchange transactions, all inequalities being liquidated by conversion or degradation of the otherwise unbalanced portions into heat or some other energy form. In the processes and transformations of electrical and mechanical energy that constitute the practical applications of energy flow in those fields, the otherwise unbalanced portions are converted or degraded into another form of energy the amount of which is called the "heat loss." This means, of course, not that the unbalanced portions of energy are lost in any absolute sense but only out of *that particular system* of mechanical or electrical energy conversion or exchange. In fact, when it is desired to convert these other forms of energy into heat, it is the otherwise unbalanced portions of mechanical or electrical energy and not the heat that is considered as lost. The efficiencies of all energy exchange systems are expressed in the quotients obtained by dividing the total energy put out into the quantity of energy that is converted into the particular form desired.

Now, in the social organism, a portion of the energy of environment that it derives from the plant and animal world and incorporates into its individual units is transformed by them somewhat differently from the transformation that takes place in an individual who is not incorporated into the structure of a social organism.

In his pre-social, non-social or anti-social state, the individual puts out his energies with sole view to his own satisfactions, including those of his own blood-bonded or emotion-bound, restricted group, the energy not yet coming under the broader and more universalized bonds of a general society. But in the social organization, while these more primitive bonds still in large measure remain, a portion of the energy that flows through the individual undergoes, in addition, a higher flow—measured, impersonal, more general and wider in its scope. He *social-izes* a portion of his energy; that is, he devotes it to the interest and places it at the disposal not merely of himself or his narrow tribal or blood-bonded group but of the membership in general of an organization not thus restricted—a *social* organization, a *societal* group. He devotes this portion of his energies either directly or indirectly (as by taking employment with others) to the performing of services or production of goods (called capital goods) so as to satisfy the needs and desires of *others*. And he does this regardless of blood relationships, thus inducing to him from many directions a voluntary counter-flow of satisfactions in the form of highly specialized services and goods.

Basically essential to the system of exchange are the services of negotiating the manifold exchanges that the preparation of goods and performing of services for others necessarily involves. To distinguish these last from the physical process of producing goods and, also, from other forms of intangible services, these services of negotiation are very properly called the services of *distribution*. They appertain to the distribution of land no less than to the distribution of those things to which physical energy or "labor" has been applied.

All the energy thus social-ized by being extended outwardly towards the satisfaction of others is a special development of energy having the same order of difference above other human energy that electrical energy has above the mechanical energy that generates it in the physical world; or that the energy of vital metabolism has above the cruder forms of energy, chemical and electrical, out of which it proceeds; or that the energy of thought has above the merely physiological energy upon which it depends. This social or social-ized energy, this social metabolism, is properly called the energy of exchange. It lies at the base of the social physiology just as basic metabolism is fundamental to the physiology of animal structures. And just as this basic animal energy flowing through differentiated physiological structures gives rise to all the coördinated activities and higher powers of the animal (or human) organism, so does this social-ized energy of exchange take the place of un-social-ized, merely self-serving energy. Just as the physiological metabolism, by converting chemical into vital energy, is the basis of all merely bodily functioning, both physiological and mechanical, so does the social metabolism of exchange transform the crude individual energy of self-service into vastly efficient social energy. In this it liberates distinctively human and unique creative powers out of the bonds of necessity and limitations that beset the whole animal world—and the merely animal in man—into the spontaneous arts and recreations, the seeking after beauty, the pursuit and expression of ideals and dreams.

We shall now take account of the manner in which exchanges of social-ized energy take place in the physiology of society; how the multitudinous diverse contributions of individuals, as such and through their membership in business organizations, are measured against one another in the process of their interchange, and how their accounts and balances are maintained.

All goods and services placed at the disposal of or performed for others in a society constitute the subject-matters upon which operate the great and unique social structure called the Market. This institution, as a social structure, consists of all those persons who prepare and contribute the services and goods of the Market and so administer them, by the voluntary and spontaneous processes of exchange, as to bring about a general unanimity of mind and harmony of will concerning their disposition or use.

These social energies, including those incorporated in commodities, are subjected to the operation of an automatic measuring process called *competition* which ascertains, in terms of value-units, the relative equivalence of things in exchange. This measuring instrument of social energy is to the Market what a watt-meter or other form of dynamometer is in a field where physical energy is being measured and its equivalences ascertained.

As in the case of physical measurements, it is indifferent what units be employed, so that the same or interconvertible units be used throughout. It is therefore immaterial what unit of measure the Market employs as its standard of value, so it be the same throughout all the exchanges that take place. Let the unit be what it will—a given weight of metal or what not—as soon as it is adopted as the unit of the exchange or value scale and all the things being exchanged take, by common consent, their respective positions on this value or exchange scale, then the equivalences among themselves of all things proposed for exchange are ascertained and determined by reference to their positions on this common scale.

What is being measured is, of course, not the commodities or properties themselves, but their social-ized energy content. Their physical properties must be measured by physical instruments and tests, and these, of course, are employed. But when it comes to measuring the energy of exchange, competition is the social instrument employed. It is the means by which social-ized energy is balanced and exchanged creatively in accordance with the social will.

The customary term for a measure of social-ized energy is *value*. All accountancy is but the balancing of values in terms of the units employed in the measurements of services as social-ized energy. For example, a physically distinguishable quantity of human energy, either as a service or as conveyed in a commodity, is social-ized and, by the contractual process, contributed to the general Market. Under the prevailing custom or common law of the Market, its instrument of competition automatically measures this social-ized energy in terms of the prevailing measuring unit and indicates it to be of a certain quantity of those units, say ten dollars. This then becomes numerically and symbolically its value, for it means that the service or commodity in question has a one-to-one or similarly proportionate exchange equivalence with all other services or commodities equally or similarly measured. It thus enters into the balanced interflow of energy by which the societal structure and organization grows and is maintained.

A customary general term in designating social energy is *service,* and the specific term for its measurement is *value*. A service may, in fact, be defined as a quantity of energy that is social-ized and therefore has value, that is, an equivalence in terms of other social-ized energy—as evidenced by the two being interchanged—either as a present fact or symbolically for a future consummation on the one or the other side. This measurement of energy continuously in terms of some value unit is what keeps up the interflow that constitutes the basic metabolism of the social body. So far as this process is carried on, the social organism has the power to grow and to maintain itself through the interfunctioning of its specialized individuals, organized business groups, institutions, etc., and also to direct its higher energies to the reorganization of its environing world.

The energy of exchange, however, does not flow without resistance. It is retarded by restrictive "regulations," usually approved by popular sentiment and chiefly applied by political authorities, that take it out of the system of free exchange and reduce it to the subsocial level of manifestation in a compulsive or coercive form. But as the social system of men matures, its collisions will be averted, its frictions overcome, by the growth of the voluntary and truly social mode into that realm now occupied by force.

The *social-ized* human energy is that part of the whole that flows in accordance with the common will of all concerned. Such energy is called *service,* and the characteristic that distinguishes it from all other human energy is that it induces a *value* or equivalent counter-flow by way of free and voluntary exchange. The *social* relationship —that of common will and consent—under which this occurs is called *contract.* The energy that is not social-ized is that which flows in opposition to the will of others, thereby involving collision and the weakening or dissolution of social bonds. There does not exist among men any relationship or process, *society-wide in its scope,* other than these two. All the general and interrelated activities of a population are either contractual and social or they are coercive and compulsive—antisocial.[1] The life and growth of a society depends upon the extension of its *contractual* processes and relationships.

The practical application of the science of society must consist in the conscious and rational extension of the contractual or service process into those areas of association where opposite and contrary relationships generally prevail, which is to say, the field of public services, so called. This is made possible by the discovery herein variously set out that the social institution of property in land has in modern times evolved a purely contractual technique with respect to certain public services which it performs and for which it is recompensed on the basis of contract and consent as is normal to all Market transactions. This means that the ordinary transactions of this institution are, fundamentally, exchanges of social-ized energy as services. And the services performed by this institution of property in land, not only are they public and general; they are the basic and primary public services. These services, and only these, bring the inhabitants of a community into peaceable, non-violent relationships with respect to their occupancies or changes of occupancy of the

---

1. For definition of the necessary restraints upon antisocial activities—violence and crime, force and fraud, see Chapter 11.

community sites and resources, or lands. These *contractual* services provide the physical security of possession the inhabitants must have before they can produce commodities and perform services for others, and thus constitute themselves into a society.

Only in recent history has this institution of property in land been differentiated out of the realm of government as force. In its present state of development, it performs only rudimentary—yet fundamental—services. It leaves public affairs for the most part under political and compulsive instead of proprietary and contractual administration, both as to what the inhabitants shall yield up to the political authority (however established) and as to what they shall accept from or endure under it. This large field of compulsive, anti-social activity necessarily infringes that of the free contractual or social-ized energy exchange and thus accounts for the collisions and friction that retard and inhibit the free interflow of energies among men. This causes them to be dissipated at lower levels in the stagnation and decay of economic depressions and in the violences of crimes and wars. These harsh hindrances and even reversals of social progress are patently to be obviated by extending the proprietary contractual technique of public services more fully into the field of common and public affairs. The institution of property in land, once it becomes conscious of its function, will afford the adequate administrative and exchange mechanism for this.

For it is the potential function of property in land, when rightly understood as the contractual distribution of a community's sites and resources and of access to its public advantages, not only to distribute these things peaceably and impartially to the most productive occupiers and users but also to provide the sites, and those who shall physically occupy them, with such protection and security and other services as will induce the voluntary recompense or value called *land value* or ground rent. This affords a purely contractual, non-political and non-compulsive process—a purely business and voluntary exchange method—of providing public services and of being abundantly recompensed for them without infringing the liberties or seizing the properties of those being served, even in the slightest degree. On the contrary, it is the prime responsibility of the community owners (once they discover it) to protect and defend the occupiers of their properties against such taxation and "regulation" as is already known to be unnecessary and therefore wholly harmful. Such alleviatory public services, to whatever extent carried on, would be a flow of social-ized energy automatically recompensed by a counter-flow of the community rent otherwise pent up by friction and collisions and repressions by governmental force.

By such extension of responsible services, as a function of ownership, into the field of the supposed public services that are so precariously based upon political depredations, the friction and collisions of the social system of energy exchange can be diminished and finally removed. Such development by the institution of property in land of its now dormant powers, in addition to the basic distributive function that it already performs, can quietly and *without resistance* gradually dissolve the deadly relationship that now exists between productive industry and the unproductive political state that depends parasitically upon it and that must itself always perish when its destructive work is done. Not only will proprietary protection and amelioration check the actual or imminent decline; its extension into the positive administration of the public and common capital and lands will resolve the frictions and collisions of unsocial-ized energy and thus liberate the social organization to grow into an enduring system of balanced and harmonious energy exchange. Such consummation will raise the social system of mankind to that level of majestic beauty possessed by the vastly older organizations of mass, motion and time—of balanced energy exchange—that constitute the enduring systems of the planets, suns and stars.

CHAPTER 22

## Private Property in Land Explained

### Its Public Administrative Function

THROUGHOUT the nineteenth century, no great social institution was so widely or so inconclusively mooted as that of private property in land. The great rise in private capital and the steady advance of political domination and restriction upon its ownership and administration has tended in the twentieth century to draw interest and attention away from the fundamental, the far broader question of property in land. But in the preceding century, this great institution of civilized mankind came under the severest scrutiny. Minds of great influence and authority were arrayed against it, and its profound modification or its outright abolition was powerfully urged.

In most controversies, both attack and defense rest on premises questioned or disputed by the other side. But the attacks on property in land were based on assumptions that its apologists did not deny; and its defense rested rather upon its existence as a fact than upon any sound justification or any reasoned refutation of the arguments with which it was assailed. Thus a kind of stalemate ensued, little ground being given or taken by either side. In fact, such conspicuous assailants as Herbert Spencer, John Stuart Mill and Henry George came either to withdraw their more drastic proposals and insist that existing values and titles be not disturbed or at least that the structure and framework, "the shell," of the institution be retained in the interest of practical convenience and a stable social order. And so, while the closing of the nineteenth and the opening of the twentieth century witnessed persistent attack on most forms of property, no other great social institution has been so little overtly challenged or openly condemned.

Yet the ownership of land, property in land, undoubtedly went into decline. With the multiplying political assaults on other property, and the mounting penalizations of the processes of its creation and use, the income to land and locations not only ceased to advance but in depressed periods so far went down that even urban locations were no sound security for loans, and country land had little or no sales value, if indeed any value, as land, apart from the improvements or such other property as its owner might possess. With its useful employment—and thus the income to land—so inhibited, its ownership so widely became a burden and a liability that through wide and populous regions it was forced out of the amenities of private use and ownership into the arbitrary administration of political authority, with its necessary implications of corruption, incompetence and political discrimination. In this country, the taxing policies of the states destroyed title to vast properties in rural and even in city and suburban lands. And the Federal Government has now extended its arbitrary and increasingly burdensome jurisdiction over more than a third of the entire nation's lands.[1]

Thus land ownership, in its practical aspect, is defensive and in retreat. With no known theory to justify it, no recognition of its essential function in the social order, and therefore without any constructive program or policy of organized defense, property in land continues, far and wide, to crumble away. Its decline in all lands is hailed, high and low, as "social gains," and its continual erosion by so-called "liberal" measures today is the subtly hidden process that leads to full "*land communism*" without which no totalitarian power can be final or complete.

The present purpose is to show how this institution distributes, without political discrimination, the productive occupancy of land and is thus society's first and last and its only automatic resistance to enslavement by a totalitarian state.

Any social institution, until its *rationale* is disclosed, is empirical, subject to subversion, ignorant and blind. Men habitually accept unthinkingly the blessings of the institution of property, its security and peace, although their traditional and emotional concept of property in general and of property in land in particular, is as a privilege or personal indulgence from which mankind in general are disin-

---

1. *United States Government Organization Manual 1955-56*, pp. 203, 238.

herited and none but the fortunate owner can enjoy. It is as though all property and wealth were personal goods owned only to be consumed or destroyed in self-gratification or sinister and anti-social designs. This is the persistent heritage of the modern mentality from its ancient and totalitarian past, when there was no free exchange economy and few if any free men. The minds of men are yet but little adjusted to the modern fact that the great community of wealth, apart from government, is nearly all of it capital goods and facilities in the course of flow by exchange towards their consummation as satisfactions in consumers' hands where they rapidly dissolve. These flowing goods, together with the fixed and the moving facilities that transform them and accelerate their flow, this *capital wealth,* is the only substantial wealth there is. None of it can be owned as mere gratification or indulgence but only administratively, for the bringing of fully finished services and goods to the condition, place and possession where they can be used or last exchanged and consumed. This *administrative* ownership is the only dominion that an owner can exercise over his capital wealth, whether in land or in goods, and its value not flee.[2]

Thus it is with land. Primitive ownership consists in getting satisfactions directly from it, as the ox gets the grass. But in an exchange society, with its highly specialized services, land, like other property, comes to be owned more and more for the benefits and satisfactions of others. Except when it is used for the owner's personal subsistence, private recreation or place of residence, it is only as a social agency, as a means of giving secure possession and of supplying community services and satisfactions to users, and in no other way, that an owner can practice any dominion over his land. Thus land ownership, except as noted, is not a personal indulgence or enjoyment but a social responsibility, an opportunity of giving services in exchange for recompense in ground rent—in such measure as that responsibility is met and those services are performed.

Land, then, may be, and the most valuable land generally is, owned by one interest and occupied or used by other interests, as tenants,

---

2. A lender of wealth is still its owner. He and the borrower become, in effect, co-administrators on shares, the lender's share being fixed usually in advance.

for the performance of services or the production of goods or services destined for others by their sale or exchange. An exchange economy, where most highly developed, tends to discover the advantages of private capital administration dissociated from the ownership of land. This is seen in the great metropolitan centers and in the practice of nation-wide sales and service organizations so efficient in their own special fields they cannot without loss invest any part of their working capital and specialized skills in the administration of land, even of the land and often the buildings that they themselves use. For the owner cannot be also the occupant or user of his own land except he act in two capacities:—once as the owner whose concern it is that the occupant shall receive valuable services through his location and, again, as his own tenant receiving these services, which he of course takes directly instead of their equivalent in ground rent. Here are very unlike functions devolving on the same person. As owner he is responsible, in common with other owners, for those public and general benefits that give the land its desirability to the tenant and hence its location value. But as a tenant, he is administratively responsible only for the specific and particular services he provides for the patrons of his own enterprise; and this is true even if his enterprise or his employment be elsewhere and even though he may use the public and general services available at the site only for their residential advantages or similar self-advantages to him. As owner, he is a provider and merchandizer of public services; as tenant, he is the purchaser and user or consumer of them.

The combination in one of both owner and user is not found in early societies. It does not characterize ancient society in the Old World fertile valleys of the south; for here the holders of the soil are sharply defined from the users whom in that climate they have from old time by compulsive tribute or taxation enslaved. Nor is it found in early social integrations of the rugged north, where untaxed *free men* rendered *rents* to their land lords by custom of consent, under measure of the market, in exchange for possession and protection and such other common services as the lords supplied. In the south, the proprietor owns both land and man; in the north, until taxation and politics is introduced, he owns only the land. But in either case, the *original* public authority is in the proprietary hands. The ambiguous combination of owner and user makes its appearance in the later slave-supported and tax-based democracies and republics in which the proprietors have yielded their public authority into political and thus irresponsible hands.

When the proprietary authority of northern lands or of northern origins, corrupted by contact with slavery and taxation in the south, fails of its obligation to protect its free men and assumes a coercive power over them, then its members war upon each other until at last they surrender all their power to a king by "divine right" of conquest over them and eventually to transitory elective sovereignties called popular governments. Then the condition of the land lords under *political* "public servants" is but little if any better than that of their once free men. They, too, come under constantly increasing deceits and depredations at the hands of the elected or otherwise accepted political authority. New discoveries and productive technologies delay the fall, but, as the burdens of taxation, "social services" and deficit financing and inflation continue to grow, enterprise at last becomes unprofitable and unsafe, employment shrinks, production falls and the income and value of land necessarily declines. And then the totalitarian state is at hand.

This failure of owners to function as such, publicly and separately from the mere use of land, gives semblance of truth to the wholly fallacious ideas that taxation instead of rent is the normal and honest public revenue of a community; that private use instead of public administration over land is the true function of its ownership; and that tenancy, but not taxation, somehow beguiles free men into a servile state. It is forgotten that with no institution of slavery or taxation, as in Saxon England, land lord and free man are correlative and reciprocal terms, and that serfdom—*servile* feudalism—in England was a consequence of Roman taxation re-imposed, after five free centuries, under Norman arms and rule.

Just as do all private free enterprises, to be effective, require direct or, at the least, supervisory administration by their private owners, so must the public proprietors organize themselves and administer, if they would be secure, the public enterprises through which the private ones must be served instead of being ruled and thereby destroyed. In both kinds of enterprise, public and private, and whether they function little or much, the owners are sharply marked off, and success depends upon actual or at least supervisory administration by them. Looking at the owners of the community lands exclusively in their capacity as such, it is clear that their function in the exchange system has to do with the common services of the community, for these are what they purvey to their tenants to the value and amount measured by the ground rent they receive in exchange.

This ownership of land or sites, apart from the ownership of capital improvements on them, does not involve the administration of any property or enterprise directly on the sites themselves. It does, however, place the owners in an administrative relationship to the *community capital* and services. Their ownership, in the functional sense of obtaining revenue by serving others and thus creating value, has to do only with the public capital and enterprises the services and products of which they sell to their tenants or lessees. But only so far as these public services or improvements are profitable or useful to the lessees will they enhance value and demand. The land owner performs a sales service with regard to all the *net* balance of community benefits, above detriments, that come to the locations occupied by his tenants. Likewise, the land owners taken together, in any community, however small or large, perform this important sales function with regard to all the public services for which there is any actual need and demand—this demand depending on and being limited by the amount of business that can be done and wealth produced under the existing burdens of taxation and the restrictions on business and employment that taxes on business are spent to enforce.

All wealth that is used to prepare and provide any products or services for others is capital wealth. So also are all the materials and commodities that in the course of exchange are being prepared for and moved towards and into consumers' hands. All properties being so used or being so prepared and distributed are social-ized properties or *capital*. Capital, then, is any wealth or property that is owned and used for the benefit of others, and all capital, from the very nature of its administrative ownership and use, is, of necessity, *socialized* property or wealth. Such wealth is not to be confounded with those negligible properties privately produced and consumed that never come into the exchange system, nor with those relatively small amounts of goods that have passed out of that system into individual use and are in process of being consumed or otherwise destroyed. Anything that does not come into the exchange system but is otherwise disposed of or remains in the hand of its producer or appropriator is not social-ized and therefore not capital, for it does not become the instrument of any societal relationship through exchange of services. The same is true of goods that have passed by trade through all the processes of measured exchange and into consumers' hands. These have ceased to be capital or social-ized goods; for their present owners do not engage them in the performance of any social or administrative function. They are not owned as capital is owned. So only that they come to their possessors through the legitimate processes of voluntary exchange, without force or fraud, and that they are then not used for any injury to others, they are not of any public or general concern. Before they enter or after they pass out of the exchange system, they move under no law of social demand; they accumulate no social utility or value and their lapse back into the substance of the earth whence they came is, in the absence of criminal or political coercion, only a matter of individual and not of social control or concern.

It is the same with land. So far as its ownership and its enjoyment or use are by the same person or interest, it is not social-ized; for either it has not entered into or it has passed out of the exchange system. An owner-user is his own land lord and his own tenant, standing in two different relationships to two kinds of property. As owner, his interest is in the public capital and services that give desirability to his location; as user, he is interested in those private properties and improvements that are requisite to his enjoyment or use of the services his location affords. He is like the lawyer who is his own client, the doctor who is his own patient; he is the merchant who is his own customer; he does not, in virtue of his land ownership, give any services to others, and so he foregoes all the advantages of such division of labor and exchange.

Land ownership therefore, as a social function, is a very special division of labor that must be considered with reference to the public properties and services upon which its values depend. This implies a special administration of these community properties by the community owners, separate and apart from any private administration that the user of the land may give to his private properties and improvements. This field of public administration, belonging historically and most fitly, as Adam Smith so strongly suggested,[3] to the land owners collectively is very wide; but, as property in land has modernly developed, this administrative field is far from being fully occupied by them. Nevertheless, one part of this public administration, and that its fundamental and most essential part, they do faithfully, albeit unknowingly, perform. This is the distributive, the merchandising and sales function—that wherein all administration of capital, be it public or private, culminates and fulfills its end.

Merchandising—making sales—is the only manner in which goods or services can be transferred for value received. It is, therefore, the only equitable mode of distribution, the only true exchange. Moreover, it is an administrative process that *none but owners themselves* can perform, for they alone can convey the *ownership* of a thing or service sold. Others may arrange sales, but only the acts of owners can give them force and effect. Transfers without owner consent, such as by taxation or other violence or by crimes, cannot be sales, for such transfers can be accomplished only by force or fraud. Social peace and stability require, therefore, not only that the common services and goods come into being, but also that they be administered and sold by their *owners* and thus distributed equitably to the community inhabitants on the basis of value received. This is the final and wholly indispensable feature of owner-administration over *any* property or services. It applies no less to the distribution of public services than to any other; and this is where the service of merchandising of these services by the community owners plays its supremely

---

3. *Wealth of Nations*, New York, Modern Library, 1937, pp. 248–249.

important role. Most properties, including those of a community character such as hotels, are definitely administered by their *owners* so that salable goods or services are brought forth. The owners then consummate all their prior administrative functions by making sales. But in the public enterprises of *political* communities, this merchandising function is just about the only administrative activity that the owners worthily perform. The community services other than the service of selling them, come into being under haphazard political arrangements in which all the property employed in them is the result of seizures, more or less systematized, on the part of "public servants" and employees, who, being non-owners, can give no responsible administration to this "public capital" nor make any sales or exchanges of public products or services. Indeed, the undoubted owners (title holders) of the political communities so far neglect all supervision of and responsibility for the common services supplied to their properties, other than the sale of them to their tenants, that the "servants" in the larger communities, unlike those in a hotel, are neither hired by the owners nor furnished with any funds for the conduct of their services. For their recompense and expenses, therefore, these "servants of the people" both pledge and seize in advance the monies, credits and properties of the population and disburse these first to themselves (their salaries) and then largely for purposes tending to insure their re-election or otherwise perpetuate their arbitrary power. Throughout all history, the practice of such non-owning and therefore quite irresponsible community servants has been to expand beyond measure their predatory processes, using their takings more and more to subsidize the dependence and the poverty that they cause and thus induce tolerance of and even popular demand for further extensions of their coercive powers.

But protection of the societal, the non-political, system of property and exchange against unauthorized violence or theft is left to the same public authority whose depredations destroy it. So it comes about that its antisocial effects must be weighed off against the benefits and public services that are supposed to arise out of the violence of political operations. This weighing off is effected and takes place in the open market wherein are set, by consent of all and coercion of none, the price equivalents of all the net public services that have any salable or exchange value at the locations to which they are supplied. These prices (rents) are the market determinations of the *net* community values that emerge in virtue of the difference between all the benefits conferred by public authority and all the depredations and distresses sanctioned by and suffered under it.

It is here that the indispensable function of the ownership of land appears. So long and so far as this *social* institution is sustained, just so long and so far, whatever actual net benefits and values of public services there are will come into the scheme of social relationships; for these public advantages will have owners, and these owners, as landowners, will distribute them to the occupiers, as their tenants, for equal values by the pro-social process of sale and exchange. These social benefits and services, being owned, can thus be purchased and securely enjoyed by the tenants to whom they are sold.

First and foremost of these benefits will be security of possession. The occupant obtains this security by an exchange process that is inviolate only so far as private property in land is respected and upheld. While this institution stands, a civilized society with secure and definite places of work and abode and exchange is possible; when it is destroyed, there can be no security either of ownership or possession, no respecting of property or freedom in any form; for then no occupancy or possession can rest on any sanction but the arbitrary will and power of a self-constituted or an elected coercive authority. Respecting the prerogative of ownership, and thereby of the exchange relationship between owners and tenants, is all that stands between the peaceable possession and use of land, between the amenities of civilized relationships and finally the dearth and darkness of utter slavery or a nomadic barbarism. These dire alternatives to private ownership and, thereby, security in the possession of land make plain the absolute indispensability of that institution to any social or civilized order of life.

Beyond seeing its indispensability, it remains to ascertain and measure the social value of the services rendered to society by the institution of property in land. Rather, it remains to be observed how, in the functioning of the social organism, this value is measured and its equivalent rendered in exchange. If it be suggested that the labor of land owners is very light, it should be remembered that not the onerousness but the need and *social utility* of a service is the gauge of its market value. Land owners may not even be conscious that their acts of ownership which confer security and services upon their tenants are an indispensable service to the society; nevertheless, they do cause whatever there is of net public services, less public disservices, to be distributed without favor and for value received. Ground rents, then, taken in the aggregate, are the exchange equivalent that a community renders to the institution of property in land for the security of possession and access to public benefits that its members thus enjoy. This is the social value and justification of the institution as it now stands. So far as it is permitted to operate, so far as the owners are not taxed out of their values and thus out of their ownership, it is the instrument of society whereby security of possession is guaranteed to land users and the net benefits of public services, such as they may be, are apportioned impartially among those most capable of their productive use.

It being accepted that property in land is the social device that confers security and thus makes other exchange relationships possible, it still remains to discern why the recompense that it yields should be precisely what it is, namely, the whole *ground rent* remaining after taxes. Here a striking automatism of adjustment appears. When, as is now usual, land owners perform no administrative services beyond providing the security of possession that is implicit in their orderly merchandising of the rights of occupancy, then the rent that springs up by the open and unforced operations of the market is a recompense that is socially determined and automatically awarded to them for this limited service.

Any public benefit that is not merchandised to the recipient for its full value in exchange must be a favor or a privilege and therefore a social detriment and of no social value. No exchange value can arise from it. The benefit to one becomes a detriment to others, and no social purpose is served. But the merchandising function converts public benefits into public values and services. It distributes them equitably, makes them legitimate, and also provides their recipients with the security necessary to enjoy them or to use them for the benefit of others in the course of business and exchange. There is no way in which public benefits can become services, not exploitations, except they be treated as the land owners' properties and measured out by them in exchange for rent. Because this merchandising process lifts public benefits from what must otherwise be privileges and exploitations into their character as services, this process may be said to *create* them as and into services. The rent received for them is then seen as no more than the due recompense for creating them.

With no other authority but location owners can this exchange relationship arise. The consequence is that when political activities are so carried on that there is any residue of benefits between the good and the evil of all public operations, then this positive residue of public advantage can be rightly obtained by no other means than by purchasing possession and use of the territory and locations to which these net benefits and advantages are served. The value, then, of security of possession is in reality the value of the services by which that security is obtained and assured. This security and its equitable distribution the private ownership of land alone creates and guarantees. The rents paid are the social values voluntarily and automatically rendered for this prime and vital public service.

It may be objected that some part or all of the rent should be passed on to the "public servants" (government) the *net* benefits of whose operations are the foundation—the raw material, as it were—of the services that land owners perform. The answer is that without the function of land ownership being performed in sales services, any public benefit or advantage to one would rest on even greater detriments to others, and because of this there would not be any net benefits. It is by this sales service alone that any public advantage can enter a market and thereby come into legitimate existence as a service or value given in exchange.

Moreover, all community "servants," other than land owners, are already *self*-recompensed for all that they do. They receive no income and exercise no powers, have no instruments of work or weapons of war, but what they derive from the forcible appropriation of property and services. Thus they recompense themselves in advance for all that they do. But they advance no public costs, make no public investments, create no public values. Because they are *ex*-propriators of others, and not owners of what they seize, they can give it no productive administration, and it yields them no income. The *ex*-propriated wealth (government seizures), for want of authentic ownership, ceases to function as productive capital and melts away, to be replenished only by further seizures which, in their turn, are consumed and destroyed.

The only pro-social and constructive public administration is that which is normally performed, albeit unknowingly, by the owners of community sites or lands. By their services alone are any political benefits raised from private privileges into public values through open bargain and sale. To them alone comes public revenue gauged to the value of the services received and not appropriated by force. Only through them can political actions result in social or public values. And only so far as this non-political administration and distribution is first performed by community owners can there be any other security of ownership, any measure of freedom from political administration of sites and resources and all that it entails, any general coöperation by free exchange, any free society at all.

The indispensability of property in land should be sufficiently clear, but the social potentialities of that institution have hardly been touched. When land owners extend their administration beyond the mere sale of possession and of the public benefits appurtenant thereto, when they organize themselves so as to enter into the *conduct* of community affairs as true and worthy lords (Anglo-Saxon: the guardians, the givers) of their lands, their first public service will be to procure reduction in some of the least necessary and more destructive forms of tax taking and of tax spending that are degrading into tax-enslaved bondmen the men of business who strive to make productive use of the sites and resources of the land. Such tax reduction, especially when seen as a continuing policy, will so release the frozen energies and facilities of production and exchange, and so replenish wages and profits out of the expanding production, that the demand for sites and lands, and therewith their value and income, will enormously rise. And it will rise at a rate far beyond the rate at which the tax burden on their use will be removed.

When this occurs, then the institution of property in land will rise from its present lethargy and come into its own, the largest, the most productive, and the most profitable business in the world. The merely negative services of relief, of even partial restoration of freedom inviolably to own and manage one's business and property, will bring the whole exchange economy into such enormous productivity as to raise rents and land values permanently to heights undreamed. This will give the land owning interest—the organized land lords—a new, sound and abundant basis for the maintenance and operation of the existing community capital and services and for the financing of every new public enterprise that can justify itself by raising either the productivity or the cultural attractiveness of the community and so realize for land ownership, organized as a business, increasing profits and dividends by the creation of rent.

In this *proprietary* administration of the community services and properties by the organized owners themselves, the slightest neglect of the public interest or lapse in the form of corruption or oppression would itself penalize them by decline in rents and values. Enterprise and efficiency will respond not only to the allurement of profit but will reap also the high satisfactions of honor and public acclaim. From region to region, the proprietary organizations, looking even beyond all material gains, will rival one another in the health and beauty of their communities and their peoples' wealth and joy. Government by seizures and repressions and penalizations will emerge into the civilized technique of mutual service by voluntary exchange. Public administration will become at last a high emprise that may rise and attain even to a new world of beauty through creative artistry.

For this mighty transformation, it is only necessary that the site-owning interest, or substantial portions of it duly organized in corporate or similarly effective form, merge their separate titles and interests and take in exchange corresponding undivided interests in the whole. To do this, they will have their separate interests appraised and vested in the corporate organization as trustee and certificates of stock or beneficial ownership issued back to them according to the appraised values of their respective contributions. This working organization will then, as it were, manufacture public benefits and services, beginning, doubtless, with protection against excessive taxation and over-regulation, and merchandise them to the rent-paying inhabitants. In this way public as well as private services will be produced and distributed by free enterprise to free men. The profits earned by such community organizations will surely grow to be enormous. Their common voting shares will come into wide popular demand, and the free and prosperous inhabitants will thus become the happily enfranchised *owners as well as participants* in the community properties and services that they own and enjoy. Thus will public proprietorship become available to all, and the voting of free men, duly qualified according to their ownership, will realize, in substance and in fact through popular proprietorship, the long-sought democratic dream.

In the beginning, some owners will hold out for a time. They will benefit with the rest, but they and their unincluded properties will naturally receive second consideration in all matters of public benefit or preferment. Unenfranchised as owners, their influence and advantages all will be of second rate, and self-interest will impel them to prefer and to bid for undivided interests and enfranchisement through ownership in the whole.

Pending the necessary enlightenment for these happy consummations through community land owners acting as business organizations, it is only possible to regard with sorrow how they are allowing the freedom and the free enterprises of their inhabitants to be strangled and the income and value of their own properties thus to be destroyed under their very eyes.

When one has no wrongs to avenge and no axes to grind, it is quite possible to observe objectively and describe correctly the structures in any accessible field of phenomena and the manner in which the diverse parts act with reference to one another to promote the growth of the structure and maintain the total functioning and integrity of the whole.

Society is an *organization* of living units. It is therefore organic and alive. Its members, singly and in specialized groups, perform unlike functions or services in the satisfaction of each other's needs and desires. This exchange process goes on only in places where common services that are necessary to the exchange relationship are performed upon the common and public parts of the community by some kind of public authority and through these public parts of the territory conveyed to and made appurtenant to the private parts held in exclusive possession. These private parts are under the social, non-coercive jurisdiction of publicly constituted *owners* as the *proprietary* officers and, except in the early stages of a modern exchange economy, are chiefly in possession of tenants or lessees in a free exchange relation to them. The political authority, however, is observed to do not only needful and necessary things but also, and in ever increasing quantity and variety, things that are so harmful to the society that the net balance of good above the evil in the public administration ever tends toward zero. Exchange, and in consequence production, is inhibited and the diminished productivity causes at once a diminished use, need and demand for lands or locations with a diminished ability to pay for the diminished benefits of possessing them. But the net benefits of public operations, whether great or small, come to have an exchange value and to be distributed otherwise than as special privileges only through the merchandising of them by the owners of the sites and lands. The proprietors are recompensed in rents for the beneficial acts they perform in being the active agents of society by which security of possession, including all other public services, as such, are obtained. The value of this distributive service, performed by proprietors, is attested by its being paid to them in open market with free competition on every side, and by the further consideration that without this service of contractual distribution by land lords, possession by or dispossession of any occupant would rest on nothing but the force or favor of politically elected and obligated persons and all safety and security would be gone.

In conclusion, it may be noted that no attempt has been made to lay the ghostly "moral" arguments against property in land. The ponderous syllogisms of the early Herbert Spencer and the myopic formulations of Malthus, Ricardo and Henry George have a kind of formal symmetry within their premised settings; but they are not at all relevant even as partial descriptions of a functioning society or community organization. They are premised on the supposed subjectivity of an individual, his "rights" and desires and how he is supposed to feel about them, or their supposed infringement. No social institution can be evaluated or appraised on any such premises. Arguments so based can have no revealing pertinency in a picturing of the free and voluntary interactions among its units by means of which a society evolves and is sustained. This discussion therefore avoids both argument and refutation in its somewhat detached description of how, in a social organization, human services, public as well as private, are incorporated in property and distributed by exchange.

When the real nature and the necessary services of property in land become better known and understood, land and site owners will organize themselves into agencies of much wider administrative service, authority and responsibility than they now assume. They will then be able to confer upon their respective communities almost unimaginable relief and advantages, and the production and exchanges of their populations, so freed and so served, can then lift them all into all the plenty and peace they now so sadly lack and deeply crave. And these true lords of the land, guardians of its free men and public servants of all, will find themselves recompensed in such abundance of rent and capital values as were never known and in such finer satisfactions to themselves as only dreamers can conceive. With this wider service, the institution of private property in land will be in splendor redeemed and its blessings fully enjoyed; without this, it will continue to be governmentally destroyed and social progress cease.

## Specific Conclusions

LAND OWNERS, in their capacity as publicly authorized officers renting sites and locations to land users, afford the only market there is in which publicly created benefits can be distributed justly for value received and at rates socially and not arbitrarily set and determined.

All public benefits allocated otherwise, and not in accordance with value received, are beneficial to some only by being detrimental to others. No social values can thus arise.

The only values resulting from government are those that manifest themselves in the values of sites and locations within the community or the territory served by it. The value of land, as expressed in net rent actually received and retained, is the only net value that arises out of public or governmental operations.

Changes in the amount, scope or form of governmental activity can be socially beneficial only when they lift some of the limitations on the use of and demand for land and thus raise rental values.

Land administration, landlord-ism, by merchandising natural advantages and publicly created benefits, transforms them from special and private privileges, precariously held, into social and public values justly apportioned and securely enjoyed.

Modern civilization has risen upon the development of free enterprise through the private ownership and thereby the contractual administration and exchange of property and services, superseding the old-time slave jurisdiction of governments over the production and distribution of personal services and goods.

Its further advance depends upon extension of this non-political, free enterprise system of property and contract into the field of community or public services through development of community proprietary authorities to promote public welfare by the self-supporting process of providing needful community services—primarily some degree of common protection (*com-munitio*) against taxation—for the creation of community rent. The rent thus created will recompense automatically the community services that create it.

The organic society that, in the field of individual services—that of production and distribution for other than the common use—, has in recent centuries evolved a proprietary system of free enterprise, is destined to evolve a corresponding free proprietary system, in lieu of coercive political administration, for all those properties and services that are common to all.

With the public system thus become reciprocal and coöperative, instead of predatory and piratical upon the private system, society will become permanent, and the livings and the lives of civilized men become secure.

CHAPTER 23

## The Business of Community Economics

ECONOMICS means the management of a house, a city or a state as a community.

A social-ized or civilized condition of men is one in which they coöperate by division of labor in democratic or willing exchange of services one with another.

Civilized men must live in communities because it is only in community life that there can be any voluntary exchange of services; here there must be community services and property in order that private services and property may be created, owned or exchanged.

A hotel or apartment house, an office or professional building or an industrial building is a community because a portion of its space and occupants is designated and given over to the common use and service of all. This refers to means of communication, corridors, stairways, elevators, etc., with all proper furnishings, equipment, services, protections, etc., needful to the inhabitants for their *common* use and enjoyment, often including heat and air conditioning, light, power, water and gas, and even recreational and educational facilities and other cultural attractions supplied by the proprietors of the community property or under their consent and control.

The community property, with all its services, is under the *proprietary* jurisdiction and therefore *contractual* administration of its organized owners, each of whom owns not a separate portion but an undivided and therefore united interest in the entire property, in the community as a whole. Thus organized, the proprietors finance and maintain and otherwise administer the whole property and all its services out of the proceeds from their services in renting or leasing particular portions and thereby merchandising to their tenants the entire community services and advantages in the proportions that these appertain to each particular portion and are so distributed.

For this purpose, particular portions of the community property are set apart for separate and exclusive occupancy and use. The exclusive occupants, present and prospective, themselves determine the value and proper recompense to the proprietors for such of the community services as come to them through their exclusive possessions of these parts. They do this by, in effect, bidding upwards for the occupancies of these separate parts while the proprietors of different communities offer them at downward prices until the highest biddings and the lowest offers meet.

The organized proprietors through their officers supervise the employees and thus administer the community property as their capital. And out of the rents they receive from the separate occupants, the proprietors meet all the costs of current labor and other services, interest on their investment and all other necessary expenses. The balance they retain as profits of administration, or the earnings from their administrative services.[1]

So it is with the basic though but little developed organization of the out-of-doors communities called towns, cities, states and nations. These public communities also are *owned* by proprietors who hold their proprietary jurisdiction, their title and authority, under power of public opinion—a social institution of property by common consent that is prior to all legislation. But the owners of these larger and older communities are not organized in any merger of their properties. Each still holds his separate and divided interest. There is no concentrated owning interest organized to administer the community as a whole by providing the inhabitants with services in such manner as to induce a voluntary and a profitable revenue from them. And these larger communities, though essential to civilization, have been notorious throughout history for their lack of permanence

---

1. Strictly speaking, only such services as the *owner* or owners of property devote directly or indirectly to the use or service of others (capital or capital-ized property) are administrative services. Authority over property delegated to an agent as officer or employee is not strictly administrative, for he is not an owner and his recompense is stipendiary, not contingent on earnings as profits are. Profits are recompense for services performed by owners. All other recompenses are for subordinate, delegated or directed services.

and success. All but the more recent of them have decayed and fallen, and signs are not wanting that these are now on the downward path of their predecessors.

Seldom if ever has any great community gone down except from or after much internal decay, and small communities are no exception to the rule. Let us examine, then, what are the essentials of the successful and profitable conduct and keeping of the small communities referred to. The whole may be summed up in the one word, *management*.

Practical persons know that in a community housekeeping, such as a hotel, management above all else is vital to its success. Good management can overcome great adversities, but under no amount of favorable conditions can a business long continue under management that is bad, neglectful or lacking on the part of its owners.

The great social function of ownership is—*administration*. This has to do with all of the property and capital, including the purchases and sales of services and products and supervision over the services of all non-owners or employees engaged in the enterprise.

These non-owners, however high in rank, can exercise no original but only the delegated authority of the owners. They come, therefore, rightly under such supervision. In all successful enterprises of ordinary size, this supervision by owners is definitely performed. But in large-scale business, especially where there is monopoly or governmental control, ownership and management are frequently "divorced"; and high-ranking employees, coming under no adequate supervision, assume original instead of delegated powers and proceed to operate the property and business in disregard alike of the interests of its owners and the welfare of those to whom its products and services are sold. This is a condition of internal decay that no small business, community or otherwise, can or ever does long survive.

A large business, however, is like a large organism; it is longer lived. It takes longer to grow and longer to die. This is especially observed in community business. Let a small private community like a hotel spring up; if ownership is divorced from management, it quickly goes down. Let a city or a state arise, and under like conditions it grows more slowly and more slowly declines. And an empire may take centuries to compass its career.

A community organization may exist indoors or out of doors; it may be a building or collection of buildings or it may be a territory. If a building, it may be a hotel or an office or industrial building. If it is a territory, it is a community, a town, city, county or state.

A community must have space, population, services and property. The occupants must have private properties and services and be free to exchange these or the use of them among themselves; and they must own and administer these properties in order to exchange them.

In like manner, the property and services which are common to the community must have community owners to administer and exchange them, the same as individual properties and services must have private or individual owners to administer and exchange them.

In exchange for the community services they receive, the occupants of the community give to the owners of the community properties and services a portion of their private properties and services. Such private property and services, rendered by accepted custom or voluntary exchange for community services, is called *rent*.

The rent paid by the occupants of a hotel or other community building is paid in exchange for the common and general services the occupants enjoy. Special and particular services, not open to all, are purchased and paid for separately as received, and not in the rent.

The rent paid by the occupants of a town, city, state or other territory is paid in exchange for the common and general or public services that the community affords. The amount of rent paid for community services depends upon their exchange or market value as it appears in connection with different plots, according to their size and location, and the demand for them. This is ascertained and fixed by the owners in different communities and different owners in the same community offering their community services (as supplied to their respective plots) in competition with one another. This presses rents downward, while those who would occupy the plots and enjoy the services they afford bid upwards against one another until the two sides of the market, the asking and the bidding, are in agreement as to the rent.

## THE BUSINESS OF COMMUNITY ECONOMICS    145

In a hotel community, the owners of the community properties, facilities and services administer them for the benefit of the occupants. In this way they cause the occupants willingly to pay rent for them to an amount adequate to meet all the costs of maintaining this community and its services and also a profit to the owners to the full value of their administrative services. A hotel not so conducted for the benefit of its occupants will have much of its space either unused or rented at unprofitable rates. Hotel owners, therefore, do administer their properties and do supervise all the servants of the hotel community primarily in the interest of the occupants and thus in their own interest of receiving adequate rent to meet all the costs of the business and assure them their rightful profits besides.

The owners of outdoor communities, towns, cities and states, do not seem to know that their ownership of the space and the area includes also the public capital and services of the communities, and that they are capital owners by the fact that their income from their lands is the earnings of that public capital and comes to them by virtue of such capital ownership, however acquired. These public community owners, therefore, do not consciously administer their property. They leave its management almost entirely in the hands of unsupervised community servants and employees of all degrees, high and low, who hold office and power by getting themselves elected, honestly or otherwise, or by other usurpation.

Since the community owners neither supervise these community servants, as hotel owners always supervise theirs, nor actively administer the community capital and properties vested in them by their ownership of the land, the community income from rents very properly does not pay the owners for any services beyond those that they do perform. Beyond paying the land owners for the services and benefits which, on the whole, the community does receive from them, the net rent does not suffice to pay the cost of the hired services and the carrying charges on the borrowed capital engaged in the community enterprises.

In consequence of their failure to administer and supervise their community properties and servants, the community owners have no funds wherewith to hire public labor and capital. For not taking the authority and responsibility of owners, they forfeit the income and so lose the financial ability to make good their proper authority. The "public servants," therefore, have excuse, and in fact no alternative but to exact taxes by compulsion and make seizures of the private properties of the inhabitants in order to maintain themselves and their public operations, whether beneficial or otherwise. The occupants of the public communities are thus exposed not only to the devastation of constantly increasing seizures of their property, but also to having the public servants impose their unbridled activities and operations upon them, with but little reference to the public interest and welfare beyond a meretricious popularity as the means of maintaining themselves in place and power.

Although in all respects a public community is, in principle, the same as a hotel, the default of the owners of the community territory, who are also, in effect, the owners of the community property and capital, permits the community welfare and affairs to fall into the hands of elected or self-constituted political "public servants" without ownership of, and therefore without responsibility for, the community properties, welfare and values. In the resulting confusion, violence and distress, the despairing population falls at last into the iron arms of dictatorship and a military despotism in which all properties and values are destroyed and barbarism returns.

Civilized life is community life. And community values are the foundation of all other civilized values. The value and income of sites and lands is the value and income from all the community properties, public capital and services that are used in common by the community inhabitants. Failure of the owners to administer these properties and supervise these services so that their income will rise spells the inevitable decline. Rent—the value of land—is the sole index of community services and community values. Upon its rise the progress of civilization depends.

The great social need is a conscious union of ownership and administration in the large community enterprises that are called towns and cities, states and nations. In such union, when happily it comes, these communities will be crowned in strength and beauty, in a peace and glory that will never die.

CHAPTER 24

## Questions for the Consideration of Land Owners[1]

BEING THE PROPRIETARY OFFICERS BY AND THROUGH WHOM SOCIETY EXERCISES A SOCIAL JURISDICTION OVER ITS TERRITORY

### 1. *Dependence of Value Upon Income*

DOES not the value of your properties, like the value of any other investment, depend finally upon the income that they return to you?

Is not their present actual value the capitalized net rent that they yield and is not their prospective or speculative value merely the capitalization of prospective rent or prospective increase in the rent yield?

Is not all your capital enhancement due, finally, to the enhancement of rent and to the prospects for its enhancement?

Is not the value of occupied land made up of the actual rent capitalized, plus or minus the prospective increase or the prospective shrinkage in the actual income from rent?

And is not the "value" of all unoccupied or non-income-bearing lands merely a *speculative* value—the capitalization of the prospects for *future* rent being received?

### 2. *Public Services in Excess of Public Disservices Necessary to Land Value: Effective Demand Also No Less Necessary*

Are not public services indispensable to the existence of all civilized values and, therefore, does not your land have a value only so long as public authority, as a whole, does less harm to your territory and its inhabitants than it does good, and thus makes ground value and ground rent possible?

---

[1]. This Chapter, in the form of questions, is an introduction to and a condensed treatment of the same general theme more fully developed in the next Chapter.

Is not your *net* ground rent (the basis of present land value) merely the market expression of the difference between what public authority creates and what public authority destroys; i.e., between what it does to and what it does for the inhabitants of your territory?

Is not *net* ground rent the measure of what is left to you and your tenants (the rent to you and its market equivalent to them) between the right hand of community service and the left hand of property seizure by taxation, with its consequent public distress?

When rising taxation and governmental restrictions make business and production unprofitable, does not this destroy the *demand* for your sites and locations?

If the *demand* for your property is being destroyed, what does it avail that it be rich in natural resources or advantages or that it be well supplied with public improvements and services—even though it be located in the midst of population?

### 3. *Public Business Now Poorly Organized—Destroying Values Instead of Creating Them*

Is not government the only business in the world that is conducted exclusively by persons on wages or salaries and carried on without any proprietary supervision?

Do you as the community proprietors who merchandise all public advantages or services to your customers (tenants or purchasers) take any conscious, willing or active part in either the administering or the financing of them?

Are not the community servants (servants of your territory) in need of proprietors to supervise and finance them and sell their services to the public—just as the employees in a private business are?

Is it not your proper interest as the land lords of your communities to finance and administer the services you sell to your tenants, the same as it is for the land lords of a hotel to do so?

If the owners who collect in rents the value of all the general services performed, either in an open community or in a hotel, fail to administer the properties and supervise the services and permit the servants to seize the property, regulate the affairs and prostrate the business of the occupants, will not the one as surely as the other go bankrupt and eventually lose all income?

4. *Land Value a Service Value—Rent the Automatic Recompense to Land Owners for Services*

Do you think your tenants pay rent merely for earth or space, or do they pay you for the net balance between the advantages enjoyed and the disadvantages that must be suffered by those who occupy that space?

Is not your *net* ground rent really the income from the community business remaining to you after all labor and material and public debt costs have been deducted in advance by taxation?

Do you not suffer in your own rents and values from the taxation and restrictions on your tenants—restrictions that smother their business and hinder them from producing the wealth out of which to pay rent—even more than you suffer from the taxes that fall directly on your values and incomes after you receive them—and prevent you from keeping very much out of the little rents that your tenants *can* pay?

5. *Income to Land Owners (Rent) Arises from the Administration of Public Capital and Sale of its Services*

Since your final net income is really what the public business earns for you as the public proprietors, after its costs—both necessary and unnecessary, proper and improper—have been deducted by taxation, then is not your income really and precisely what the public capital yields to you above the cost of public labor and public debt?

When each of you became, as land owners, the public proprietors, did you not, in effect, make investment in the public capital with a view to the net income then yielded or then expected to be yielded by it?

6. *Land Owners the Equity Owners of the Public Capital and Income—The Real Owners*

Is it not the order of nature and of society that land owners, as the public proprietors, must receive collectively in ground rent whatever *net* income is yielded by the public capital?[2]

Does not this fact constitute you the beneficial owners and therefore, in a business sense, the *real* owners of that public capital?

Is it not highly advantageous to all parties that the real owners of the capital engaged in any service or enterprise should direct and administer that enterprise?

And does this not apply to you, as the proprietors of the public capital that is engaged in the public enterprises, as much as it applies to the private owners of the private capital that is engaged in private enterprises?

### 7. *Obligations of Land Owners to Themselves and to Their Communities*

If you were the proprietors of a hotel instead of an open community, you would know that you owned the capital invested in that hotel and that your income was the earnings of that capital, after deducting all costs.

Would you permit the servants in that hotel to destroy your income by the seizing of property, controlling and destroying their business and violating the liberties of the occupants of your hotel?

Would it not be your very first and obvious duty to yourselves and to your tenants not to sanction these abuses but, rather, to protect them against such fatal exploitation?

Is it not now your corresponding obligation to yourselves and to your tenants to stand between them and further seizures of their property and destruction of their business by taxation, in order to revive demand and thus restore the values of your holdings by making saleable the public advantages that your locations afford?

### 8. *General Tax Relief a Public Service and Advantage to Tenants*

Does not taxation now stifle business, inhibit its expansion and thus enforce both under-employment and under-production?

---

2. The conventional manner of speech is here employed. Not capital itself, but the administration of capital, including the sale of its use—lending or leasing it—creates earnings or income.

Is not much of this taxation wholly unnecessary to essential community operations and is it not expended often for purposes injurious to your present and prospective tenants and purchasers—prejudicial alike to their welfare and to your values?

Would not the removal or reduction of such unnecessary taxes be a positive boon, a public benefit, service and advantage, to every business that occupies or uses land and pays rent to obtain and enjoy community advantages?

Would not your tenants be benefited first, by the direct amount of their exemption from taxation; second, by relief from the indirect discouragement of enterprise and curtailment of production caused by the imposition of unnecessary taxation; third, by their relief from those regulative, restrictive and destructive activities on the part of government that give excuse for needless taxation and which unnecessary taxation is imposed to support; and, finally, by their relief from uncertainties as to changes in the tax policies, which so greatly discourage the growth of free and forward-looking enterprise?

## 9. Tax Reduction the Key to Restoring and Raising Land Values

Do you think that with all the foregoing benefits and advantages to the conduct of their businesses, that with all your unburdening of industry and wealth production from restrictions and penalizations, your tenants would not bid eagerly for sites and public services until the amount of new rent created would far exceed in amount all of the taxation abolished and all present rents combined?

Would you not receive the entire amount of new rent so created as your proper recompense for your services to your tenants in lifting such burdens from them and safe-guarding their prosperity?

Would not this eventually result in all public values coming to you as rents and all public costs flowing through your hands, making you the paymasters and thus establishing *you* as the natural supervisors of the community servants, the proper administrators of the community capital and the honorable distributors and merchandisers of its services to the public throughout your communities?

### 10. *Public or Community Service—Administration of Community Capital—The Only Business Proper to Land Owners*

As owners, administrators and supervisors of the public capital and labor, would not every act and policy of good administration be rewarded and recompensed to you in superior rents for your location, while any lapses from good administration would be penalized by diminishing your returns?

Would not such conduct of your business redeem your now precarious fortunes and at the same time put the providing of public services upon a value-received basis instead of a privilege basis and redeem government from its present practices of force and indirection in obtaining its revenues and from the restrictive policies that impair all revenues and values and so thrust idleness upon land, upon capital and upon men? If you organize yourselves as the public proprietors and guardians of the public welfare in your communities and, exercising your virtual ownership of the public capital, you knowingly administer it—if thus organized and, as responsible owners of the community capital as well as of its lands, you safeguard your tenants, patrons and purchasers against public violence and expropriation and provide efficient administration of the public services that you sell—will not this far greatest and highest business enterprise in an increasingly prosperous land then yield to you magnificent profits and build for you property values incalculably high?

Great as are these material rewards, you will merit, in addition, the highest civic honor and public acclaim—the lasting gratitude of mankind.

CHAPTER 25

# The Administration of Real Property as Community Services

### REAL ESTATE ADMINISTRATION FOR PROFIT

I

ALL BUSINESS consists in the administration of property, and all net revenue or profit from business is the product of administrative services.

The real estate business comprises the administration of two different kinds of property: (1) land, with the public improvements and services—the *public capital*—appurtenant to it, and (2) the private improvements and services—the *private capital*—appurtenant to it. Strictly speaking, in neither case is it *land* that is owned. In the one case what is distributed or sold is the use of public capital. In the other it is the use of private capital that is distributed and sold. The public capital is appurtenant to the land laterally or horizontally, touching the sides of and lying between the various parcels and plots. The private capital is attached vertically and is appurtenant perpendicularly to the site. The public capital is public because it improves, appertains to and is common to many sites, whereas a private improvement appertains to and is attached to only one site.

The land with its public improvements yields to its owner, above taxes, a net revenue that is called ground rent. The private improvements yield to their owner, above ordinary interest and expenses, a net revenue that is properly called the profits of administration, or the earnings of administrative labor.

The ownership and management of real estate, then, is a special division of general business in the fact that it is the administration of fixed instead of movable and personal properties. It differs from a commercial, manufacturing or industrial business only in that the property being administered, with the services incorporated in it, is not being passed from hand to hand as in these industries, but the services of it are divided up into periods of time and sold piecemeal, as it were, under various tenancies, and, except where full title is transferred, the physical turnover of the business takes the form of renewals and replacements, instead of transfers of ownership outright.

In a very primitive economy, the owner-administrator, such as a farmer, merchant or manufacturer, is commonly the owner of and must administer different kinds of property. He owns personal property in his products, which are his moving capital, or turnover, and also in his movable equipment and appliances. He owns real estate in all his fixed equipment and improvements. This is his fixed capital. And he also owns real estate in his land, and in this he has the services of public capital as the basis of its value. Not only must he administer all these various kinds of property, but he must supervise all the subordinate labor he engages to assist him in his enterprise. Such organization of industry is simple only in the sense of there being but little division of labor; from the standpoint of the multiplicity and wide diversity of the functions the owner must perform, his situation is not simple but highly complex.

The whole development of industry consists in its being divided up into many different kinds of units that are structurally separate and distinct but that are connected together by the system of commercial exchange. This division takes place along the lines of the different kinds of properties and services to be administered. The more highly the type of administration suitable for one kind of property is developed, the less such an owner or organization of owners can afford to have its capital tied up in properties requiring a different type of administration. This is exemplified in chain sales organizations, the owners of which cannot afford to have their capital tied up in, or to give administrative services to, the buildings they occupy, much less the land and the public improvements appurtenant to it. In like manner, the most highly specialized business and professional persons seldom own the premises they occupy, not because they lack the necessary resources but because they cannot give effectively the special administrative services that such properties require.

So it comes to pass that in an advanced economy, and especially in metropolitan communities, the different types of properties are held generally under separate ownership and administration. The movables, in both turnover and appliances, are owned and managed by tenants of buildings or of other private improvements on land. These buildings, with all their fixed appliances and services, are owned and administered by persons or organizations who are themselves tenants of the lands they occupy. And these lands, with all the public appliances and services appurtenant to them, are administered by persons and organizations who own them and who, because of their titles as proprietors and the services they perform, are, in effect, public officers distributing the use and benefits of public capital—servants of the community as a whole.

Every tenant in a building, residing or carrying on business there, is a purchaser of the services that the building provides. It is the proper and useful business of those who own and administer the building to see that all the services of the building to its tenants are adequately and efficiently supplied. Their whole profit from the building is the product of this administrative activity. This includes general upkeep and maintenance, the purchase of materials and supplies and the payment of wages for labor engaged in upkeep and in all the services that are provided for the tenants. All of this, and the interest paid on or credited to the fixed investment, is the current capital turnover. The only profit of the enterprise, the only return for administrative services, will be the amount by which the returns from rentals exceed all these current costs.

Now, since building space and services are sold in open market, it is clear that the rentals represent the market value of the space and services. It is the aim and duty of good administration to make and maintain this value at the highest level. This requires, first, that the services be supplied and maintained, but over and above this, it also requires that everything that is possible be done to keep up the public demand. This branch of building or hotel administration extends to such matters as protecting the tenants from all theft, injury or insubordination on the part of the service personnel, as well as policing the premises and guarding the tenants against everything inimical to their comfort and prosperity. All of these negative services maintain the demand and therefore the value of the positive services supplied.

Now just as the building owners depend for their market upon the demand for building services by the owners of movable goods and services, so do the owners of land depend upon the demand of those who own and administer building properties and services. The building or hotel owner sells services; so does the land owner; and good administration has in both cases two aspects: not only the keeping up and improvement of the services themselves, but also the building up and maintaining of a proper and sufficient demand for them.

It must be granted that building owners have thus far shown a keener consciousness of the essentials of their business. They have not at great cost purchased buildings, only partly tenanted or yielding but little income, and then abandoned them to the mercies of the servants and employees without supervision or control or sufficient funds, permitting them to find the costs and deficiencies by levies on the properties and operations of the tenants. Building owners are too wise for this. But the owners of lands and locations do something very similar. They purchase costly sites, idle or only partly tenanted and yielding little income. They contribute a portion of the cost of the public benefits received by their properties, yet they leave the conduct of these services entirely unsupervised in the hands of the public servants themselves. But, instead of doing anything to protect their present or prospective tenants in the quiet use and enjoyment of buildings or other improvements, the site owners acquiesce and even encourage the public servants and authorities in their practice of levying on and seizing the properties and demoralizing the business and belongings of the occupants of the buildings. Land owners do not know or do not realize that all these charges laid against the tenants of buildings and against the tenants of the land, who own the buildings—that all these respectable depredations against both kinds of tenants *drastically limit their rent-paying power* and cancel out the advantages for which all these tenants pay.

This condition manifests itself in two ways: first, as to the lands and the buildings actually occupied, it cuts down the amount of rent that can be offered or paid by the occupants, and, second, by its deterrent effect upon new tenants and new occupancies, it limits and tends to hold down the entire demand for land and building services to that of present occupants alone. The result is that only the lands and buildings that are in present use have any present or income value, and all those potential properties kept out of use in this manner have no present actual value at all, however much may be the investment in them without income—unless they be allowed a mere gambler's value, the value of speculative hopes or expectations. And the carrying of all such idle properties without income as often happens through long periods of depression is a heavy loss of capital earnings and profits for all owners of land and buildings, besides the actual melting away of capital in obsolescence and depreciation.

This vast disemployment of potentially valuable land because of the destruction of all demand for it—because of the limitation on the demand for and earning capacity of buildings, which, in turn, comes from the hazards and poor earnings on the part of those who use building space and services (which again reflect *their* low production due to the scant purchasing power of all *their* customers)— this places an enormous burden upon land ownership such as no other one kind of property ever has to bear. In fact, this burden is the reflex of the burdens borne by every kind of property and business that there is, *for it is only the profit arising out of every other kind of business and services that creates and constitutes any demand for the use and services of land.*

It is well, therefore, to consider just what service it is that land owners have to sell. To do this, let us first look at the building owner. He does not sell mere space, but the services with which he surrounds and conditions the space, these comprising the administrative services that he directly performs and all the services that he hires and purchases from others, including the use of the public capital that he receives from the owner of the land. Thus, the building owner shows the true pattern for the value of the land:[1] *For it is not*

---

[1]. It must be remembered that we are considering only the real value of land—of the services to it that are at present existing and in demand—without reference to anything paid or offered in the mere hope or expectation of revenue or profit to arise only in the future, if, indeed, any shall arise.

*the land itself but the supply of public advantages, amenities and immunities surrounding and enjoyed at the site that constitutes the basis of all its present value.*

But the mere presence of public advantages is not enough. Every kind of service, including commodities, comes into being through human activity, but no service or commodity has any value except in the presence of human demand, and this demand must itself consist of other services or commodities that are offered (through open market) in exchange.

The real value of the land, then, like any other value, depends first upon the kind and amount of services and advantages the tenant will receive, and, second, it depends upon the effective demand on the part of actual or immediately prospective tenants. This effective demand arises out of the amount of services and commodities (wealth) that the occupants are permitted to create and control in connection with their use of the land, and the rent they offer to pay (which is the current value of the land) is that portion of this wealth which goes in open market in exchange for the public advantages that come to them through possession of the land. The land value, therefore, as seen by the occupier, is the value of the public services he receives and pays for; as seen by the owner it is the value of the rent—wealth—that is given by the occupier in exchange for the services he receives.

It is the right of the occupier to receive public services, and the right of the owner, as public distributor, to receive rent for distributing these services. The rent is, in fact, the only thing of value that the owner (as land owner) receives or has any right to receive. This right is expressly conferred upon him by the spontaneous will and power of the whole society. In virtue of his position thus established, he is, taken collectively, the proprietary department of the society. Because of his official proprietorship, there must flow into his collective hands the control and disposition by sale to tenants of the *net* services resulting from all the activities, both good and bad, of the current political or public service department of society. These public servants and officers, as such, are not proprietors. They own no part of the territory. Out of property publicly seized, they receive stipulated wages and salaries as distinguished from profits arising out of ownership and administration. The proprietor, on the contrary, depends for his earnings or profits upon the net income remaining to him after all the labor costs (wages and salaries) and all the capital costs (interest) of the public services have been met.

With the administrative position of the land-owning proprietor thus seen to be similar to the position of the proprietor in the conduct of any other business, it remains to point out the ways in which he is accustomed to exercise his administrative functions and the direction in which such activity on his part can be most profitably extended. And since the public services must extend, in varying degree, to the whole territory and so serve the interest of all the proprietors of a community, it is necessary that they associate themselves together and act, for the most part, collectively and in their organized capacity. This is essential, alike for unity and consistency of action, and to constitute a solvent, and thereby a responsible, public authority.

## II

Business consists in nothing but the contractual and proprietary (non-political) administration of property, and of services connected therewith, by its owners on behalf, presently and prospectively, of others. Property and services so administered is called capital, and the net recompense to owners, above costs, for such services is called profit. As regards manipulation and maintenance of capital, business administration is technological and physical; as regards the making and performing of contracts, it is psychological and social. All administration culminates in the transfer of jurisdiction over property or the use of property or of services, in exchange for money or other instruments of debt and credit whereby equivalent other property or services, similarly administered, is obtained. All owner-administration culminates in sales, and only by owners can either ownership or use be rightly transferred.

What the proprietors of land have to sell, and do sell, is the net public services received by the occupants of their sites. Tenants and lessees are their patrons and customers. The "public servants" (political) operate the service and production department whence arise the physical services that are sold. Each proprietor is custodian and distributor of so much of these as attach to and give rental value to his particular site. Individually, he distributes to the tenant who can make the most productive use of, and thereby pay the highest rent (or price) for, the services the site affords.[2] Collectively, he owes to his tenants and to himself the duty of *protecting them from property seizures and political domination,* all in the interest of higher productivity and purchasing power and consequent further demand for locations.

The land-owning proprietary interest, as a group, have relations with two classes of persons, public and private—political persons who perform public services (and disservices) upon the public territory (both directly and through toll-taking public corporations created and controlled by them) and provide them publicly through the public rights of way, using public capital for this; and private persons who carry on production and all private services upon the private territory, using private capital in connection therewith and distributing these goods and services among themselves by private contracts. These last, exchanging their products and services, constitute all private industry and trade. But private industry must have public security of property and possession,[3] public rights of way for communications and exchange, and other common services that can be supplied only by or under a united public authority, either political or proprietary.

Since such services can be delivered only through highways and to nothing but the locations served by them, it is the function of the publicly established (and recorded) proprietors to make these services (such as they are) available to the private occupants and users. Free bargaining to pay ground rent establishes the market value of the

---

2. It would be hard to imagine such services being equally well performed by salaried officers receiving their pay by way of taxation and not having the amount of their pay in any way dependent upon their selling the public services efficiently or even honestly.

3. Historically, security of property has rested fundamentally upon general acceptance of the common law institution of property which is prior to and independent of statutory enactments.

services supplied to each location and provides a just and proper basis for payment according to the measure of public services (less disservices) that each occupier individually receives. Thus, through the proprietors, even in their unorganized condition, the rent-paying occupants obtain access to all the community advantages, whatever they may be, by free negotiation and without either party in any way coercing the other.

But the relation of the public proprietors to those public persons who are assumed to perform services that are of value to the occupiers is wholly different. Notwithstanding that these are properly a service class, they act and assert themselves virtually as masters. For in the course of development of "free institutions," they have inherited the kingly power of seizing private property, a power unknown to Anglo–Saxons for centuries until their Norman conquerors laid upon them the slave technique of despotic Rome. This right to *seize* property that the Norman kings fought for, and the Tudors and Stuarts so freely and fatally practiced, has been carefully preserved to their present-day successors in power, whether by popular election or otherwise, in what is now tamely tolerated, for want of any known alternative public revenue, as the power of taxation and regulation.

So we have in the business of community administration today the anomalous condition of the proprietors, who purvey all the net public value that there is, standing idly by while the "service" department, uncontrolled by any responsible supervisory authority, seizes increasingly the production and private property of the population and so imperils not alone the freedom but all the values of the land. Taxation is said now to be seizing more than a third of all the wealth and income—rent, wages, interest and profits—now with so much hazard and under so many restrictions produced. The public "servants," taken in the aggregate, are permitted to set their own wages and other expenses and to be paid not by way of recompense for services, as other servants are, but out of their seizures by taxation and out of their public borrowings on the faith of future seizures. They are under no definite or effective responsibility to any authority apart from themselves. Their practice, in the main, consists in legislating special privileges and more and more public funds and plunder into the hands of special groups and classes whose support they seek for their continuance in office and in power.

Such is the body of servants over whom the proprietors of each community, beginning at the local level, must take supervisory control. And this is imperative to them, for, *as taxation mounts ever higher, rent cannot fail to decline*. This must follow so long as public revenue is raised by force and spent on favored classes and groups.

As public revenue is now raised and expended, there can be no long-term outlook for anything but decline in land values and rent. This is so, not simply because the whole of present taxation is forced tribute instead of payment by voluntary exchange, but because it diverts funds from rent. In addition, seizures by taxation create an indirect charge against the public services, and thereby against rent, owing to the loss and damage it inflicts upon all users of land by hampering and demoralizing their business and productivity. It is necessary to deduct from the advantages of the public services in gross all taxes or other compulsory charges, direct and indirect, laid on those who receive the services, in order to arrive at the residuum which is their net value. This *net* value is precisely what is sold to the occupants of the served sites and paid for by them willingly for value received.

*Since this net value of the public services to land is all that its proprietors can sell, it is only by enlarging this net value that their income can be increased.*

This is just where land owners should organize and give their best powers of supervision and constructive administration. It is a field highly potential for profit and in which there is a tragic need for such services. It is enormously inviting. It can be made fruitful to the community and thereby of unexampled profit to the whole land-owning interest in return for whatever cultivation they shall give to it.

Considering the peculiar manner in which the *political* public revenue is raised—precisely contrary from what is desirable and legitimate in any other field—it would be a matter of surprise if it did not have its well-known devastating effects upon the whole system of measured and balanced and thereby reciprocal exchange. The underlying evil is that taxation diverts out of the goods and services contributed to the common pool for exchange very large and increasing proportions of the goods and services that, but for this, would be distributed back to those who have contributed them. Not only this, but by establishing fictitious bank deposits and otherwise counterfeiting the numerical instruments and symbols of exchange, government pretends to an opulence that is not its own. Government not only diverts to itself the proper purchasing power of the tax payers; it creates also an artificial plethora of fictitious purchase instruments in nowise dependent on the quantity of goods and services to be bought. More dollars have to buy less goods. The goods value per dollar goes down and prices thus rise. Government finance creates the illusion that money is wealth, and wealth, in terms of money, seems to increase. Traders, seeing prices rise, are tempted to trade the same actual wealth back and forth among themselves and thus "make money" without producing any goods to buy with it. They even buy "on margin" wherewith to increase the volume and velocity of their exchanges and of their imaginary values, keeping swift pace with parallel government borrowings, until at last their "money" will buy but little if anything at all. Money values collapse and the losses are "written off," except as government underwrites them by subsidies and loans or other fictions that bring actual goods and services to the hands of its favorites to the detriment and loss, soon or late, of everyone else. The process is cyclical, just as alternations of chill and fever mark the reactions of biological organisms in general when their basic metabolism is seriously impaired.

During the inflation, almost everybody wants to buy and nobody wants to sell—except at a higher price. Such "profits" are not created by any productive administration of property or any increase of wealth but only by doing as government does—treating money as though it were wealth instead of counters of wealth, rising prices as though creating riches. During the deflation that follows, almost everybody wants to sell and nobody wants to buy—except at a lowered price and at forced sales. That is what is generally the matter with land values. They cannot have any long-term rise except it be on the basis of actual services rendered in the administration of them—of the community services that are automatically recompensed by them. So long as services that are common to entire communities, large or small, are relinquished to politicians organized not productively but politically as government, there is no way for them to finance the public needs except by seizing private money and credits—which are titles to property—and by writing themselves fictitious titles and credits wherewith to seize more and more out of the common pool. The alternative is for the community owners themselves unitedly to administer the common services wherewith their properties must be in common and unitedly served.

It is well known that practically all of the supposed public services, as well as public disservices, are supplied and maintained out of the proceeds of direct and indirect taxation in all its thousand-fold rigors and insidious forms. Political public works are not supplied in response to any economic demand on the part of those who are compelled to meet the usually extravagant cost of them, nor are these "services" distributed in proportion to the contributions of those who are forced to provide their cost. There is no balanced relation of exchange between what anyone surrenders in taxes and what he receives in public protection or other benefits. It is a fact of nature and of society that politically administered public advantages cannot be returned in the same manner or proportion as their cost is collected. And any attempt by tax payers to get value-in-exchange for what is taken from them could lead only to further violence and confusion.

But the societal organization in any settled community affords the institution of property in land, with its incidence of rent, to provide for the fair and orderly distribution of public benefits by free and voluntary exchange on the *measured* basis—the market basis—of value received. This is the *great office, the societal function, of land ownership*—the just and fruitful distribution by free contract of all the special advantages, natural resources and public services of the community as they appertain to its particular parts. Any benefits not distributed to the territory of the society through its common ways

## THE ADMINISTRATION OF REAL PROPERTY

and communications, and therefore not attaching to and reflected in the rent of land, are necessarily private services. All private services are provided by and exchanged between and among private persons, so far as this distribution is not discouraged and prevented by prohibitory laws. These private services, performed by the occupants of the private parts of the community, constitute all private wealth and create all the demand that there is for land—for the *public services* to land for which rent is paid. Any benefit or property conferred upon a private person, class or group by political authority is, *ipso facto,* not a community service but a private service, a special privilege, conferred at public cost and expense. This is all to the detriment of public service and thereby a deduction against rent.

Public services can be distributed in exchange for rent only to the extent that the private demand for them is active and alive. Whatever burdens private industry must bear, whatever restrictions upon its voluntary operations and exchanges are imposed, whatever inhibitions it suffers by reason of the hazards and uncertainties with which it is beset; all these influences, both directly and indirectly, destroy its capacity to make profitable use of community resources and services, thus paralyzing the demand for land. Considering the magnitude of taxation, the violent and vexatious manner in which it is imposed and the destructive purposes for which its proceeds are so largely used, it may be wondered how long any demand for land can continue and that far more of it is not idle and unused. Paradoxical as it may seem, the taxation which supports the public servants and all their works so bears upon industry and trade as eventually to all but destroy the demand for public services and with it their value, as measured in the value of land. But what value *does* remain, whatever rent *is* paid represents the final residuum, the net benefit delivered to the territory, of all the services performed by or under the public authority.

Taxes are always a charge against rent. For taxes are taken always by force or by stealth, and rent can be taken only from what remains, and this only by contract and consent. If taken otherwise it is not rent; it becomes taxation, taken indirectly by stealth when not wrung by force. Modern land owners have no political or any other coercive power. They perform the great public service of merchandising the country's resources and advantages into the most productive hands. Rent is their payment for this great public service. But taxation, being imposed without regard to the value, by market measure, of any benefit conferred, is a charge against rent, for it cuts down the demand for and hence the market value of all public services and thus destroys rent.

From whatever angle viewed, it must be seen that the administration of land has to do not merely with the land as such but with the common and general services that are supplied to it. It is to the interest of organized land owners, therefore, not only to distribute the sites and resources into the hands of those capable of the most productive (value-wise) and thereby most profitable use of them, but to protect and defend their functional freedom, and thereby their productivity of the wealth out of which alone rent can be paid and land values thus rise. The implications of a positive administrative policy by the organized proprietary interest are at once a challenge to their public spirit and an invitation to almost unimaginable affluence and prosperity. The initial obstacles are small and the incentive to proceed will be fed by accumulating rewards. Success will be contagious and emulated far and wide. With land owning organized and conducted *as a business,* good administration will rise above all wishful thinking into intelligent action—the highest service to self through the greatest service to all. No other policy is progressive or profitable or sound.

### III

When men learn the art of peaceful exchange, they cease to wander in search of subsistence. Settling in communities, they rise above mere dependence on crude nature by the arts they develop in serving and exchanging with one another. This they cannot do without protection and services that are common to the community as a whole. But so far as these are maintained by taxation, their value is canceled and finally extinguished and the society dies. Meantime, whatever community values remain unextinguished by taxation attach themselves to the territory as the net value of the land. During whole periods of civilization, as long as there remain any public values, the institution of property in land determines that ground rent shall flow into the hands of proprietors in recompense for their services in making societal, non-political allocations of the land. This natural and historical fact establishes the authority of land owners to administer the community services and guarantees them adequate and automatic returns, so far as this authority is exercised and its implied obligations performed.

The alternative field of action, the political, is marked by the complete absence of any general and conscious policy of public service. In the national, the state and even local governments, public power is exercised largely at the behest or dictation of pressure groups and special interests, each seeking special advantages for itself through measures detrimental to others and to the public as a whole. A listing of these would range from trade and manufacturers' associations to the grocers' and plumbers' local unions; from learned professional societies to the organized barbers and beauticians, not forgetting the endless seekers after subsidies, pensions and doles. The multiplicity of their conflicting interests, their clamor for privileges and the demands of each for the burdening and restricting of the others turns the process of government into an orgy of conflict instead of the performance of public services. The *political* officers seize property —taxes. They levy tribute. And they use the public funds to maintain themselves in office and in the continued exercise of their deadly powers. Even such balance of benefits above public injuries as they may confer, they are not able to distribute fairly because they are not owners. There is political but not contractual ownership or authority in their hands.

The owners of lands, sites and locations, on the contrary, constitute the one group in society whose interests rise superior to all this conflict and destruction. This group, always maintained by the authority of social custom, common law, automatically disposes of all the net public advantages. They are the real purveyors of public services in exchange for rent, the only group whose primary interest is in the productiveness and prosperity of all the rest.

Community proprietors need to learn how greatly the taxes wrung out of their land users come out of their own pockets as well. For every dollar so seized cuts into the earnings and profits of their tenants and thus reduces their capacity to pay rent. Moreover, the injury to all parties is not limited in amount to the dollar seized. The uncertainty alone is heavily deterrent against commitments and plans. This reduces the employment of both labor and capital, destroying the demand for land and all that it affords. And when that tax dollar is spent, more than often it is used to finance further repressions of, and depredations upon, the productive industry and exchange whence all income to land owners must arise. An enlightened land-owning policy of service to and protection of land users would not only retrieve that dollar to present and prospective lessees, but could reverse completely this whole train of evil into freedom and prosperity for all. The increasing income to land would provide easily a margin for the continuance of any real community services that the remission of taxes might impair, and with the tax method of community finance finally discontinued, the value of the community services and amenities, and of the community itself, would become incalculably high. Out of their rising rents and values, the well organized land owning interest could easily maintain all essential services and enjoy net returns far greater than ever before.

As the necessity for taxation is outgrown, all honest profits, incomes and values will be enormously enhanced. Without the monstrous restrictions on production, both direct and indirect, that are now of necessity imposed, the splendid liberation and expansion of productive industry would carry with it a corresponding requirement for public services, and therewith a mighty expansion of demand for the use and occupancy of land. Even without any improvement physically in the public services themselves, the increase in the demand for them and in their market value as attached to land would be vast indeed. In response to the new demand, all well served lands formerly idle or but little used would be drawn into profitable use, the untaxed occupiers gladly paying rent to the owners according to the *then* market value of the public services supplied and the freedom and opportunity enjoyed.

If the organized proprietors of the land should perform such a mighty service to its inhabitants as to render all taxation unnecessary, their reward would consist in certainly a very large part of the whole excess of the previous taxation above necessary public costs and, in addition, all the increased net revenue coming to the land that had been idle or only partly or poorly improved or employed. The clear gain to the unburdened and liberated inhabitants, to active capital and labor, under full freedom of production and exchange would be unimaginably high, and the net income to land in return for community administration would be tremendous indeed. The revenue by way of rent even now springs from a public service that is essential and fundamental, even though it be unconsciously performed. It is the automatic recompense to title holders in exchange for an essential public service of distribution—for their non-political allocation of sites and resources through the social mechanism of the market and thereby into the hands of the most productive and efficient users; for only such can offer the highest rent or price. Not only do they seek out, albeit unwittingly, the most productive users. What is even more important, their negotiation of acknowledged titles provides an alternative to force and arms, to the anarchy of unorganized violence or the essential tyranny of political distribution and administration.

These reflections are not to suggest that all taxation could be abolished at one time, but to make plain the position occupied by the owners of land in relation to taxation and the public services, to illustrate the great principle involved and to point out a constructive policy benefiting both the public and themselves.

Notwithstanding that it is as yet almost wholly unorganized, the land interest has been able in many communities to procure legislation setting limits to taxation on its own kind of property. But, with mounting public budgets, this is only to shift the burden to bear upon other kinds of property and production and thus diminish the demand for real estate and make land even more idle and unproductive than before. What is required is not directly to ease the burden on real estate, but to unburden all those forms of production and exchange that create the wealth and services on which the demand for real estate depends.

If the owners of community buildings should find their tenants being impoverished by the service personnel in charge, they would not withhold the necessary supervision and control to put an end to it. Yet the public community "servants," by their seizures of property and infringements of liberty, impoverish all users and occupiers of land. Their limited productivity limits the demand for land and its public services. In depressed periods, great numbers fail in business and are unable to pay any rent at all. The burdens imposed, including the indirect effects, more than offset the advantage, if any, conferred. How much greater the injury to business and production than the amount of taxes taken, it is impossible to estimate; the inhibition on enterprise is incalculably severe. It is only when the indirect cost is considered, how this may be many times greater than the tax itself, that it can be realized what a mighty impairment is made to the advantages of occupancy for which site value is paid.

The land-owning interest, as such, is not engaged in any physical use of the land. It has no private business interest that taxation can burden or destroy. It is therefore impossible for any tax relief to site values to bring any benefit beyond the flat amount of the tax. But a tax laid on the *use* or the user of land diminishes its worth to the user not only by the amount of the tax but also by the amount of indirect damage to the business for which the land is used. It is more vital to the land owner that the use of land should be exempted than exemption of the land itself. For untaxing the use of land brings benefits to both user and owner, instead of giving the owner an exemption that can be more than canceled by the additional burden thus thrown onto the user of the land. For in the prosperity of all who are engaged in production and exchange, and in this alone, lies the demand for the public services afforded by land. It should not be supposed that these wealth-producing, land-using interests can obtain any considerable tax relief for themselves. In their many special fields, they are too far divided for effective resistance; and, like land owners, their profits come from what they do for others, not what they do for themselves.

## THE ADMINISTRATION OF REAL PROPERTY 171

Starting at the level of least resistance, the proprietary interest can extend tax benefits and exemptions to the business world of land users with corresponding enhancements of rent. With taxes on production finally abolished and ground rent thus enormously enhanced, a small part of this would suffice to support the public services at existing levels. All beyond this could be turned back for extensions and improvements after provision for liberal dividends on the original property invested. And all turned back for either maintenance or extension would be contributions to public services, voluntary and self-imposed for profit, the very opposite from taxation for public purposes, contrary in every way. Thus, the proprietary interest can come completely into its proper position of responsible supervision over its community affairs by a conscious, enlightened and profitable administration of the public capital. For even now their income, such as it is, comes from the administration of public capital—or from as much of it as serves the common needs of the community. This fact alone makes them, in effect, the equitable owners of capital that is administered by *political* trustees.

The real estate interest is, potentially, the most powerful of all business groups. When it seeks relief merely by shifting direct taxation into more indirect forms, it simply puts the business and production of its customers under increasing burdens that constantly weaken the demand for and the value of all property. But when it serves all its tenants and purchasers by lifting such restrictions upon them, then, by such public service, the real estate interest will be serving itself doubly well. That part of it which owns improvements on land will be enabled to operate these improvements to full capacity for eager tenants at rentals based upon flourishing business activity and abundant production. And those whose investments are in land will find themselves beset with demand for their formerly idle locations and with increasing bid and demand for the locations already in use. The effect upon rental and sales values can better be imagined than described. And such a boom in rents and values would be permanent and not collapse, for it would be based on the actual *production of wealth* and not upon artificial values and debts that can never be paid.

Political public officers, unlike the owners of land, have no ownership hence no business interest in the public values. Like servants and subordinates in any other business, they need to come under supervision and restraint by the proprietors of that business, whose property and income is built up by supervised services or destroyed by unsupervised default or devastation. The services of any community authority are bestowed upon the territory and thus fall into the charge of those who own that territory. It is the business, therefore, of the properly organized proprietors to administer their property by keeping up the demand for these services and to distribute them among the members of the community at rates and prices determined in open market and voluntarily paid. This last is only the sales side of the business. If the proprietors are to have for long any values to sell, they must act also on the management and production side. Efficiently and democratically organized (each member voting in proportion to his contribution) under a public trusteeship of their own creation, they will administer the largest and most important business of all—the public business—in their own communities, and ultimately, through voluntary interrelations with similar solvent and self-sustaining service organizations in other communities, become members of the public service business of the entire civilized world.

All the foregoing has been stated with a view to land ownership outgrowing all its present speculative hazards into an energetic and prosperous business for which there is an enormous public need. Sound business principles have been the constant guide, and such thorough-going application of these as is now proposed contains social implications that are deep and wide.

The progressive reduction of taxation and rapid enhancement of ground rent and land values must surely transform government from the predacious character in which it finally destroys the society it assumes to serve, into a vast agency of veritable public service. As in all small community properties, coercion will give way to *contract*—the creating of property values by voluntary exchange. That is how piracy on the seas was transformed into trade, and how the golden rule of commerce has—thus far—redeemed the world from force and war. It should encourage, even inspire, those who are eminent in the real estate world to perceive that the owning interest in sites and land is potentially able, through high service to its clientele, to emancipate their industries and arts and in so doing build magnificent profits and values of its own.

## IV

### Retrospect and Prospect

When populations migrate from lands of public debts and deficits and high taxes to a land of slight taxation and no deficits, they cause a phenomenal rise in the value of land—such as took place during the nineteenth century in North America.

The American colonists brought with them all the skill, but none of the facilities, for the production of wealth that they had in the lands from whence they fled. In their new land, when they became numerous and their trade relatively untaxed and free, there was in a single century such production of services and goods as no age or people ever saw or knew before. The institution of property in land afforded them peaceable possession. It made sites and resources freely saleable and thus available to those best prepared to make them most productive. Out of the new wealth so created sprang fabulous new values in the land. There was a full century of unexampled freedom, unrestricted production, rising land values and lengthening life.

But the twentieth century reintroduced the Old World ways. Government came to be worshipped more than feared and confined, and constitutional barriers went down. Government began absorbing all liberty and property and is now itself so looked to for welfare and freedom that insecurity, uncertainty and anxiety widely prevail.

Yet a great abatement of coercive taxation and other modes of expropriation, with all their attendant ills, would have, even now, in this once free land, the same effect as if by some mighty magic the population of today, with all its works and wonders, wealth and powers, could be removed all unknown to still another distant virgin land where government, again transformed, could serve yet not enslave.

Such release again of creative power would bring forth marvels of grace and beauty to shame even the mighty wonders of today, and build public values in the land as far beyond those known today as these exceed the dreams of those who long ago sought freedom here.

For land value—the exchange value of public services—is a reflex of all other exchange values. It is determined by the most that is offered out of the general productivity for the net services, above dis-services, that the occupancy of land affords. Without production and exchange there could be no rent, no value in the land. With free and taxless exchange, and thus unrestricted employment and production, there are no heights beyond which, under a proprietary public administration, future rents and values may not rise.

Thus the administration of real estate involves the administration of the community property—of the whole public capital and lands. So far as this administration is political, its products or benefits are politically distributed and not sold for value received—hence produce no income or value. But so far as the community administration is *proprietary,* its benefits attach to and are distributed through the community sites and lands, hence can be sold for an income or value called rent—a free *contractual,* instead of a political, distribution among free men. Thus proprietary administration is the one manner and form under which government can be the servant of the people and they not be in servitude to it. Public services so administered create their own revenues, their own proper values—the value of the real property, the real *estate*—the value of the commonwealth, the common weal and welfare, of the social and civilized realm.

CHAPTER 26

## *Towards the Utopian Dream*

### A Hypothetical Distribution of National Income under Proprietary Public Administration

IN THE FOREGOING PAGES, the primary relationship that exists between the owners of labor and of private capital on the one hand, and the owners of land and its public capital on the other, has been described in general terms and in the light of there being a general system of exchange into which the specialized services of the respective parties are being constantly pooled *en masse* for exchange; and then *selectively* withdrawn in full variety as dictated by the need and desire and in the proportions of recompense to contribution that the open voting of the market as to prices and terms democratically allows.

This social process of democratic distribution by consent and exchange has been shown to apply to such services and goods as remain under the social jurisdiction and free disposition of the market after the part required by the political authority has been forcibly or coercively withdrawn. The annual contribution of services coming from the owners of labor, capital and land, measured by the exchange appraisements of the market in terms of money or bank credits, is collected by statisticians and footed up as the national income. Of this total national income, the part taken by government, including its borrowings, is subject to *political* distribution not in exchange for any contributions made to the market, but to consumers who, in peace as in war, do not make any corresponding contributions to the general exchange system. This depletes the market. What remains, the market socially distributes by contract and exchange back to the owners of labor, capital and land in the proportion of their respective contributions.

The diagram and table annexed at the end of this chapter have been prepared for the more graphic illustration of the distribution of social income under present-existing conditions and of what the volume and the distribution might become under a proprietary administration by public owners of the public services, beginning with the new public service of abolishing unnecessary waste and taxation and, finally, all taxation. It is assumed that in response to such services, labor, capital and land, released from the penalization of their services and products, would come into full employment, thus causing the national income progressively to rise from a figure ranging between 75 and 100 billions, as in the late nineteen-thirties, to twice the latter figure (assuming no further debasement of the dollar) at the point where taxation would be entirely superseded and far more than replaced by the newly created and enhanced ground rent accrued to the Proprietary Community-Service Authority out of the magnified national income consequent upon its new and enhanced public services.

It is further assumed that upon the final abolition of the restrictions upon employment and production resulting from taxation—and of the unbalanced distribution of national income thus caused—and upon replacement of the dis-services of politics and government by the exchange services of public proprietorship, consciously and intentionally performed, there would continue to be a progressive increase of real social income.[1] This increase is indicated by the heights of the successive columns in the diagram and in the series of totals set at the bottom of the table.

Placed in the left vertical column of the table are the three factors, Labor, Capital and Land, contributing their respective services into the common pool of the exchange system before receiving any exchange recompense therefor; and at the bottom is a fourth, Government, which participates forcibly in the joint product without making any present or subsequent return to the exchange system.

It should be noted that in the table, *Labor* refers not at all to self-services but to services to others, to social or societal services. *Capital,* likewise, refers not to ownership for the use of the owner—for one's

---

[1]. Not a mere increase in the money income, such as has taken place under increasing monetary inflation.

own use—but to ownership for the service of others. In a similar manner, *Land,* as an economic factor, refers to the ownership and administration of sites, locations, natural advantages and resources, including the artificial advantages of public capital, for the public and general service of others by making a social—a contractual—distribution and not a forcible, arbitrary or irresponsible distribution of public advantages, both natural and artificial. *Land,* as a social or economic factor, refers to the persons who distribute and administer land through contractual relations, in the same manner as the products of Labor and Capital are distributed. It does not refer to those who hold land merely for self use. Nor do Labor and Capital, as *economic factors* contributing to the exchange system, hold land, or indeed anything else, otherwise than for the service of others. In all categories, only the services performed or property owned for the *service of others* has any societal import or social or economic significance.

The second vertical column in the table lists, opposite the three factors in production, the kind of services contributed by them to the exchange system and the kinds of recompenses, as exchange values, received for them. However, in the space opposite *Government,* it is necessary to list service and recompense more darkly and in reverse, since political government, as distinguished from the Proprietary Community-Service Authority, impinges upon but does not operate within the general democratic and non-compulsive societal system of voluntary services and exchange.

In the third and subsequent vertical columns, footed by the figures for successively increasing national incomes from 75 to 400 billions, the services contributed by each factor have numerical assignments, and under these are lesser numbers to represent the values or recompenses received in return, the service contributions and value recompenses becoming one and the same and set in a single line only from the point in progress where Government, with its crude financing by taxation and inflation, ceases to impinge.

There are thus formed six horizontal columns marked off by Roman numerals I to VI. The first two service factors, Labor and Capital, occupy respectively horizontal columns I and II, but to the factor Land, as the Proprietary Public-Service Authority, the three horizontal columns III, IV and V are assigned. This is for the purpose of making very clear the three kinds of services, actual and potential, that this public authority can provide.

The first of these proprietary services (horizontal column III) has reference only to the gifts of nature with which a population, as a community, is endowed. Ground rent, so long thought to be unearned, is, in the first instance, the value received for making *social* distribution of these natural things. When taxation is relatively high, and the production contributed to the market therefore relatively low, land, like other things, is but little distributed and but little if any ground rent is actually received. Leases default, voluntary sales cease to be made, and there is little or no return or value in real estate, except from the improvements upon it, at such times.

Horizontal column IV refers to the second kind of services contributed to the exchange system by the public owners. This has reference to the social distribution not of natural but of artificial advantages arising from the presence of public capital in a community, such as water supply, street paving, public sanitation, educational and cultural facilities, etc., the advantages of which in any degree or for a time outweigh the disadvantages of increasing taxation and its concomitant dis-services. This field of public capital services under political and predatory public administration is of questionable, transitory and abortive value, but under public proprietary administration it is open to enormous desirable and profitable developments. With expanding national production providing abundant proprietary profits and income from the maintenance of existing public facilities for reinvestment in further public capital services, it could surpass such literary (as in libraries), artistic and recreational public services as are now supplied in cities and in many hotels. It might be extended even so far as to include the supplying of food in the form of a community service as is now done in "American plan" hotels, where the rents paid for the various rooms or occupancies include dining room and food service as appurtenant to the rooms.

The third category of public services is described briefly in horizontal column V. This service at present is only *potential*. Unlike

## TOWARDS THE UTOPIAN DREAM

those of horizontal columns III and IV, it is not automatically performed in the ordinary course of selling and leasing of the community advantages appurtenant to its lands. In a hotel, the owning interest not only distributes and dispenses its public and general benefits and advantages to its rent-paying occupants, but along with this it supervises and directs the community servants from the general managers down, not omitting those who police the premises, and thus it protects the liberty and property of all who there abide. This protective service in a hotel is supplied by the proprietors as a matter of course.

But in the great out-of-door communities, now dominated and being broken down by the political techniques of their putative public servants, no corresponding protective service by the proprietary interest is being performed. The political authority, not being socially—that is, by contract and consent—integrated with the voluntary exchange system, is always bankrupt, in the sense of having no ownership or income of its own. Pending its evolution into the proprietary pattern of services for recompense by exchange, it is therefore of necessity predacious upon the national income and ultimately inimical to the solvency and continued existence of the exchange system itself.

In the graphic diagram at the left of the table, the line $B$-$B$ represents the base on which all the services and goods contributed to and pooled in the general exchange system rest, upon which all the market or exchange values are built and below which all things de-social-ized out of the market by a contrary or compulsive technique, and therefore having no market or exchange value, must fall. The fourteen vertical columns correspond with the fourteen national incomes of the table. The first five drop below the exchange level by the amount that taxation takes out of the exchange system by compulsory process and thus makes unavailable for free contractual distribution by exchange. The portion below the base line need not be here analyzed into the multiplicity of political expenditures that do not create any exchange values or otherwise reappear into and restore the broken balances of the exchange system. The portion remaining within the exchange system is projected upward in each column and divided into three segments corresponding with the three divisions in the tabular analysis: *Land* and *Public Capital* at the base, *Private Capital* next above, and *Labor* completing the column height. The first column shows only two divisions. Land, under this national income, is too depressed to have any income; but in the second and succeeding columns all three divisions are shown.

It must not be supposed that any of the figures given are held to be based on exact statistical data or to be otherwise quantitatively correct. The first two columns of national incomes are, indeed, rough approximations to a known experience, and the distribution indicated here is at least roughly in the known order of recompense; for it is known that under ordinary conditions, the largest share goes to Labor, the next largest to Capital, and the least, if any, to Land. The figures are offered therefore as being only schematically correct and for the purpose of showing the general relationships that commonly prevail and how these relationships will develop and improve under the expanding national production that such extension of the proprietary public services as is indicated in horizontal column V can release. The table and diagram are offered not for the setting out of specific figures and facts but as the pattern of distribution that is inherent in the present economy—the system of production and exchange—that supports civilization and upon which its continuance depends.

As set out in detail in the preceding chapter, it is the golden but unseen opportunity of the land-owning interest in any political community to take unified action of service in defense and protection of the exchange system that now only occupies its properties through striving, manfully, to utilize both the resources inherent therein and the public capital appurtenant thereto. For in the vast flow of production and income thus released the landed interest would become, in its recompense and values, the prime participant. And what is equally to be desired, the public servants and employees would then be well and abundantly, instead of improperly and insufficiently, financed.

In the first two vertical columns of national income, under the heading *Service Contributions and Exchange Values Received,* it is taken that the total income may be either 75 or 100 billions (depending on the trade-cycle phase) without any of the protective services described in horizontal column V being performed.

But in the third column of national income (125 billions), the proprietary interest has begun to waken and embrace its golden opportunity for public service and magnificent reward. The increase from 100 to 125 billions is attributed to the initial new services of the proprietary interest, Land, in procuring for its tenants and customers a reduction of 25%, from 20 billions to 15 billions, in the exchange deficit due to taxation. The addition of 25 billions to the total income is assumed to be due to an increase of 10 billions (20%) in the productivity of Labor, and an increase of 10 billions ($33\frac{1}{3}\%$) in the productivity of Capital, and an increase from a total of 20 billions to a total of 25 billions (25%) in the productivity of Land and Public Capital administration. Labor, Capital and Land, each and all of them, are now receiving out of the exchange system greater percentages of their respective contributions in the order listed, Labor being rewarded with 55 out of 60 billions of production instead of 45 out of 50 as before. Capital getting back 35 out of 40 instead of 25 out of 30, and Land receiving 20 out of a total contribution of 25 instead of 10 out of a total contribution of 20 to the previous lower national income.

The next four vertical columns proceed upon the supposition that the proprietary interest continues its third category of services, namely, protective services (horizontal column V), until a national income of 200 billions is reached, at which point the exchange deficit due to taxation is entirely extinguished and the proprietary interest creates and receives a total income of 50 billions, which is an increase of 40 billions over its maximum total income before it began to perform these services. This shows the proprietary interest in receipt of additional earned income, out of which to maintain and finance its public enterprises, two and one-half times as great as the taxes taken forcibly before the new services were undertaken and performed.

It is assumed that during this change from a 100 billions to a 200 billions national income, private capital has reinvested much of its income progressively in private enterprises and that the proprietary interest has likewise made increasing investment of its returns back into new and enlarged enterprises of public capital. The increasing productivity and income of both private and public capital guarantees this. And if both are and remain equally efficient, and therefore equally profitable, doubtless both will continue to reinvest their accumulations and thereby come into receipt of continuously increasing returns. This is shown graphically in the diagram and by figures and notations on the right-hand side of the table where similar efficiency of private and public capital is assumed. This is taken as the ground for their coördinate development as shown.

There is, however, much reason to anticipate that under equally skillful administration *by its owners,* the capital invested in *public* enterprises would be the more efficient and therefore more productive of income and values. Assuming this to be true, there would be a natural tendency towards free capital investment in the public and more profitable enterprises. The old socialist argument against the alleged wastefulness of multiple deliveries of such things as groceries or milk to variously located customers by numerous competing enterprises, and in favor of a unified public service, would have here a legitimate application not through any compulsive abolishment of "wasteful competition" but by the benign operation of competition itself. As the public enterprises became more profitable, the investing public, being the owners of private capital, would be more and more disposed to sell out of private enterprises and buy into the public and more profitable ones, thus providing the proprietary interest with additional funds for buying into the assets of and thus taking over private enterprises in due course by the wish and will of all concerned. Nor could the public owners wish or afford to take over any private enterprise unless or until they could make the public administration of it more serviceable and efficient and therefore more profitable. Not only would it be costly to purchase a highly productive private business, but to do so would deprive the proprietary interest of a valuable rent-payer as a customer of its own public services. From the standpoint of the public proprietors, the question would be: "How can we obtain the highest rent revenues? Will it be by continuing to serve this private enterprise as a desirable rent-paying customer of our services or by acquiring its securities or assets and seeking to administer them so much the better publicly that the rent revenue in general will rise by a greater amount than the particular rent lost through acquisition of this private enterprise?"

There can be no doubt that, with an enormously increasing abundance of services and supplies of every kind, economy and efficiency would lie more and more in the direction of the public administration of and a general participation in them. As an example of this, the unprecedented abundance of food in nineteenth-century America was probably the chief reason for its being dispensed in hotels usually as a generalized service, instead of by the sale of specific items or menus. When the public proprietors of America awake to the profitableness of releasing the potential productivity of their rent-paying inhabitants, it may well be that the resulting enormous abundance will come under a veritable "American plan" of a more and more generalized system. There has, indeed, already appeared a tendency for the public to purchase at a rental or use charge the service or use of many articles and commodities rather than taking full ownership themselves, leaving upon the highly specialized owners, in addition to the usual services of production and distribution, also the responsibilities of continued maintenance and the general duties and obligations of capital administration. The extension of living facilities through apartment housing, the community use of business and professional premises and facilities, including shopping centers as business communities under unified proprietary administration, group medical and surgical services and even installment buying (so-called)[2] with trade-in allowances have been among the distinct evidences of the trend, under a high abundance of production, towards a general distribution of the services of both public and private capital on a rental basis, leaving ownership and its adminis-

2. Installment buying, sometimes known as "the hire system," suffers ill repute only because of its mis-use when credit is employed unduly to finance consumption instead of production. Borrowing to finance production and, thereby, to raise the general productivity, is a legitimate part of the creative social process.

trative responsibilities concentrated in better organized and more competent hands.

From these and similar considerations it is taken that such increasing abundances of national income as are indicated towards the right-hand columns of the table would carry with them a corresponding tendency towards the public and general use of things on an inclusive rental basis, just as many things now are supplied in office buildings, highly developed hotels and the like community properties. Accordingly, it is taken that if, as seems likely, the public and general administration of enterprises, *when administered by the proprietary public authority,* should prove the more profitable, there would be a tendency for them to outgrow the private ones by attracting capital investment at a greater rate. This could occur through the investing public selling out of private enterprises and buying into the public ones, or by the direct exchange of private for the public securities, by which method private enterprises would become at once public and take on the advantages of community-wide administration.

This probable development is indicated in the diagram at the left of the table by the dotted lines beginning at the dividing line between the public proprietary income and that of the private capital in the column for 200 billions national income. These dotted lines indicate an increasing proportion of the entire capital income arising out of the public capital, leaving the relatively diminished private capital at first with less and eventually with a relatively declining return.

The tendency thus indicated might be supposed to lead ultimately to all private capital coming under the public proprietary administration. This would of course realize, in effect, although not in method, the socialist ideal. All industry might gravitate towards a public and general administration by the responsible community owners, of both the natural and the artificial means and instruments of production, service and exchange. Private employment would become public, and in this extreme development (if it can be imagined) commodities and services would be distributed largely if not entirely as appurtenances and perquisites of the sites and occupancies for which the consuming public would pay such voluntary rents as the open market would set or allow.

Thus, by the mere emancipation of the owners of private capital from tax-expropriation of their private incomes and assets, there is permitted to arise and develop a free evolution of capital ownership and administration with its resulting production in such abundance that it may become feasible and more efficient to produce and distribute in a general fashion, on a community-wide scale, services and goods of many varieties and kinds in addition to those which are now commonly accepted as public or community services.

This evolutionary advance would spring from the enormously expanded community services being not merely *distributed,* as now, but also being created and financed by the proprietary authorities out of their own property and income. This capacity of a veritable *public service* to evolve on the basis of its own earnings is in the highest contrast to that of a compulsive authority that for its revenues must seize not only the property of conquered and subject peoples but even the properties and incomes of its own citizens whom it is assumed, and whom it professes especially, to represent and serve.

But the conversion of private into public capital could never become absolute and complete. The relative efficiency of private administration *versus* public administration would determine the allocation, finally, of all capital income—profits to private owners and net rents to the public owners and community administrators. But at all stages of such development, some private capital services would be in constant competition with some corresponding public capital service and would be brought under the latter mode of administration *only* as it became more profitable to all concerned for them to do so. Even if a full cessation of private capital administration could occur, there would remain always potential private capital competition (there being no political restrictions creating monopolies) ready to spring up and correct with its higher efficiency any very serious deficiency in the public administration—even as, under present conditions, superior water and other services are privately supplied to those who can afford them when the public supply is meager or falls short or its quality falls low.

There are forms of community service that require the occupancy of streets or highways and other public domain and cannot be performed by a multiplicity of agencies without conflict of authority or impractical duplication of facilities, such as police or military protection, public transportation and communications, the supplying of water and drainage service or of power or heat through installations occupying public domain. All such as these are necessarily as public, from their inception, as is the domain delegated to them by the public charter or franchise in which the services are prescribed and the manner and amount of their recompense fixed. Such services at inception and during their development, and especially when the direct use and benefit of them can be measured out, are recompensed usually by authorized graded tolls or a system of fees levied on the immediate beneficiaries. In most cases, their installation is initially financed by the capitalization of these prospective tolls or fees. Notwithstanding that they are publicly created agencies, the persons or companies performing these services are often regarded as "private" or merely *quasi* public because "affected with a public interest." When such public agencies are transformed through financing them with public debt, and those persons who formerly had a limited direction over them become, or are displaced by, public employees with only political and no proprietary responsibility, this change is commonly regarded as a change from private ownership to public ownership.

In either case, any economic advantage to the inhabitants of the community, *above the disadvantages of the tolls, fees or taxes politically prescribed and imposed to maintain them,* is contractually distributed among the inhabitants by the community owners, just as all the merely natural advantages are. Their recompense for this social distribution is included in their ground rent, or land values. It is the prime economic interest of land owners not alone to distribute these benefits but to insure administration of these public facilities to the utmost advantage and least detriment or inconvenience to the inhabitants of their communities.

However completely and inclusively the public capital facilities may come to be administered by the enlightened proprietary interest, and however high their honors and rich their rewards, there would always be at least a modicum of private services, especially those growing out of fresh discoveries in science and thus likely to begin tentatively and on a small scale. Certainly those services which become most widely distributed and participated in are most likely to be "free," payment for them being included in the rent or other general service charge for the location, occupancy or community membership to which they appertain.

In any case, it is highly apparent that the present existing exchange economy of "free enterprise," rightly understood, and when redeemed from the governmental depredations that destroy it, holds all that is essential not only to an enormous growth and expansion of its private and individual services but also an inherent capability of indefinite development and transformation in the general direction of a completely unified system under the free contractual technique of proprietary public administration. A total transformation is probably impossible, but it could remain the ideal end-point or condition towards which the societal evolution under full freedom of contract would tend.

The present discussion of a universalized proprietary public service —the socialist ideal—as a possible and probable outgrowth from the present existing system of capital services, once it is emancipated from unnecessary and destructive taxation, has not been with purpose to advocate the imposition or adoption of any unified collective system. It is only to point out how the collectivist *ideal* is inherent in the existing capitalist system, once its creative technique of contractual services for voluntary recompense and automatic values is permitted to expand. There is no fallacy in the socialistic ideal; only the *methods* proposed have been futile and false. Ages of indoctrination in the worship of organized force have impressed great masses of "intellectual" men with an almost inexpugnable faith in the essential benevolence of political and governmental power—so only it be "democratic" in form and his submission to it be without physical or political revolt. Believing that free contractual relationships are somehow essentially dangerous and depraved, these pseudo-intellectuals make the Citadel their Altar, despite the warning clanking of its chains. Not in slavish traditions, not in submission nor in revolt, but in new awakenings to the basic realities and the high potentialities of the societal heritage as it *now* exists, is the social ideal to be attained.

Free enterprise is so called not because the persons and organizations engaged in it are free from the burdens and compulsions imposed by political power, but because the parties contractually engaged are in exclusively free and voluntary relations with one another, no force or compulsion being applied on either side—except as some of the parties or interests jeopardize their own freedom by contriving governmental abridgements of the economic freedom of other members of the voluntary system. Yet with all such defections from it, and notwithstanding the huge political burdens that it bears, the creative and productive power of free enterprise is the miracle of the modern age. In the two decades, 1935 to 1955, it increased the national income (gross national product) for the United States from 75 billions to 175 billions, in the dollars of 1939, at a very nearly uniform rate. On this basis it may reach as much as 225 billions in the same dollars by 1965. Current forecasts indicate that the population will then be about 170 millions. This will amount to about $1,300 per capita or $6,500 per family of five, equivalent, doubtless, to $15,000 or $20,000 per family in the dollars of 1965.

These figures reflect the enormous productivity of the non-political form of organization. If they seem extravagant as to the future, they are certainly not more so than were those that have been actually attained, when these are viewed from almost any standpoint in the past. And when this free system of administration has developed so far as to take not only agriculture and industry out of governmental operation and control, as it has done in the historic past, and carries its technique of proprietary administration into the public and common services as well, no bounds can be imagined beyond which the national income and the public welfare may not rise.

The foundation of all life, not to say all progress and all attainment, lies in the environment of mankind and the welfare that it affords. Unlike any other creatures, human beings have learned to practice, in a limited way, a universal relationship that of itself creates favorable *human* environment and at the same time gives them productive and creative power over their material world. Production is creative. A national income is a numerical expression of the extent to which a population, with each member serving many others, has modified into wealth and satisfactions its environing world. And these material things are not without higher significance. They flow out of a spiritual, a golden rule relationship of services reciprocally performed —services that create an ever new and renewing world environment, fit for the self-creation of a higher, a longer living, a less and less mortal, mankind.

As services and supplies become abundant and assured, human nature exhibits less and less tendency towards separate and exclusive possessions. Things are enjoyed by participation more than by possession, and the habits and manners of the drawing room and banquet hall become the rule. Ownership thus takes the form less and less of personal possessions and more and more of capital enterprises in the service of others by those who enjoy the responsibilities of ownership and administration and rejoice in the development of previsioned plans and ends and the winning of contingent recompenses above mere wages or stipendiary rewards; while those more numerous persons, who care but little for the burdens of administrative policies and plans will prefer to engage themselves to the former with variously skilled but subordinate services at customary or specially negotiated rates. Under a growing abundance, this latter class comes into increasing leisure and freedom for the spontaneous activities of personal and social recreation, and of those esthetic and creative arts that spring directly from the individual and constitute the soul of a society; while the owning administrators of public and private capital enterprises and properties through employment of talented executives create, in gracious architecture and design, the noble habiliments of material environment in which alone a spiritualized society can be both nourished and clothed.

VICE CONTRIBUTIONS and EXCHANGE VALUES RECEIVED

| 50 | 60 | 70 | 80 |    |     |     |     |     |     |     |     |     |
|----|----|----|----|----|-----|-----|-----|-----|-----|-----|-----|-----|
|    |    |    |    | 90 | 100 | 110 | 120 | 130 | 140 | 150 | 160 | 170 |
|    |    |    |    |    |     Increasing income to Labor          |
| 45 | 55 | 65 | 75 |    |     |     |     |     |     |     |     |     |

| 30 | 40 | 50 |    |    |    |    |    |    |    |    |    |
|----|----|----|----|----|----|----|----|----|----|----|----|
|    |    |    | 55 | 60 | 65 | 70 | 75 | 80 | 85 | 90 | 95 | 100 |
|    |    |    |    |    | Increasing income to Capital        |
| 25 | 35 | 45 |    |    |    |    |    |    |    |    |    |

| 15 |    |    |    |    |    |    |    |    |    |    |    |
|----|----|----|----|----|----|----|----|----|----|----|----|
|    | 15 | 20 | 25 | 30 | 35 | 40 | 45 | 50 | 55 | 60 | 65 | 70 |
| 10 |    |    |    |    |    |    |    |    |    |    |    |

Increasing income to organized proprietary
authority, available for all public expenses
and for extending public services, facilities, etc.

| 5 | 5 |   |    |    |    |    |    |    |    |    |    |
|---|---|---|----|----|----|----|----|----|----|----|----|
|   |   | 5 | 10 | 15 | 25 | 30 | 35 | 40 | 45 | 50 | 55 | 60 |
| 0 | 0 |   |    |    |    |    |    |    |    |    |    |

| 0 |   |   |   |   |
|---|---|---|---|---|
|   | 5 | 5 | 5 | 5 |
| 0 |   |   |   |   |

B —

| DEFICITS |    |    |   |
|----------|----|----|---|
| 20       | 15 | 10 | 5 |

100  125  150  175  200  225  250  275  300  325  350  375  400
AL NATIONAL INCOME (cost and value in billions)

PART III

# General Survey

SPIRITUAL AND PSYCHOLOGICAL IMPLICATIONS

*When a seeker after knowledge of the earth discovers a whole new continent or world his first concern is that its parts shall be well described, the pattern of their relationships and configurations well disclosed, their plant and animal riches, rainfall and fertility, mineral and other resources made plain. He may then propose that mankind take over this new possession, avail themselves of its riches and bounties and build in it for themselves a world of affluence and abundance for all men—a milk-and-honey-flowing land.*

*So it is with him who discovers a new world of man, a new continent of conceptions, fresh knowledge and thought. He is at pains to describe its parts, delineate their conformations and point out their relationships and their potentialities. He may then well propose an application of them, a utilization of the new knowledge, the practice of its potentialities, the building of new values through new sciences, a new fellowship in production and creation and, incidentally, peace.*

*But having thus acquitted himself in the manner of the discoverers of material worlds, he may be permitted to stand on the pinnacle of his own thought and from this vantage point survey to its furthest horizon the world of nature and of mankind.*

CHAPTER 27

## *The Qualitative Transformation*

PHYSICAL SCIENCE teaches that all nature consists of one universal energy and that this energy is organized from primary and elementary units or particles called quanta, photons, electrons, etc. These are the prime individuals, the fundamental units of nature, by the multiplication and in the combinations of which are organized all the actions and events, all the substances and all the structures and manifestations of energy that occur and thus are said to exist.

This casts nature in her role as the Great Collectivist. She brings her ultimate quanta together in myriad forms and her children are the atoms, the molecules, the cells, the structured plants and animals, the societies of men, the stars and the systems of stars. In all these forms of "action" and in us, nature organizes her ultimate elements in all the terror and in all the creative beauty we behold. This is the creative collectivism in which the cosmos evolves.

Shall we say, then, that nature has regard for the mass and not for the individual?—for the whole and not for the part?—that she destroys the unit that the structure may grow? Rather, we may perceive at every stage that only through combinations of their lesser units do organized individuals come into being, and in this being they are not lost; their natures are fulfilled. Nature works always away from undifferentiated mass towards higher organic unities of the individualized components. It is the nature of individuals to combine and fulfill themselves always in the growth and being of a higher organic unity. Being so created makes them acceptable in this higher membership. In this they are not lost, but their own nature is realized and self-found. Thus alone can they be "saved" from their own disintegration. For it is the law of each individual being that it shall attain such harmony of self-hood, such integrity of life and being, as qualifies it for the associative relationships that constitute a higher order of existence. This is the true collectivism.

Trace this law of nature in the life of man. As his nature grows in balance and beauty, in the fullness and integrity of his own being, does he not become more acceptable for associative relationships, for social integration into a society composed of him and his fellow men? And in this higher, this more complex mode of existence, this community life, does not the social environment and the freedom it brings condition him for still higher growth and realization of self in his individual being? Out of his own beauty and perfections, however unconsciously, man builds his social world, and here he is far more than requited for his individual gifts in that higher freedom and abundance that only the providence of social organization and exchange can bestow. In the Great Society man builds his heaven, for it is the function of the social organization to serve and minister him into the perfection of his individual life.

An individual may be defined as finite energy having its three attributes organized into a limited number of mass units endowed with a limited rate of motion or potential for a limited number of durational units or time. The individual's mass and his potential or rate of activity appear to be predetermined for him. In general, they seem to be inversely related, the individuals of lesser mass having the higher activity rate and *vice versa,* as the extremes are exhibited between the small but dynamic man and the phlegmatic giant. The duration of the individual, however, depends upon the manner in which the mass-motion activity takes place. If the parts act together in freedom, each without restraint of another, there is harmony and mutuality of action and the duration is long. But in proportion as there is conflict or restraint upon the harmonious energy transfers within the organization, its duration is limited and brief. The internal activity or functioning takes the form of adjustment to environment—adjustment of "internal relations to external relations" —the individual being subordinate to and not dominant upon the environment.

But when the human individual becomes the unit of organization, as in a general society he does, then the continuity and duration of the society depends upon the inter-activity of its members being without conflict or restraint of one by another or among numerous groups. These free inter-activities are functional; they are manifested in the division and exchange of services that take place under voluntary engagements with one another. These functionings result in such modifications of the environment that a higher degree and efficiency of adjustment is achieved. This conserves the individual energies, releasing them into length of days and for activities that are not mere adjustments—mere reactions to stimuli—but are original and spontaneous to the individual in his practice of the progressive enterprises and creative arts that transform his world. The greater duration, the longer rhythm of life thus socially attained, is the qualitative transformation and advancement of human life into powers that are more free and creative, hence more spiritual, more divine.

The implications springing from this concept of populations' rhythmic energy rising out of environment are thus wide and deep. By its purely inductive and quantitative approach it brings the societal life-form within the scope of the objective sciences. So doing, it discovers in those populations in which the units of living energy are organized in the free relations that lengthen their generations as pulsations between birth and death, the power to modify and refashion the system of environment whence they spring. In this positive technique it glimpses a creative, and in that sense a spiritual world. Here it seems to discover organized mankind as derived from a self-existent universe and, through its powers so derived, able itself to become self-existent and self-creating, through its power of recreating its environment into its own likeness and desire. It seems to place and reconcile philosophy and science upon a common ground at the point where, in the organization of vital energy into waves of less frequency and longer duration, positively qualitative and creative powers arise out of and upon the merely quantitative. It lays the groundwork for objective examinations and adequate appraisals of the positive and creative, the harmonious and power-giving contractual relationships among men, that the institution of property and its administration by voluntary services under free contract and exchange affords.

And such examination under the energy concept discovers in the conduct of public community affairs a singular, tragic and almost total failure of the political as distinguished from the proprietary officers, to practice the social technique of administering community services under the social freedom and productivity that can be realized only within the relationships of contract and consent. It leaves little doubt that the long suffering of men from the practice of arbitrary and the absence of contractual relationships between them and their "public servants" or rulers, is due to no scientific analysis in basic quantitative terms having heretofore been made, and hence to insufficient intellectual illumination in this field of phenomena where mass emotion and national hysteria have almost exclusively prevailed.

The social organization raises the individual member from the state of being as a *creature,* dependent on and arbitrarily enslaved to environment, into freedom and abundance, dependent on but not enslaved by the society of which he is a functioning part. Without the services of his fellow social units, his whole life is ruled by the exigencies of environment and circumstance. His life is determined without regard to his choice or will, and he must obey, under penalty of his death and the extinction of his race. But when he enters into the social relationship of serving many persons and being by many served, the productivity, the creativeness of this golden rule of exchange lifts him out of an almost completely necessitous state and into a relative abundance that relieves him from the compulsions of an un-social-ized environment and endows him with wide alternatives and options for the exercise of his spontaneous will. And when he has so entered, his acts of service and exchange are by voluntary contracts under consent of his own will in accord with that of his fellow man—the "social will"—as its unforced expressions arise in the forums of exchange. Out of the fruitfulness of the services performed and exchanged, this as yet too limited mutual freedom and accord of individual wills, the energies of men are emancipated to activities not prescribed by necessities from without but by preference and choice—by realizations of the intrinsic and spontaneous will. For this gift of freedom to its members, the society is requited with all spontaneous researches, discoveries and recreations and the practice and enjoyment of the esthetic and creative arts.

It is in these esthetic and artistic creations that the intrinsic will of man is most completely fulfilled. In his necessitous world of imperative needs, conduct is in the main prescribed, with almost no liberty as to what he must do, and choice only as to how. But in the communion of service with his fellow men that constitutes his social world, the imperative needs are so much more adequately met that a large part of his life becomes emancipated from these compulsions, and with this unprisoned power, he is not driven, but is free to move in what direction he will and to follow such leading as most inspires and brings fulfillments of supreme desires. For the free heart of man knows no love so high, no desire so strong, as the passion towards that Beauty whose inspiration lifts and leads it ever on.

Man is composite of myriad fluid and fluent elements and parts forming and reforming themselves in ever-changing figures and patterns of relationship and change. This organization of energy in the individual is unique; it possesses a continuing positive or constructive entropy unpredictable in pattern apart from itself and non-reversible in direction. It is capable of statistical formulation but not of any other, and therefore where large numbers are concerned it yields to practical although not to absolute prediction. How it came or comes to be what it is has no relevance in any consideration of the freedom of the individual will, for it constitutes the personality of the individual, his very will itself. Since only the state of society, the kingdom of the golden rule of life and power by consent and exchange, gives men the freedoms of contractual as against compulsive relationships, here his spontaneous will becomes a determinant factor in the selection and succession of events. In the degree that he extends these free relations, they supervene upon compulsive ones, and man comes into his heritage of, and creative dominion over, the environment whence he draws the energy that is his life. And thus, in the measure that his will determines the outer world that conditions him, in that measure does he attain and participate not alone in the universal creation but also in that *self-realization* which he imputes to the Universal Reality as the unconditioned and divine.

CHAPTER 28

## *Mind and the Cosmos*

EVERY OBSERVATION or experience is a duality. It has two sides—action and reaction, objective and subjective. When the objective, the external, is dominant and compulsive, the subjective effect is in the form of feeling, negative feelings, prompting reactions in habit pattern of attack or escape, under biologic reflexes previously acquired. As the subjective, the individual, by aid of the social system of exchange, becomes dominant over circumstance and environment, feeling then becomes positive and amenable to external harmonies. Now it rises into inspiration, and actions follow designedly, creatively and unerringly to heart's desire.

Without vision there is no understanding. Comprehension comes always as illumination of the mind, a light that beams also in the countenance and in the eyes. A new organization of neurons has taken place and become integrated with what was before. Each new conception is valid and can be verified in experience only as it is conceived in terms of what has been grasped and verified before.

The social order, therefore, can be validly conceived and understood only in terms of those verified and finite conceptions of the universal reality upon which the natural sciences are based. Mass, motion and duration; substance, activity and period, or continuity of time; these are the three terms, in the unity of which reality, in the natural sciences, is experienced and conceived. The units of physical measurement corresponding to these are the objective standards to which the descriptions and formulations of the sciences finally refer.

These three units, taken together, constitute a unit of reality, a unit of "action," or of energy-in-action, such as the kilowatt-hour, the pound-foot-minute, and the dyne (inertial mass of one gram)-centimeter-second, called the erg-second. There is no known limit in nature beyond which these units are not multiplied and combined; energy is believed to be universal and, by many, infinite. But physical science does find that there is a limit to the divisibility of energy, that there is a definite bottom limit, an extremely small quantity, in less than which the all-embracing trinity of mass, motion and duration is not to be and cannot be experienced. This unit of action, or *quantum of action,* as it is called, is a very definite but almost infinitesimal fraction of an erg-second. From this it follows that energy as action can manifest itself to us at any quantitative level upward, beginning with the quantum, but that it does not manifest itself objectively to us in any less or fractional part of this small quantity of action or event. It thus constitutes an indivisible unit in multiples of which all organization of energy proceeds without any necessary limitations, which unit is also the bottom limit below which disorganization can not take place. It follows from these fundamentals of physical science that it is the nature of reality, of the cosmos as universal energy, to be ever progressive, without any necessary limitation, into ever higher complexities of organization. And by the same token all disintegrative and retrograde movements or trends, by reason of their direction and of their own nature, cannot prevail but must come to a definite end. It would seem, therefore, that indefinite progression is the essential attribute of the universal energy or reality as it comes into human experience.

As the erg-second is a compound of mass, motion and duration, so also is its smallest fraction, the quantum, so compounded. Quanta, therefore, are not simple but complex, and instead of being every one alike, they can be as variable as may be the ratios in which their three elements are composed. It follows from this that any integration of quanta can be and probably is entirely unique, even though there may be a quantitative equivalence through equal numbers of quanta being combined. Even a combination so simple as only two quanta can possess properties very different from those of any other binary compound of quanta unless the latter are not only quantitative equivalents but also alike in the proportions in which their elements of mass, motion and duration are composed.

Thus, at the very base of physical science, the "building blocks of the universe" have, or at least may be presumed to possess, the same qualitative differences that are found in all the higher structures into which they are wrought. This qualitative property may be defined as interior, and independent of any over-all quantitative relationship or equivalence, being that property of energy whereby its diverse organizations are qualified to interact. All are qualitative; but the type or kind most qualified to prevail and endure—as the *societal* organization of men—is most positive, most creative and most *real*. And it possesses this property through the preponderance of duration or eternality among the three elements of which it is composed. Thus natural science and the Christian theology, in their ultimate conceptions of *reality*, are essentially the same. Each is founded on its basic trinity—the one composed of elements finite and measurable, the other of the same elements infinite and immeasurable; and there is within each the same ascending order of reality—mass, motion, duration—Substance, Power, Eternity.

As in physics, so in mathematics, there can be no organization of indivisible units below the unit taken as *one,* whether symbolized as digit or fractional part. From that base, however, an indefinite organization and evolution of numbers without any necessary end can proceed; but any reverse process or involution, as it is called, can regress only to the primary unit, upon reaching which it must and does abruptly end. From this point of view, it may be said that mathematics, so far as it has been developed, is an abstract reflection of the processes and organization of energy that constitute the universal reality in concrete form. If this speculation is sound, it accounts for the fact of so many processes of nature, from the atomic to the astronomical, being describable by abstract and general mathematical formulations and terms. It was no accident, then, that the formula of Galileo that described the movement of falling bodies should also describe the path of a projectile, the orbit of the moon and the path of Neptune all unseen. If it seems strange that the abstract processes of the mind should so faithfully parallel and portray the processes of the concrete world, we may reflect that the whole mind and organization of man is a product, a by-product, if we like, finite but still no less a part, of the total organization of the reality that constitutes the concrete world. Whatever man is or has he derives from the universal, and whatever is particular in him, as the child of the universe, must be in the veritable likeness of his objective and universal world.

These thoughts leave no ground to doubt that the rational mind of man has the wit to come into conscious understanding of, and to formulate into general principles and mathematical laws, the special organization of universal energy that constitutes and maintains a population of men into a societal life-form. The scientific *reason*, the rational intellect of man is, within itself, wholly subjective, an order and process existing only in him; but when it is based on sound induction, on objective and verifiable experience, then it becomes one with the cosmic reality and has the power to *create*, for it gives foreknowledge of events and things to come.

The concept of energy, that is, energy-in-action, as the ultimate reality, affords the key to the kingdom of man's understanding and conscious mastery over his social world. Just as it reveals the basic life-functioning of the individual man in the balanced energy transfers among his ultimate units or cells, so it discloses the free energy transfers among the ultimate social units and organized groups as the fundamental function that maintains a population as a societal life-form. Just as the energy concept shows the three-fold nature of the individual man in his material substance, in his nutritional energy-supply and activation, and his neural coördination, these three—mass, motion, continuity—so does it reveal the three great divisions and departments of society: its mass manifestation in government as the organization of coercive and compulsive power, its service and exchange activity that supports its life and enables it continuously to re-create its environment and thereby increasingly to subsist, and its cultural department that gives coördination and continuity of functioning and thereby advances the organized life of the whole. It shows that the growth and development of human society is the gradual differentiation of these three departments—the state; the exchange system; and the system of religion and creative arts, imagination and intellect—each sustaining the other in the rising order of their development and each, in proportion as it is differentiated from the others, serving, refining and elevating them in the reverse and descending order, the order of their beauty and beneficence upon men.

The basic and general pattern of the whole system of society thus is clear. But it is not full blown; it is seen only in the bud; it is far from mature. The rational exchange system is still in the toils of arbitrary power, in bonds to the Citadel, slave of the state. The world of the imponderables in religion and in the arts, the realms of fancy—and especially of pure intellect—are in large part enthralled to the political power. And in the commercialization of religion and of the arts and sports, its rude perversions of the Market stain also the graces and soil the outer vestments of the Altar. But the pure spirit of the Altar haunts the marts of trade and exchange, bringing the light of new knowledge, refining the ethics and raising the practice of those who function there. And the Market thus inspired is destined to cleanse the Citadel even of war and transform it into a thing of beauty and love, a solvent, serving, and a divinely protective power.

The modern social-ization of land ownership, of community sites and resources, out of the Citadel, out of the power to tax and rule, that began during the period of political revolution toward the end of the eighteenth century, and the more recent widespread aspirations for a more business-like administration of community affairs, are among the many manifestations of the influence of the exchange system upon the system of force—the influence of the Market upon the Citadel. Silently and unobtrusively, it offers for the administration of public affairs the exclusively social technique of exchange by *contract* and consent—in the further functional extension and development of the institution of property in land as the proprietary public agency and authority to maintain and exercise responsible supervision over the community servants and to give constructive administration to the public capital of the community, as it now unconsciously administers and distributes the community lands. For if civilization is to advance, this it is destined to do through land-ownership acting primarily in the interest of community members as tenants and purchasers and for community rewards to itself in rising rents and permanent values on such a scale as few now can conceive.

This is the impending great step or leap forward in the evolution and self-development of the social organism. The intellectual light for it shines even now upon the Altar; it may soon spread to the Market-place; and then, through the administration of property in land and in pursuit of honorable recompense and profit, the Market will take all tyranny out of the Citadel by social-izing it into services and investing it with highest honors and rewards. This further light needs only to be seen; all the enlightened instincts of men, selfish and altruistic, will prompt and urge them to make avail.

The energy concept of population affords the necessary ground for a truly rational and scientific approach to the three basic institutions of associated men: The Citadel, the place first of protection, then of compulsive tyranny, government, enslavement and war. The Market, where freedom's first gift is peace, as force and stealth give way to contract and accord. And lastly the Altar, realm of the non-necessitous, where dwell the imponderables of spirit and mind, religion and the esthetic arts and all spontaneous play; where inspiration descends and aspirations rise; where temples cradle muses and cathedrals foster colleges and schools; where faith flowers in the arts, philosophy sparks the torch of science, and creative mind and spirit find their ancient and their native home.

These living institutions of men are in and of the cosmic system no less than are the atoms and the stars. They constitute the whole organic society. They are peculiar to men alone and to none but socialized men. They develop in an ascending order; as their separate structures differentiate and separately evolve, their successively higher functions are performed, and they are reunited in the supreme function of conferring upon men the ever larger and longer life to which men in society unitedly attain. These basic social structures came into being without the conscious will or ken of man; so, they serve his needs and desires only to the extent that they have empirically evolved. Only for want of vision, of conscious understanding and development of them, do they but incompletely serve. Without such understanding, the Citadel fails to protect, violates the Market and enslaves it with the chains and wheels of government and war; and the realm of the imponderables, the Altar, is violated with false religion, intellect and art governmentally prescribed. But the Science of Society, new wonder child of the Altar, begins now to reveal the rational harmony implicit in the basic institutions of men no less than in the physical and natural world whose several sciences have made so many dreams come true and the creative will of man so near supreme.

Citadel, Market, Altar: these are the social symbols of protection and stability; of nourishment, maintenance and growth; and of increasing freedom of creative and thus spiritual advance. In their rational development into differentiations of form with integration of functions, the organic society will bless its members with higher lives and length of days and invite them ever more into the perfect and ideal Unity of "Substance, Power and Eternity," the Ultimate Reality, the mystic's perfect dream and crowning joy.

CHAPTER 29

## Society the Crown of Creation

ALL SCIENCE is founded on observation, comparison and measurement—that is, upon induction. What constitutes the science is not the body or mass of data with which it deals, but the order and relationships that are found to prevail throughout the field in which the data are observed. This order and these relationships, when first apprehended, are called generalizations or hypotheses, and when later they are independently verified, they become truly established and accepted as theories, principles or natural laws. It is in this way that the separate sciences, each within its special and restricted field of observation, first appear; and each new science, as separate from the others, occupies a different field of observation. Thus the foundation sciences—mathematics, astronomy, physics, chemistry, biology, psychology, etc.—all have primary reference to existing and enduring relationships in particular fields. But each of these sciences, roughly in the order given, in addition to its own special field and data of observation, involves the inclusion and use of the principles and theories previously won. The factual parts of astronomy and physics possess no great significance except as they exhibit correlations with mathematical principles and laws. Chemistry assumes the relationships accepted as mechanical and physical laws, and biology accepts all of chemistry and physics as the frame and foundation upon which its special phenomena are superimposed. In the like way, psychology rests upon physiology as its necessary antecedent in the biological field.

All of these sciences are founded primarily on the inductive data of present observation; they are, first of all, descriptive. When, in the descriptive data, relationships that repeat themselves are discerned, or assumed and finally verified, the principles and laws appear as invariable; and a consistency with the mind of man is found in the relationships of the phenomenal world. All of this comes about from science making a rational and objective (contra-emotional) examination of things as they are.

But the observation of things as they *are* renders up many evidences of much previous development and change—that there has been a sequence in nature similar to the order in which the various sciences themselves have evolved. The scientific examination of these successive sequences and steps in nature at last leads to the hypothesis, not alone of invariable relationships, but also of a definite order in which these successively arise. From this the theory of evolution was born and, upon verification, accepted, bringing into the purview of science not only the relationships of things as they exist, but also the order, method and process by which they came. At first this was thought, in the living world at least, to have been by increments of variation within the otherwise relatively invariable relationships. It is now known that while minor variations do take place in the structures and functions of living things, great and significant changes came about through the emergence and growth of new organizational forms. This frequently takes place through the association of previously independent or even antagonistic units or individuals in relationships tending towards stability and permanence in the new organism and giving it functions and powers far transcending those of the units or parts composing it. This is called creative synthesis or emergent evolution.

Going beyond the static and looking upon nature from the dynamic and genetic points of view, science sees that which was once formless and void evolving into units called electrons, protons, neutrons, etc. These it conceives as organizations of primordial energy that have come to possess a degree of structural stability. These evolved units science sees as coming into group relations, through energy transfer and balance, until new and highly stable groups known as atoms emerge. Repeating this process, but now using atoms as the units to be balanced and reconciled to each other, nature puts them together in still higher organizational forms and the world of molecules comes to be. The time involved can only with difficulty be conceived. The paths of possibility vainly sought and attempted we can only faintly imagine; but undaunted nature still pursues her inherently creative way. She frames the atomic constellations in her molecules at last into that triumph and mystery, the biological unit, the living cell. Its complexities are extreme; its constituents are chiefly carbon and water, and its molecules are the most complex of which chemistry gives any account. It has the protection of a garment as versatile as its needs; it is capable of ingestion, excretion and even locomotion; and it achieves that supreme function in which the cell becomes lost in its own progeny, in its self reproduced.

What shall nature do now with so wondrous a creation? Shall she rest from her labors? Or is the essence of her own being that she must evolve—that she herself is not entity but really energy and process? We know the answer; it lies in the layers of the rocks throughout the vastness of geologic time; in the tragedy of endless trying and almost endless non-success. The myriad extant forms of organized cell life in the plant and animal world are those that have been weighed in the balance of changing environments—and *not* found wanting. The plant world itself only became secure by specializing in the molecular organization of carbon from the air by utilizing energy from the sun. From this has come all structures of the animal world and the peculiar modes of energy and higher powers that distinguish all the animal forms.

It was a great emergence when nature began to organize her cells, and again when she achieved her world-wide symbiosis in the universal coöperation between plant and animal life.

The plant, throughout its existence, converts its energy into structure and ceases to grow only when it dies. But the animal reconverts its structure into the energy of physical and neural activity that continues throughout its life, though after maturity it ceases to grow. The plant accumulates energy for the animal. Through the animal flows the energy that the plant captures from the sunlight. But the animal structure is constantly consumed and constantly renewed. It takes as food the stored energy of the plant and puts it out again in the complex functions that constitute its higher life. Its myriad coöperating somatic cells constantly proliferate, give up their energy and die. Those that reach a critical maturity multiply by division (fission); and thus the animal structure is maintained until at last the capacity of the cells for integrated coöperation, in some vital organ or part, is lost; the interdependent parts can no longer serve each other; the structure disintegrates back to environment. The animal dies. But this does not occur with all; there are highly specialized cells called genetic that have the somatic structures as their special environment. Such of them as meet and unite with others that are contra-specialized as to sex set up new trains of cell multiplication and organization that constitute the individuals of the renewed and successive generations.

It is to its much higher complexity that the animal organism owes its unique and transcendent functions and powers. This indebtedness it must repay in sensitivity and susceptibility to adverse environmental factors. To maintain its higher functions and complex forms, it must modify them in such ways as the necessities of its environment impose; it must build up within itself such flexible powers of response and adjustment as will compensate the environmental changes that the individual and the race must withstand. The records left by extinct and surviving species tell this story of nature's strivings in the animal world. Those extant are the animals of fixed habitat that have successfully modified and adjusted themselves to conditions that remained nearly uniform, and also those animals that have such versatile and compensating powers as have enabled them successfully to withstand wide changes within their habitat and, finally, without essential change in themselves, to inhabit the most diverse environments that the earth affords.

The animals best modified and adjusted to fixed habitats and, therefore, most dependent on continuity of present unchanged conditions have hostaged themselves to the future. Changes in their environment they must meet by changes of structure or perish, and the more completely adapted and adjusted they are the more difficult or impossible it is for them to change. For animals that are not able to modify their behavior or to compensate within their existing structures, the future is not bright. As external conditions change, they must perish completely.

The only animal whose versatility and compensating powers

enable him to inhabit the whole earth is man. Even in a relatively primitive state he lives at almost any altitude and in every clime, and he exhibits as an individual always the same essential structure with the same functions and modes of action. This power of internal adjustment and compensation without any permanent change of structure is, doubtless, what has enabled man to occupy the earth and out-survive all other animal forms.

At this point, the story of man and his capacity is not half told; for, as a social being, in an organic and symbiotic or exchange relationship with his fellows, he achieves an organization and powers by which he not only inhabits and occupies the whole earth, but actually inherits—makes it his property in the sense that he brings it under the dominion of his will and can remold it to his heart's desires.

It was a great emergence when a creature like man was lifted into powers of adjustment and compensation so far above his fellow animals. But his attempts throughout history to social-ize himself into a successful and permanent, organic relationship of free exchange with his fellows (dis-junctive symbiosis) presage a vaster and a higher emergence still. The one was the creation of a new animal form by higher synthesis of the original biological cells. But the emergence now going on is no less than the synthesis of a new living form in which the essentially similar units are the individual men themselves; an organization of life and therefore an organic being that stands in relation to its units as a living animal body stands in relation to the living and coöperating biological cells of which it is composed, but whose individual capacities the animal body so far transcends.

In like manner, the living social organism exhibits capacities far transcending those of any of its units, either as isolated individuals or in any unsocial-ized mass or horde not organized upon the symbiotic basis of service by exchange. Yet more, the social organization releases, in its individuals, powers and potentialities that under no other state of being could be exercised or fulfilled. In fact, the ultimate function of social-ization, of the human society unlike that of insects and animals, is the fulfillment of itself through service to, and the self-realization and fulfillment of, the individual units of which it is composed.

It is the peculiar glory of man that nature has wrought into his being so much of her own modes of action and organization that through the eye of his mind she can look back and trace her own evolvement from mere primordial energy through all the structured systems, suns and stars, atoms, crystals and cells—through the myriad organic forms that lead, at last, to man, her most complex and most completed offspring, gifted with versatile powers of internal adjustment to the widest habitat or environmental change, and endowed through his social and coöperative nature with power to modify conditions external to him, to shape environment to need and desire and, measurably at least, to rebuild his world to the pattern of his dreams.

But just as man's marvelous powers of internal adjustment derive from the fine coöperation that exists between the component organs and parts of his individual organization, so does his building of his world depend upon the like coöperation of the individuals and groups, the specialized organs and parts, of which the Great Society of mankind, the social organism itself, is composed.

Into this Great Society of man, nature combines the best fruits of her tree of evolving life. Creation cannot rest with the building merely of the animal man. In the long nights of barbarism, nature may rest from her labors; but still she must move on to the building of society, of organized mankind. "Saith Life, 'I am that which must always transcend itself.'"

With lesser creatures, nature has made experiments resembling but not rising into social organizations. Herds, hives, flocks and schools are advantageous modes of life. The creatures thus united come better to withstand the rigors of environment. They multiply and prosper, but unlike man they do not refashion their environment and make it increasingly serviceable to their lives. On the contrary, as their numbers increase, their environment becomes impoverished and their place in the living world less secure. To this hazard nature responds, in general, by giving them higher reproductivity. As the insufficiency of food and other factors shorten their lives, fecundity, at the expense of other capacities, increases the number of the shorter lives. Thus the vital balance is maintained. But increased numbers again press upon a declining subsistence until the stronger are compelled either to kill and eat, or to starve out the weaker, lest all should expire. This downward spiral must lead to complete extinction or to an increasing number of increasingly shortened lives—a reversion to the bacterial form and condition—but for the circumstance that elimination by conflict and starvation raises the vital resistance and virility of those who are thus able to survive.

Nature here again resorts to an improvement in the individual units before better and stabler organization can be evolved. Her attempts in the form of herds, flocks and hives, all falling short of social organization, have been complicated by climatic and other environmental changes and by cross conflict between variant forms and species. But the general process of increasing the numbers with depletion of environment, higher fecundity to compensate a shortening vital span and selection of the superior to improve the race, has still gone on.

At last, in man, a creature appeared who, in addition to his previous animal techniques possessed a new and further instinct—that of social organization. In him, the services between individuals and social groups are not entirely unconscious. Although, consciously, men do act primarily with regard to their individual advantage and only secondarily with a view to the advantage of the social group as a whole, unconsciously they enter into reciprocal relationships, biologically in their intimate and familial groups, and economically with other persons who are not so related. Distinguishing him from all other creatures, man's social instincts lead him gradually to abandon force and the relationships of dominance and subservience and to enter into a voluntary democratic relationship of exchanges measured by value and price with a system of charges and credits for the keeping and adjustment of accounts, so that the utmost division of labor and elaboration of service and exchange can be engaged in throughout an entire and extensive population. This highly productive and creative relationship, corresponding as it does with the symbiotic relationships in the lower forms of life and also between the individual cells that constitute these forms, leads to a social metabolism that guides the individual energies of men into their special participant functions in the society, the social organism.

Society thus becomes the universal servant of the individual by maintaining for him an exchange relationship in which his special services are most abundantly performed for all, and in which he, in turn, is most richly and abundantly served. The preponderance of this new intimate and intricate relationship is what constitutes all the life and power of the organic society. Upon its rise or its decline hangs the fate of civilized nations and men.

The question may arise, why will not this social-ized population of men also be compelled to exhaust its environment, consume its substance, and, in the ensuing hazards of shortened lives, multiply its numbers into the necessity of starving, exterminating and finally devouring each other until only the ruthless and resistant survive?

The answer is that these more perfect and widespread exchange relationships of men give them the unique power of improving and rebuilding their environment and thereby raising their substance far above anything that their increasing numbers can require. The further answer is that the high biological security that such socialization provides lengthens the days of the individuals and thus relieves nature of the need to multiply the units of life to compensate for a shortening of the span. Thus, a far higher biological economy and efficiency is obtained through prolonging the individual life and thereby putting forth vital energy more in functional and less in maintenance and reproductive forms; for all the years of each individual leading to maturity are years of cost to, and dependence on, the vital power of the race. The society or race in which the lives are many and brief is the least efficient. In a social condition of but little division of labor and exchange of services, the span of life is but little more than the time taken to mature. This condition is but little above that of those ephemeral plants and insects that live only to bloom, bear seeds and die.

The function of the social organization is to bring about, through its exchange relationships, that higher subsistence and biologic security under which not more, but more perfect individuals may grow and come into being and in which there is a longer span for the exercise of their mature powers and for the utmost development of the potentialities of their individual lives.

In the evolution of living forms, clearly such is the condition and achievement towards which the integrative processes of nature have long conspired. It is as though Nature, with justifiable pride in man as the highly organized and efficient unit that crowns her commendable labor from an infinite past, in whom she combines and confides her most precious powers and delectable dreams, leads him now into the household of social creation, endowed with creative, and thereby spiritual, powers. By exercise of these powers society evolves. By the practice of exchange, men grow into cities, states and nations—creations of ephemeral glory that seem to rise only to decline. As voluntary service and exchange raise wealth and subsistence, so does the coercive public power increasingly penalize and pervert this vital process. Instability and insecurity set man against man, group against group, race against race, nation against nation. Divisions arise, barriers are set. Deadly agencies and instruments of attack and defense are piled up. The "nationalized" states penalize and paralyze their peoples' exchange, both within and without. Impoverishment follows. They blindly destroy themselves and fall by each other's hand.

By her rigorous penalties, nature has taught men and groups of men to divide their labors and exchange with each other in order to survive. Under the like penalty of death she commands the same upon her public communities—her cities and states. The conduct of the public business, of community service, which is the only proper reason for government, must be lifted above the barbaric practice of force and violence against the property and social relationships of the community members; it must be established on the firm and enduring principle of the golden rule, the principle of voluntary exchange, as any other successful business is.

As in the long barbaric past myriad millions of men must have perished from failure to follow the principle of peaceable exchange in their private relations, so have countless communities gone down from their failure to practice exchange instead of compulsion and force in the conduct of their public, their community affairs.

By what our predecessors have learned, we exist merely as we are. Only as we ourselves learn can we make any advance. Standing now before the threshold of a social glory the realization of which will dwarf all poets' dreams, men must again choose whether in their community affairs the practice of force shall cast them from the House of Life into outer darkness or the practice of public service by profitable exchange shall lift them into its awaiting freedom and fullness of life. The great social mutation that awaits and impends is the social-ization of public force into public service by exchange.

When the great business of community service is carried on *as a business* and not by depredation upon business, it will be magnificent above all other business in the world. In one country alone it will have a hundred and sixty million customers, every one a consumer of its community services. For its capital structure, it will have all of the existing public works, facilities and materials now employed in public and governmental activities. In its executive positions, from highest to lowest, it will have the most creative and constructive officers and experts that the owners of the land, the now potential administrative owners of all the public capital, can engage. Most of all, it will create its products and services with greatest facility, for it will bear no crushing burden of tribute or taxation. It will have no expenses and make no payment except for its needs in the conduct of its business. And the value of the public services thus performed will be commensurate with their great utility, for they will be sold to tenants and customers who likewise will be free from all burdens of tribute and compulsory taxation, and whose economic productivity and effective purchasing power and demand for public services will therefore be higher than was ever known or dreamed.

Society, thus, will have a free and unrestrained economic system including a free, efficient and self-supporting system of public services. Each will exchange its wealth and services with and thus enhance the productivity of the other. Nature will have achieved a form of integrated life in which the component individuals will be circumstanced in completest freedom to give and to receive. The consequent abundance of economic goods will come to them almost as automatically as the filling of the lungs with air.

Emancipated alike from the environmental compulsions that beset and enslave the whole primitive world, and from the political and governmental repressions and restrictions that bind and burden the functioning of the social realm, the spirit of man will leap upward in the free practice and culture of all the artistic, esthetic and spiritual powers with which it is essentially endowed.

CHAPTER 30

## *The Inspiration of Beauty*

### Human Emergence into the Divine by Creative Artistry

IN THE NATURAL WORLD great discoveries are made by men who delve into the order of nature and her laws under the inspiration of the beauty that they seek and find. Such labors are esthetic; art and beauty for their own sake, and for no other reward; fruits of the creative spirit of man.

But these spiritual gifts come into the practical service of men only through the operations of production and exchange. The engineers, the technicians, the men of business who buy and sell, must give bodies to these gifts of the spirit and market them to the populace in tangible forms—and for great tangible rewards.

So also is it with nature as she manifests herself in the living societies of men. The working of her laws in the social organization can be discovered only by pursuit of the beauty that in them lies. This done, practical business alone can embody them in forms of utmost service to man.

What distinguishes human from other beings is that they are endowed with a spiritual and creative power that gives them dominion over the whole earth and makes them the "children of God." This power has lifted them into a new mode of life, a social organization, in which each member finds his enrichment indirectly through specialized service to others and, by a system of measured exchanges called business or trade, enjoys the products and services of others in vast variety, convenience and abundance. The growth of this mighty mutuality of service is the divine pathway to that transcendent state, visioned in poets' dreams, in which the highest being is attained through each becoming, in effect, the servant of all.

In their un-social-ized state, nature lays heavy restrictions alike upon animals and men. Without the power to create and exchange, their subsistence is only what nature provides, and this they cannot employ to rebuild their world but only to multiply their kind. They cannot bend the forces of nature to their needs and desires. But social-ized men, by their technique of trade and exchange, can raise their subsistence to vastly higher levels than their increasing numbers can require. So it comes about that in the animal and un-socialized world, even the existence of an individual or group is inimical to every other, and the necessary technique is to seize, violate and destroy. This crude relationship among men is the heritage of their animal past. All creativeness, all the sciences and arts, all social culture and growth, is the product of the distinctively human—the divine—technique of creation through exchange of service. However little we are aware of it, this is the divine symbiosis, the living with God through living divinely with men.

Evil is atavistic, reversion to actions no longer adaptive, and hence not enduring. When the sum total of human energy shall flow outward in functional and creative modes, then evil can no longer exist. All activity either for or against evil is creative energy misdirected, perverted and lost. But the putting out of the divine, the creative, power transcends all evil, resolving it into the beauty of the divine. This is the cosmic pageant of evolving nature, for only the positive can prevail, only the creative can abide. It brings into being relationships that endure through being synthesized into higher relationships. It is the divine business of universal life, the abiding reality. The character of evil, as such, lies in its impermanence.

Salvation from evil is not any advance but only a salvage at the best, for it does not enter into the progression of the divine. Life manifests itself in creation by growth into higher relationships. Its real business is to flow forward in forms transcending all its past. The enduring office of religion and of all the esthetic arts she has nurtured and brought forth is not to destroy nor yet to save. It is to inspire. It is to qualify the crude energy of life with the divine beauty of its creative expression.

Amid the vicissitudes of life, and above all merely negative gratification or relief, there are relationships, receptivities and appreciations that suffuse with a sense of unity, integrity and creative power. This is the sensing of beauty, the veritable inspiration, the authentic revelation of the truly divine. It is expressed outwardly in the uplifted eyes, the parted lips, the inward breath, the outstretched arms, the heightened muscular tone and the sense of being fully alive. Its recipient is at once, and for the moment, however brief, perfect and whole; a "child of God" in whom there is no guile. To cherish and cultivate this receptivity is the true "spiritual discipline," for the inspired mind cannot destroy; it is the seer, it is illumined, it alone understands. The deep and secret beauties and potencies of nature and of human nature are revealed to it. It is "at one with God" in the joyous putting forth of divine power, for it has emerged into the perpetual springtime of infinite creation.

In every age, so far as men have practiced the golden rule of service by mutual exchange, the creative "power of God" has blessed them with a measure of freedom; and with freedom, abundance; and with abundance, peace and length of days. The energies so liberated from conflict and wars on wings of inspiration divinely rise, not in flight from death, but in an eternal seeking after light and life. Touched by this esthetic perception, the children of men's lifted vision spring from their hearts and hands as works of art, evangels of the Universal Beauty whose mark and sign they bear. Under this inspiration men create objects as symbols, devise actions as ritual, weave words into melody, and sounds into symphony and song. Thus through the esthetic arts do they worship and commune with Beauty, and by their works pay homage to this, their Source divine. As its inspiration descends they clothe it in color and form, in rhythmic motion and melodic sound, and in the magic of story, poesy and song. These rouse the sense of wonder and awe, feed the awakened aspirations and release in ecstasies the potential powers of man. Thus through the esthetic arts does religion speak and move, and in ever-flowing concord bind men's hearts to creative Beauty—to the divine.

Yet more: awakened and uplifted eyes trace out heavenly beauty, and the swinging constellations make music in the rational and reflective mind of man. The world is traversed in its breadth, its summits scaled, its depths explored, its history revealed; and there also man finds order and process native to his emancipated mind. In the joy of this new light he learns the sure way of knowing and of doing that is called science, and by its employment widens all his limitations of space and time. The vision of the intellect, of the eye of the mind, gives the hand of man its grasp upon eternal power— the power wherewith to mould to heart's desire his physical and, no less, his social and therewith his spiritual world.

Those who respond to the persuasions of beauty are, so far, exempt from the rude compulsions of animal life. They enter the positive phase of existence where they strive not for less pain but for highest exaltation—where they love not possession but to be possessed. Such persons alone can clearly distinguish the integrative and creative modes of action either in the social organism or in the individual life. The ecstatic vision alone can limn to seekers and seers the patterns of living beauty that lie in the social institutions of men no less than in their essential selves. Transcending all expedience and quickening creative power, is the inspiration—the very *spirit* of religion—that consecrates the esthetic and the abstract arts and endows with visions that transform the world.

The uninspired will protest that degrading conditions of life dim the minds and dull the hearts of men against creative inspiration, casting down the weak and rousing in the strong a wrathful fury to destroy. But the appeal of the spirit is not to victims nor is it to avengers. It is to those unpretending servants and redeemers of mankind who thrill to the rationally understandable beauty that inheres in all the life-ward ways of peace, however mean or commonplace they seem. For they, of all men, are sufficiently detached from the rigors of mere animal existence and from the sweet seductions of organized brute force to discern the creative harmonies in free human relationships no less than in the singing of the stars.

When *private* persons put others under compulsion of force or deceit and thus get without giving, such actions are forbidden and punished as crimes. But precisely similar acts, systematized under governmental power, we morally approve and applaud or blindly accept and endure. Men acting as government, supposedly as servants of all, have no code of pro-social conduct such as there is for plain and private men, for those who are limited to the voluntary relationships of consent and exchange. We have not apprehended the divine beauty, the golden-rule character, the spiritual quality of the exchange process and so have scarcely yet dreamed of its potentiality, its awaiting beneficence, when extended into those territorial or community services that men must have not separately but *in common* and that are essential to community life.

And so in our blindness to the beauty of the voluntary relationships of contract and exchange, in which our creative and thus our *spiritual* power dwells, we have all too little enjoyed the blessings of this divine technology in the production and distribution of *community* services and goods. The miracle of social organization lately evolved out of ancient tyranny is the highest form of organic life; but it is very young, hardly adolescent, not yet sufficiently evolved.

The modern free society employing the process of contract and exchange took over from the ruling classes, from the governments of ancient and medieval times, agriculture and most of the services then performed by serfs and tax-ridden "free" men under domination of their ruling powers. Only a century or so ago it separated the administration of land, of community sites and resources, out of the power of government by bringing this basic property under the non-coercive jurisdiction of ownership or possession determined by free contracts sanctioned by common consent. But society has not yet so far evolved as to bring within this non-coercive administration the providing of general community services (other than the mere distribution of them) which are appurtenant to the sites and lands and available to the public only through its occupancy or use of them. Under this evolutionary lag, ancient political power now so moves forward as to threaten complete reversion to the slave technique. In this adventure, mountainous public debt mortgages future production to past dissipation while advancing seizures of property and curtailments of freedom prevent the *productive* employment of lands, of capital and of men. Thus stalks the warning shadow of a completely political or "socialized" society which, of course, would be no society at all.

All of the social and spiritual energies of men spring from their divine sublimation of otherwise destructive and undifferentiated brute force. This energy cannot be destroyed. When blocked in its creative flow, it finds expression in public and private violence and crime. Every social perversion, every business depression and the downward trend of production and exchange that marks the social decline, can be traced to cumulative repressions of the social process by political authority. This dries the very springs of public revenue, bankrupts the productive economy and destroys all the values that society creates. Yet a higher public technology waits, and it must evolve. Just as the whole organization of private enterprise can serve its myriad customers with no need to enslave them, so must society evolve the like system of public enterprise through the organization of *community owners* to provide common services to their habitants without ruling or enslaving them.

Public services are those conferred publicly on a territory through portions set apart as rights of way for communication and for other common purposes or needs. These services enable wealth to be produced and exchanged within the territory served. The portion of this wealth that by contract and consent of all is rendered up to the territorial owners as location rent is the public revenue given in exchange for the owners' services in making contractual and thereby peaceable and productive allocations of the varying advantages appertaining to the sites and resources. This includes any balance of services above the dis-services of the political regime—if such balance there be. And as in all other transactions in which property or its use is transferred, the market is the real arbiter of the terms. For the free market, by its consensus of many minds, gauges the recompense according to the social advantages of contract above the alternative of political administration by force. And in this it is governed by all the circumstances as to present demand and the alternatives available, and not merely by the physical properties or advantages possessed by the property rented or sold.

Society can do no act otherwise than through its public officers. The owners of the land are officers of society established by custom and consent and constituting the membership of its basic institution, property in land. The functioning of this institution provides the society with the vital service of a *contractual* allocation of its sites and resources with security of possession on equal terms for all. For performing this necessary service of merchandising *socially,* by free contracts and without coercion or discrimination, the society voluntarily awards to these proprietary officers a recompense out of its resulting productivity that is called land value or ground rent. Like the owners of a lesser community such as a hotel, it is also their function, as yet undiscovered and unperformed, to supervise their community services, protect their tenants against violence at the hands of the community servants and to meet the costs of the public business out of the enormous revenues thus to be created and freely obtained. For the public business when so administered will yield rents far exceeding all present rents and present taxation combined, and the high revenues remaining above all other costs will be the earned recompense of the owners for their administrative services. Unlike mere elected officials, such owner-administrators will have everything to lose by force or fraud or any inhibitions of the social process and everything to gain, in fortune and in honors, by their fruitful and efficient administration of the public affairs in the communities they own.

The social-ization of government into a contractual agency of public services, by transforming the present practice of seizures, compulsions and restraints into one of protection and assistance to men's employment of and services to many others through their voluntary relations, will result in almost unimaginable improvement in the material and the spiritual condition of mankind. The abundance of goods can be like that of light and air, and the energy that now wastes in strife and war can flow into creative services and sublimest artistries. Fear and hate will be transformed, under inspiration, into the ministrations of love. Through loyalty and devotion to Beauty, men will find abundance and peace, and even those who sought only security and ease will awaken, God-like, in the liberty of free spirits to the majesty of creative labor and to the grandeur and the glory of the Cosmic Dream.

Deep from the rhythmic heart of Time, 'mid all
   The Cosmic Process, and the rise or wane
   Of human hopes and dreams, comes the refrain,
Betimes, of Beauty's rapture-raising call.
She led that hand on carven cavern wall,
   Those eyes of shepherds skyward on the plain;
   Inspired by her and scorning mortal pain,
Artist and seekers glory in her thrall.
For she endows with vast creative urge
   The earth-born spirit risen from the sod.
Beyond all impulse to destroy or purge,
   Her inspiration lifts the self-bound clod
From creature, as *creator,* to upsurge
   Enraptured in the song—the work—of God.

*Appendix*

# On the Meanings of Terms

> *He shall be as a god to me who can rightly
> define and divide.* —PLATO.

MEN are ever prone to construct systems of thought and of action, philosophies and laws, moralities and economics, to guide and rule other men. These always fail. For the systems of Nature in all her realms are only to be discovered as they are. They can never be constructed or imposed.

The use of terms is no exception. A writer has no valid choice but to use them as they, either obviously or by subtle implication, *are*. He cannot give them *new* meanings. The meaning of a newly formed or adopted term is seldom if ever wholly new to it. Its roots are deep in the experiences and the usages of the present and of all the past. Its meaning springs from its aptness, and this is discovered, not assigned or imposed. Words are really founded on experiences. Even words that idealize things yearned and dreamed as full blown and fulfilled are wish-projections conceiving in full-orbed splendor some good or beauty that has been in some degree attained. Ideals are happy experiences magnified in dreams.

Language reflects experience as it is and also as it is wished and hoped to be. In much human action the ends sought are gained. Here the words have single meanings (except in metaphor) easy to define in terms of what they speak *about*. We may call them *fact* words. For example, *wages* always means payment for time-gauged or piece-gauged services; *community* always means an inhabited place having *common* services.

In other fields of action the objects desired are but little attained. Here the words are *wish* words, and they are paradoxical. In one moment they signify ideals, in another they refer to a cherished means habitually attempted towards attaining them. For example, *Government*, as an agency of service and as an instrument of rulership; *Democracy*, both as equality of freedom and as equality of condition.

Socionomy searches and discovers not what has been *said* concerning a population but what *distinguishes* it as a society. It must employ words as they are found, seeking always their operative significance.

The following principal terms are defined and explained not merely in their literary or controversial and often contradictory significances but with a view to underlying objective distinctions implicit in their ordinary use but not always sufficiently understood or even known to exist. They are arranged in order from the most broadly abstract significance to the most broadly objective and concrete, from the most widely abstract activity of the mind, without regard to quality, to the most inclusive fulfillment of desires in concrete experience.

1. Reality
2. Eternality
3. Energy
4. Action
5. Mass
6. Motion
7. Duration
8. Life-year
9. Structure
10. Entropy
11. Quantitative
12. Qualitative
13. Rational
14. Socionomy
15. Service
16. Population
17. Community
18. Society
19. Social
20. Societal
21. Anti-social
22. Government
23. Law
24. Democracy
25. Ownership
26. Property
27. Wealth
28. Administration
29. Social-ization
30. Economics
31. Labor
32. Capital
33. Land
34. Public capital
35. Land administration
36. Contract
37. Competition
38. Exchange
39. Credits
40. Wages
41. Salaries
42. Fees
43. Profits
44. Price
45. Rent
46. Interest
47. Value
48. Capital value
49. Income value
50. Speculative value
51. Citadel
52. Market
53. Altar
54. Civilization

# The Meanings of Terms

1. REALITY

In its conceptual and absolute sense, transcending experience, this means the ultimate totality of universal existence, advancing by structural differentiation through infinite time into ever more enduring types and operational forms. It is the first and ultimate postulate on which all the sciences, including philosophy, are based.

In its experiential and limited sense, reality is the quality of continuity, duration or relative eternity manifested in any organization of energy, structure, process or event.

2. ETERNALITY

The absolute and infinite reality in its aspect of duration, the highest qualitative aspect or manifestation.

3. ENERGY

This is the scientific name for the cosmos or total reality. In its absolute sense, it is the totality of passing events, of action—actuality. In its relative sense, it is any finite integration of mass, motion and duration, as the horsepower-hour, kilowatt-hour, pound-foot-minute, erg-second, man-hour, life-year; or as atom, animal, object, star, system, etc., when the manifestation is of great duration, stabilized at low frequency of disintegration and recurrence, repetition or reproduction.

A *dyne* is the metric unit of force which, acting for one second against the inertia of a mass of one gram, is sufficient to accelerate the mass to a velocity of one centimeter per second. An *erg* is the metric unit of energy or work—the amount of energy expended or work done by a dyne acting through a distance of one centimeter; a *dyne-centimeter*. An erg-second is a *dyne-centimeter-second*, an erg of energy expended or work done during one second of time. It is the metric unit-rate of energy per unit of time. When this is multiplied by time—taken any number of times in succession—the product is the quantity of energy-in-action or *action* during that time. The *quantum of action* is an exceedingly small, apparently the smallest possible fraction of an *erg-second* that can be experienced.

4. ACTION

That which energy does, or can do, when or if it *acts*. Work.

Energy is treated variously as the ability, or possibility, of a stationary body or force to do work—potential energy; the work that can be done by a moving body—kinetic energy; and also at times identified with a particular quantity of work actually done or performed, which is action itself and not a mere potentiality or possibility of action, nor a mere ratio or rate of action per unit of time. Energy may be contemplated variously, but it does not enter into objective experience otherwise than as action.

5. MASS

The conception or aspect of energy as static and without change. That which resists motion or change of motion. That to which motion or change of motion appertains. That upon which, when its motion changes, a force is said to act.

6. MOTION

The aspect of energy that relates mass or inertia to extension or space.

## 7. DURATION

The aspect or conception of energy with respect to its persistence or continuity in a particular form of organization, rhythm or functioning. Period, life-span, "lease of life," etc. Inverse of frequency.

## 8. LIFE-YEAR

The unit of measurement for energy or action as manifested in a population. A single human integration of mass, motion and velocity during the period of one year.

## 9. STRUCTURE

Any organization of energy relatively stabilized; considered without reference to motion, process or change.

## 10. ENTROPY

The progressive movement or change of any organization of energy towards or into a particular pattern of relationships.

The movement of a particular organization of energy may be in either direction, towards a greater or a lesser degree of order. Scientific materialists use the term in the second sense only, meaning greater and greater disorder—randomness.

## 11. QUANTITATIVE

The characteristic of any organization of energy taken as a totality without respect to its composition as to mass, motion and duration, and having no reference to human objectives or desires.

Quantity is objective; dimension is subjective. A dimension might be defined as a quantity conceived subjectively in numerical terms.

## 12. QUALITATIVE

The characteristic of any organization of energy with respect to the relative magnitudes in its composition, respectively, of mass, motion and duration.

A transformation of these magnitudes in the ascending order, in the direction of duration, is a positively qualitative or creative change. A transformation in the descending order is negatively qualitative.

With respect to human concerns, a transformation of environment conducive of individual and thus of social continuity (duration) is a positively qualitative or creative change. Since the will to live and to live abundantly is the dominating desire, those activities and resulting conditions that tend to realize human desires, dreams, plans, aspirations and ideals are qualitative in the positive sense.

## 13. RATIONAL

All rationality is fundamentally a matter of ratios, the weighing and balancing of related magnitudes or quantities. The process of thinking is rational only in the degree that it involves comparisons under quantitative appraisements.

So far as the magnitudes, quantities or dimensions comprising any object, process or event are taken by means of specific units of measurement, the description or analysis is *numerically* quantitative, involving numerical ratios, and thereby strictly rational.

Among men, relationships and processes are rational so far as they are voluntary, balanced and reciprocal in their numerically measured quantities based on specific and accepted units of service or value. Thus, the free societal relationships of contract and exchange are rational.

Political or governmental relationships—those enforced by a dominating sovereign power—are not voluntary, reciprocal and numerically balanced. They are therefore of necessity empirical, non-rational.

### 14. SOCIONOMY

*Theory or formulation of the organic laws exemplified in the organization and development of society*—Webster's New International Dictionary.

The Science of Society.

It treats of population as organized energy or structure manifesting functional and creative energy within itself and upon its environment—social-ized mankind as an agency of creation.

### 15. SERVICE

Human energy flowing voluntarily either directly to others or indirectly through being organized and accumulated in structures called wealth, being such human energy as induces a voluntary counter-flow, recompense or value. Service, as a highly differentiated and positively qualitative form of energy, and not merely wealth, is, next to population, the principal object-noun of socionomy.

### 16. POPULATION

Any aggregation of human beings, occupying or inhabiting a specific territory, community or property, without any necessary reference to their being organized and having inter-relationships.

### 17. COMMUNITY

The territory or place occupied by a population as a society. A place having common security, and other welfare services used and enjoyed by the inhabitants generally and in common. The word is often used loosely to include or personify the inhabitants of a community.

### 18. SOCIETY

A population the individuals of which are organized in a relationship, more widespread and universal than the bonds of blood, tradition or belief, that differentiates them into a system of reciprocal services by free energy interchange called trade or economic functioning. It is a population occupying a community, its members sustaining contractual or exchange relationships towards one another with respect to services, both private and public. These services are public with respect to the use of land and all that is appurtenant to it. They are private with respect to all else.

Notwithstanding its incomplete development, a society has functions and capacities far beyond those of any or all of its members under any other relationship, and it confers upon them powers and capabilities that they cannot otherwise possess or attain. It is composed of three basic departments into which its membership is functionally although not perfectly or completely divided: *government,* the exercise of physical force; *economics,* the contractual relationship and process among men with respect to jurisdiction over property and services; and *esthetics,* the engagement in non-necessitous, spontaneous activities freely chosen by a feeling for them for their own sake without ulterior ends. Their respective symbols are: *Citadel, Market* and *Altar.*

Government, as the forcible repression of violence, is a necessary service, active or potential, to society—

a prerequisite to societal relationships. Economics is the means by which at any attained state of development the society is maintained and exists. Esthetics, which includes all spontaneous intellectual, artistic and religious activity, is the realm of creative spirit in the light and inspiration of which all social advance is made and higher development proceeds.

Culture and civilization are attainments and attributes of society. Both refer to the fact of, and to the general results flowing from social organization. Culture refers particularly to the intellectual and artistic achievements of a society and to the ornate.

### 19. SOCIAL

Having reference to a society or its processes and relationships; contractual, as opposed to coercive or compulsive. In loose language, it may mean any human or even any animal relationship.

### 20. SOCIETAL

This differs from the term *social* only in being more specific. It has reference always to the general organization of a population under the voluntary relationships whereby it functions creatively upon its environment, whereas *social* often includes any kind of human, or even animal, interrelationship.

### 21. ANTI-SOCIAL

Compulsive, coercive or fraudulent as against any person or number of persons acting as members of a society.

This term does not apply to the employment of force for protection against violent or criminal persons *as such*—persons whose anti-social conduct places them, temporarily at least, beyond the social pale. The restraint and prevention of such conduct is a necessary societal service.

When performed by the community owners, without violations of the persons or properties of the inhabitants, then such public services are highly rewarded and freely recompensed in rents and location values. All anti-social conduct, whether criminal or governmental, diminishes rent and, unless restrained, finally extinguishes all community (land) values.

Any service (so-called) that rests upon coercion and does not create its own voluntary revenue is, *ipso facto,* anti-social. Community services (when not canceled by coercions) always create their own revenues.

### 22. GOVERNMENT

That portion of the population in a community which, by custom, popular election or as a result of conquest, is accepted to practice coercion and compulsion over persons, and thereby has dominion or sovereignty over the territory and exercises rulership over the population as a whole.

The meaning of the word *government* is in process of very slow transition due to a general inability to distinguish community services from community conquest and rulership. Educated minds, no less than vulgar ones, under the influence of academic habit and classical traditions, completely confuse the predatory practice of conquerors, and of those who become their political successors, with the service-for-recompense function of community owners, of which they are only dimly if at all aware. It is not realized that conquest and rulership are alike anti-social and equally destructive of both ownership and public services. The forcible takings of despots or of their elected successors are thought of as contributions to public welfare. Tribute or taxation is patriotically and feelingly rationalized as recompense for public services and thought to be compatible with social and voluntary relationships.

The effort to combine these two antitheses under one conception persists. So the word *government* has two diametrically opposite meanings as a result of this inveterate belief that a people must be robbed and ruled in order to be served.

When superior minds discard this psychological anomaly and discover the present and potential public service power of the institution of property in land, then governments as proprietary agents will rise to utmost affluence upon the voluntary recompenses induced by their own services. Then all but the criminal or irresponsible will be free men enjoying the protection of their freedom and other public services for which they voluntarily pay. Government, in the ideal sense of public services, will then be more fully experienced and the pro-social implications of the word will become clear.

## 23. LAW

Any uniformity of process or procedure, customary conduct or behavior.

Social law, the natural or *common law* of society, is that body of voluntary custom or any part of it whereby the social relationships are practiced and maintained, and departure from which leads *automatically* to deterrent consequences and results. Because of its autonomous operation, social law is generally taken for granted and but little examined or understood.

Political or governmental "law" is the body of special enactments or statutes set up, some of them in confirmation of social custom and law, but principally in violation of or in supposedly necessary or salutary opposition to the natural law of society, and prescribing artificial penalties not naturally or directly resulting from disregard of these statutes.

Social law is the manifestation of voluntary service relationships, widespread and impersonal, throughout a population. Statute "law" originates in conquered or enslaved societies and maintains compulsory relationships. Social law can only be discovered and observed; it cannot be enacted or prescribed.

## 24. DEMOCRACY

*Democracy* is the term by which the desire for non-coercive and happy community relationships is perhaps most frequently expressed. The term is seldom used descriptively in an objective sense, but rather as a subjective ideal that in practice is only partly and precariously achieved. It is thought to be attained or maintained by resort to its contrary—struggle, conflict, war— rather than through the social device of contract, consent and exchange.

Owing to widespread feeling that social justice and well-being are somehow dependent on popular elections, democracy is often wishfully identified with "majority rule."

In the science of society, the term is applied only to the practice of the free and voluntary, the social relationships. Thus used it is practically synonymous with *social, contractual, voluntary,* etc. In this objective sense, democracy may be defined as: Doing things together by consent of all and coercion of none.

The only circumstance in which democracy in this sense is consistently practiced is in the making and performing of contracts, of self-imposed obligations. As in ancient and primitive times, the market is still the forum of democracy.

When persons contractually pool their separate titles to property by taking undivided interests in the whole, they elect servants—officers—and otherwise exercise their authority over their property by a process of voting, as partners, share owners or other beneficiaries. This is authentically democratic in that all the members exercise authority in proportion to their respective contributions. Coercion is not employed against any, and all persons are as free to withdraw their membership and property as they were to contribute it.

As a form of government or type of rulership, democracy is the exercise of coercive power, more or less limited, over persons generally, by popular decree or by persons elected and thus authorized to do so.

### 25. OWNERSHIP

The social relationship between individuals with respect to property under which the subject matter can be (1) peaceably enjoyed or (2) contractually administered for the limited use or service of others or (3) sold outright, whereby its unlimited use, and thus its ownership, is completely transferred. Ownership, if any, not sanctioned by a society would have no social, contractual or service significance.

Ownership of property as capital, as social-ized wealth, connotes the social obligation to administer it for the use and interest of others; the social penalty for failure to do so is a decline of income and value. This is always, and *especially* true of land ownership, which carries with it an obligation to protect from violence, and otherwise publicly serve the occupants or inhabitants of the land. The final liquidation (running out) of land and income value in all politically controlled communities is the historic penalty for this failure.

In its Anglo-Saxon meaning, now only dimly realized, to *own* was to *owe*. Ownership was inclusive of others, not exclusive. What was owned, chiefly land, was held in trust, as it were.

Ownership, as a social function, is the making and performing of contracts conferring the use, limited or unlimited, of either natural or artificial things as property.

Ownership, as a status, is the socially acknowledged and accepted exclusive right of possession or use, and of the unlimited disposition of any natural or artificial thing.

### 26. PROPERTY

Almost any element of human environment can be or become property. It becomes such, not alone by act of its possessor, but by the natural law or custom of the society, designating it under various circumstances and conditions as property, and resigning or appropriating it to him as the owner.

Property results only from societal custom, convention or agreement; wealth from the labor or activity called production. Property can exist, *as property,* only in a society.

The social will creates property in both natural and artificial things—so far as it holds them subject to none other but voluntary or contractual distribution or disposition. Natural things cannot themselves be created or produced; wealth is created by artifice or labor applied to what once were natural things. Neither land nor wealth is, of itself, necessarily, property.

Property may be anything that by the custom of society becomes the subject matter of ownership and thereby of the social, non-violent processes and relationships called contracts, between persons, with respect to its disposition or use.

### 27. WEALTH

In its *social* aspect, wealth is any man-made object, any natural substance or thing modified by human work or labor, that by common custom and consent is the subject of ownership, or property. When used by its owner or owners administratively, as the subject of contract and hence for the benefit of others, it is then the administrative or social-ized wealth called *capital*.

Wealth, when considered physically and without reference to the social relationships of contract or exchange, is any portion of environment (land) so affected or transformed, by human energy or agency, as to yield satisfactions.

### 28. ADMINISTRATION

The practice of ownership in the social or contractual sense of putting property or wealth to the use or service of others. To *ad*-minister is to *serve to*. By such administration, property or wealth is lifted into the category of capital in both the physical and the societal, or functional, sense of that term.

### 29. SOCIAL-IZATION

Adoption of the social or contractual process of consent and exchange with respect to property or services; the bringing of property and services into a market and thus submitting them to the social jurisdiction and common will as to their distribution or re-distribution.

Because of the constantly serious, often tragic, distortions caused by invasions and restriction of the social freedom of distribution by consent and exchange, it is the common belief that the taking of property and services out of the common pool and social jurisdiction of the market, and yielding them up entirely to government jurisdiction, will result in a social, or at least a more desirable, distribution of them. Under this fallacious belief, almost any complete change from free social to governmental and political jurisdiction is thought to be social-ization, notwithstanding that this is, in fact, *de-social-ization*.

This inversion of the term is one result of the widely prevailing disbelief in free relationships, a disbelief engendered by our classical slave-state traditions of government, and the belief that rulership by force is of the same nature as society, and not of a contrary nature, tending to destroy it.

### 30. ECONOMICS

This is the general term of reference for the subsistence department of a society. It applies to the relationships involved in the use of property as capital in the production and distribution of services and goods.

### 31. LABOR

As used in the social, economic or functional sense, the term *labor* designates collectively those *persons* who under contractual engagements perform services for others, only as servants or employees and without being the owners and administrators of the property they use in connection therewith.

In those exceptional cases where a

person serves others as an employee, but also owns and administers property for the use of others, this term labor applies to him only in respect of his interest or capacity as an employee. Such cases are common or exceptional in proportion as the society has attained structural differentiation and thereby functional organization, development and growth.

In the strictly societal sense, as a function or activity, labor is any human exertion that under a social or contractual process becomes service and thus induces a recompense or value in exchange.

In the literal, non-social and personal sense, labor is *any* human activity or exertion that is necessitous and not pursued or indulged in as an art or recreation for its own sake.

## 32. CAPITAL

In the social, economic or functional sense, *capital* is correlative to *labor*. The term designates collectively those *persons* who, as owners and administrators of the property used in connection therewith, employ labor and thereby perform services for others through contractual engagements for the sale or use of property, or of the services of themselves and their employees, to their patrons or to persons generally, without themselves being specifically engaged as servants or employees.

In the literal and physical sense, capital is any or all wealth let for hire or otherwise in course of distribution by exchange, or used to facilitate the production, use, distribution or exchange of services or of other wealth or property. Instruments of credit or obligation are neither wealth nor capital, except in a figurative or representative sense.

## 33. LAND

In the social, economic or functional sense, *land* is the term that designates those *persons* (or their services), taken collectively, who, by the law of custom and consent in a community, are entitled and authorized to make social or contractual disposition or distribution of the use of sites and natural resources, including the advantages of all artificial things appurtenant thereto as public capital, and to transfer such title and authority.

The original possessor of land, prior to title, whether by conquest or other form of occupancy or appropriation without contract or title, does not by such possession or appropriation perform any societal service, nor does he have thereby any voluntary recompense or value, any social acceptance, or recognition of his possession. But on being accepted and invested with title, he no longer holds possession by his own force but by the common law and consent of a society. This constitutes him a proprietary officer of the society, with authority to administer the land, no longer by his own personal or physical force, but by the social or contractual force of voluntary energy exchanges that constitute the functioning of the society. From this point the land becomes *property* and its possessor, now become owner, is in position to perform the contractual services of social administration, distribution or disposition of the land.

If such services are not actively or immediately required, there being no present market demand for the land or for its use, then, pending such requirement, the owner performs a passive, waiting or stand-by service, the accumulated value of which, be it little or much, is the selling price, if he sells it, or the basis of his ground rent if he puts it out on lease. In case of sale, his successor in title pays him the market appraisal of his accumulated stand-by services, or, if the land is sold while under lease, then the sales price is the capitalized value of the current net income according to the market appraisement of its probable continuance and future magnitude. In any case, after the first investiture of title, the selling value, income and increments to land are the market appraisements and awards for the services performed in the course of its social and contractual administration.

Each time unoccupied land is sold, the selling price is the net value of and recompense for the accumulated past services of a stand-by character that the owner and his predecessor, if any, have performed. This recompensing of stand-by services is of the nature of a social insurance against the land reverting to the barbaric or tyrannical dispensations of the pre-social or the anti-social coercive or tyrannical condition. During all the time that the land is under lease, the current net rent is the recompense or value of the contractual services performed in keeping the land socially placed, maintained in possession of the most productive tenants and devoted to the most productive and therefore most profitable kind of use.

As public improvements to the land, in the form of public capital, come to be placed adjacent to and between the several plots or holdings of land, the net annual value, if any, of the use of this public capital is reflected and included in the aggregate net rent.

When this public capital is maintained by the services of and its increase provided out of the net incomes of the owners of the community lands, the taxation of labor and capital or their products will be as unnecessary as it is undesirable. In such case, the value of the public capital, instead of being destroyed will be reflected enormously in the aggregate income and value of all the land.

The supplying of *any* public or community services or advantages without destroying their value by taxation is recompensed in the thereby lifted values and incomes from the community lands. This takes place on a community scale in response to the public improvements (those for the use of which there is need, purchasing power and demand) abutting, adjacent to and between the private holdings, precisely as the individual plots have their value and income enhanced by the placing of private capital improvements or advantages directly upon them, without levying forcibly on the properties or infringing the liberties of the tenants in order to do so.

And, entirely apart from the administration of public capital as such, whenever there is a rising productivity of labor and capital, remaining above taxation, for free redistribution out of the market by the contractual process, there is a correspondingly great increase in the need and in the effective demand for a societal distribution of all the advantages appertaining to the use of land. This is the explanation of high rents and land values during those times when the productivity of labor and capital is large and the tax-seizures of it out of the societal jurisdiction of the market have remained relatively small.

Land, in the merely physical sense, without reference to any social organization or societal relationships, means simply the whole natural environment of a population.

## 34. PUBLIC CAPITAL

In the physical sense, this means all of the artificial things appurtenant to land that are open to the general and common use of the occupants of a community. These constitute the lateral improvements adjacent to and between the privately held plots of land and occupying the public or common land used as highways, public health and recreational areas and as sites for public enterprises and agencies of every kind. In this physical sense, the public or community capital is the wealth that is publicly appurtenant to the individually and exclusively occupied portions of a community. It consists of the man-made public facilities with which the private parts of a community are supplied and their occupants served.

A social or contractual distribution of the advantages arising from the existence of public capital in a community —as contrasted with a more or less arbitrary distribution under political authority—can be carried out only by the *owners* of the community. For none but the community owners can make contracts with respect to community occupancy and thereby distribute *socially* its public advantages. And this remains true even though the community owners function, as at present, only to distribute its access and use and give no further administration to the public capital nor exercise any supervision over the salaried public servants to whom it is entrusted. But the community owners forfeit and forego enormous rents and property values by their failure unitedly to further supervise the common properties and services appurtenant to their lands.

## 35. LAND ADMINISTRATION

Land and its resources, together with all public appurtenances and the common use of them, is administered by sale or transfer outright of its unlimited use, or by the sale of definitely limited uses called leaseholds or tenancies. This is land ownership in the social and functional sense. It is the performing of contractual services in the transfer or distribution of ownership, or of the private and exclusive occupancy or use of land and its resources, including also the use of the public parts of the community and of the community capital wherewith the public parts are improved.

Before the Norman Conquest, the land of England was so far administered in this manner that the voluntary revenue of rent defrayed all public and governmental expense. Not until the Conquest and Doomsday Book was any permanent system of taxation in force. Under the Conqueror, the new owners of England acquired kingly and compulsive powers. Land ownership thus became a *political* institution. It so remained generally until, in the late eighteenth and early nineteenth centuries, it became re-social-ized—degovernmentalized—divested of its power to seize private property. Bereft of all political prerogative, land ownership again began to function socially as property in the administrative sense of making contractual instead of political distribution of it.

Potentially considered, and looking forward to a condition of social freedom and permanent peace, land administration comprises the ownership type of service and control, not alone over the natural locations and resources privately held, but also the like administration in connection therewith of the public domain and the entire public capital facilities with which a community is improved and with which its inhabitants are, in common, served. Public service through land ownership and administration is *consensual*—sanctioned by the societal will. It abrogates force; it gives a basis for community services without forced contributions; it makes contracts possible and thereby gives social freedom, for none but contractual relations are consensual and free.

A great step in societal evolution will be the non-political administration by the public proprietors, not only of the sites and resources, but also of the community services and the community capital appurtenant to the sites.

### 36. CONTRACT

This term, in its general sense, denotes the relationship and process under which the wills of particular persons come into voluntary accord, each with the other, and with the general will, respecting any exchanges of property or of services.

A particular contract is a mutual engagement to enter into a new or to modify an existing relationship between persons respecting any property or services. It prescribes the terms upon which services are exchanged or the use or ownership of property is transferred. Since the equivalence of things in exchange is determined by the natural law or custom of the market, the contract expresses not only a resolution of individual wills and desires, but, also and automatically, the prescription of justice and well-being by the social or community will. This contractual relationship and process is truly democratic, in the sense that it ascertains and executes the common will and welfare through measures and transactions of mutual service that are accepted by all and which none oppose.

Contract, a psychological relationship, a "meeting of minds," is the matrix or adhesive between men in society which, through the institution of ownership, relates them together into the societal organism. Civilized men as freely follow the voluntary customs of the market as, in fulfillment of its instinctive nature, the honeybee follows the law of the hive.

Contract is the social technique that, *through ownership,* puts property to the use of others.

### 37. COMPETITION

In its societal sense, competition is the measuring process whereby the exchange equivalence of services and properties is socially determined, contracts with respect to them made and exchanges of them effected. It is the voting democracy of the market in which bids and offers are harmonized at particular levels or points of exchange-equivalence called ruling prices or market values.

Without competition registering the social will as to the proportionate redistribution of the services and properties pooled in the common markets, there would be no objective basis of reference for the reconciling of individual wills in the formation of particular contracts.

Since the competition of the market guides individuals into non-coercive relationships in the distribution of properties and services, it is the reverse of conflict and in no proper or societal sense the same.

Competition is the technique by which a society, to the extent that it can function, abrogates conquest and conflict through the establishment of contract and exchange. As its root and prefix suggest, it is the mutual petitioning of persons who wish to serve and to be served.

The ill-founded moral opprobrium so often laid upon this vital social process springs from confusions of competition itself with the invidious compulsions and restrictions that cancel its benefits and distort its operation into anti-social results.

The opposite and contrary from competition is monopoly. Monopoly exists when government by its coercive power limits to a particular person or organization, or combination of them, the right to sell particular goods or services, and thereby abrogates the right of any other person or organization to compete. It is an infringement of the right to make a living, for it limits the right of the general public both to sell and to buy. Where the liberty to sell and opportunity to buy are not forcibly infringed, there can be no invasion of any rights. Neither bigness nor singleness can be injurious, so far as it results from the unforced preferences of purchasers and freedom of competition prevails.

### 38. EXCHANGE

The social metabolism or general function that transforms a population into and maintains it as a society—the process by which population energy is social-ized into services.

Exchange is not the forming but the carrying out of contractual engagements. Conducted otherwise than in accordance with contract, it ceases to be a societal phenomenon.

Exchange of services is the basis of every societal relationship.

### 39. CREDITS

Parties to contracts not immediately and completely performed become mutual creditors and debtors. When one party performs his obligation before the other, the numerical token or promise he takes is called his credit or the other party's debt or obligation.

Tokens and instruments of credit are not wealth or services; they are signs and measures of property or wealth to be delivered or services performed. Credits can be liquidated or promises performed. As between the parties to them, this may be effected by transfer to and substitution of a new party, when done by the consent of all.

Credit tokens that are treated as a charge against the general market are called *money*. Credit tokens issued or prescribed by a government as the medium in which publicly enforced payments of private debts must be made become thereby *legal tender* and are so called. Legal tender is based on the governmental enforcement of private obligations.

### 40. WAGES

The credits or drafts against the general market that are received immediately in exchange for time-gauged or piece-gauged personal services.

"Real wages" are the actual wealth and services that these credits presently or finally command.

### 41. SALARIES

Recompense received in exchange for continuing personal services not gauged strictly by time nor measured by any specific output.

### 42. FEES

Recompense for highly specialized or professional services, usually involving the exercise of discretion and being such services as the recipients themselves have but little ability to understand or perform.

The performance of some kinds of specialized services is limited by statutes prescribing effectively deterrent penalties upon the acceptance of fees in recompense therefor by any but special persons or classes designated by political authority and having, presumably, superior capacities or qualifications.

### 43. PROFITS

The recompense for owner-administrative services performed in the production of wealth or services for others. The recompense to an owner for the services he combines with property or services owned by him, including the service or services of selling them—of bringing such property or its use into the market and making a *social,* or contractual, distribution of it.

Profits are stated usually in terms of increase in credits or assets above debts. Stated in terms of money, as a charge against the general market, they are called cash or liquidated profits. Like wages, profits are not "real" profits unless or until they are liquidated into property or services.

Profits are distinguished from wages, salaries, fees, etc. in this, that although they are recompenses for services, they are obtained only as residues after meeting all contractual obligations. They are nowhere prescribed in the terms of any particular contract. Hence, the services recompensed by profits are often called "independent enterprises."

### 44. PRICE—

SALES PRICE OR PURCHASE PRICE

The exchange recompense received by an owner from a purchaser of specific property in exchange for its unlimited use—for the transfer of his entire ownership and title to it.

Prices are stated almost invariably in terms of money. They are indices of the voluntary social will as to the exchangeability and hence as to the distribution of goods and services—so far as the social will can operate within the governmental regulations and limitations under which it is bound.

### 45. RENT

Rent is the term almost invariably used to designate the recompense to the owner for the time-limited use of specific property of any kind.

The property may be the owner's physical wealth or capital or it may be land, either with or without improvements upon it, but always including the use of any public improvements appurtenant to it. The owner usually maintains the property; he parts with only a time-limited use; and it is always fully returnable to him.

### 46. INTEREST

The contractually determined recompense received by the holder of credits or money (drafts against the general market) for the limited use (as to time) of these credits or money to draw from the market property or services of any kind, usually as actual capital for productive administration or use, and the creation thereby of new capital and credits.

Just as rent is paid for the use of specific property, so interest is paid for the use of *generalized* property, as credits or money, returnable only in the generalized form of credits or money, and not in any specific property as in the case of rent.

47. VALUE

That property or service which, in the course of exchange, is received for property or services given. When two things are exchanged, each is the value of the other.

In all those exchanges that are not immediately completed in property or services, the term *value* is applied to the credit or money-token by which the actual value or recompense must be measured when finally received.

Value is often thought of as being intrinsic or inherent in property. Any such "value" is only an estimate or anticipation of what credits or recompense the property would command in case of sale or exchange.

The word "value" is used also in a great variety of figurative, metaphysical and subjective senses in no way connected with exchange or any societal process.

48. CAPITAL VALUE

The over-all value of capital wealth or property, in outright exchange, as distinguished from its annual value or the annual recompense for its use.

49. INCOME VALUE

Recompense for the use of capital wealth or property in terms of its annual use, as distinguished from its sale outright or unlimited use.

50. SPECULATIVE VALUE

Any estimate or anticipation of a future exchange value, as distinguished from a present or actual value in hand.

51. CITADEL

The symbol of physical force or its equivalent in duress or coercion, practiced principally but not exclusively by public authority, such as the taking of taxes, imposing of penalties, the waging of wars, and the prevention or punishment of crimes, as well as the perpetrating of them.

The social and legitimate function of the Citadel, as a community service, is the suppression of violence or other contra-social behavior by persons attacking the social organization from within or from without, and not the imposition of force upon the society itself, its processes or its functioning members. From the standpoint of society, the office of the Citadel is to protect and serve; not to dominate or control. To the extent that community services are performed and recompensed by exchange, without domination, the Citadel is *social-ized* by the Market. Such services are maintained out of the voluntary revenues called ground rent.

52. MARKET

The symbol for that department of society whence its subsistence is derived—in which contracts are made and performed, goods and services pooled, social-ized or commun-(ity)-ized for redistribution to the contracting parties or interests in accord with the social election and will, as registered publicly in the common scale of prices and terms, and carried out by their respective contracts and exchanges.

53. ALTAR

This term is the symbol for that department of society concerned with the intangibles of intellect, feeling and imagination, and with the spontaneous activities of scientific research and discovery, artistic creation, and of the inspirational, spiritual and recreational life—things done by unforced election, selection and choice, recompensing in themselves, and not to be measured or exchanged.

This department of a society is often referred to as its culture.

## 54. CIVILIZATION

The functioning of the social organization.

Civilization develops through the progressive differentiation of three modes of human behavior into Citadel, Market and Altar, and the interfunctioning of these departments of society to raise a population from coercion, through coöperation, into creative consecration.

It is any state of being that a society achieves in consequence of its capacity *to modify and rebuild and thus to create its environment* and thereby to extend its numbers and its power to serve all its members, liberating them into length of days with growth of individual capacities and powers.

INDEX OF PRINCIPAL TERMS

|  | Page |  | Page |  | Page |
|---|---|---|---|---|---|
| Action | 229 | Fees | 240 | Public Capital | 238 |
| Administration | 235 | Government | 232 | Qualitative | 230 |
| Altar | 242 | Income Value | 242 | Quantitative | 230 |
| Anti-Social | 232 | Interest | 241 | Rational | 230 |
| Capital | 236 | Labor | 235 | Reality | 229 |
| Capital Value | 242 | Land | 236 | Real Wages | |
| Citadel | 242 | Land Administration | 238 | See Wages | |
| Civilization | 243 | Law | 233 | Rent | 241 |
| Community | 231 | Legal Tender | | See also Land and | |
| Competition | 239 | See Credits | | Land Administration | |
| Contract | 239 | Life-year | 230 | Salaries | 240 |
| Credits | 240 | Market | 242 | Service | 231 |
| Democracy | 233 | Mass | 229 | Social | 232 |
| De-social-ization | | Money, See Credits | | Social-ization | 235 |
| See Social-ization | | Monopoly | | Societal | 232 |
| Duration | 230 | See Competition | | Society | 231 |
| Economics | 235 | Motion | 229 | Socionomy | 231 |
| See also Society | | Ownership | 234 | Speculative Value | 242 |
| Energy | 229 | Population | 231 | Structure | 230 |
| Entropy | 230 | Price | 241 | Value | 242 |
| Eternality | 229 | Profits | 241 | Wages | 240 |
| Exchange | 240 | Property | 234 | Wealth | 235 |

# Bibliographic Note

ANCIENT AND CONTEMPORARY, there is a rich bibliography of "the good life" from the conceptual and subjective point of view. But these writings propose none but subjective technologies—the trusting heart, submission to divine will, triumphant love, all being conditions attained within the personal consciousness of the individual mind.

Against all this, there is a vast literature of revolt and of "reform" by *the re-enthroning of old tyrannies* under popular slogans and signs. For in "reform" and revolution alike, there is no process but coercion by government and by war. Apart from the natural sciences, there are no specific and workable procedures for the externalization of dreams and ideals.

The literature of the natural sciences, in recent times, is the first to reflect untrammeled adventures of the mind into realms of order and beauty in the natural world. But until now, the rational mind of man has not risen to the impersonal system of order and beauty that exists in the societal realm.

Here is the unique and original contribution of the present work: It discloses the creative and durational character of the contractual, the free processes among men, and it shows how infinite realizations of human hopes and ideals await only the proprietary administration of community affairs through the business-like development and growth of the modern institution of property in land and of the community services and properties accessory and appurtenant thereto.

Of this there is no bibliography. For original discoveries, no precursors are known.

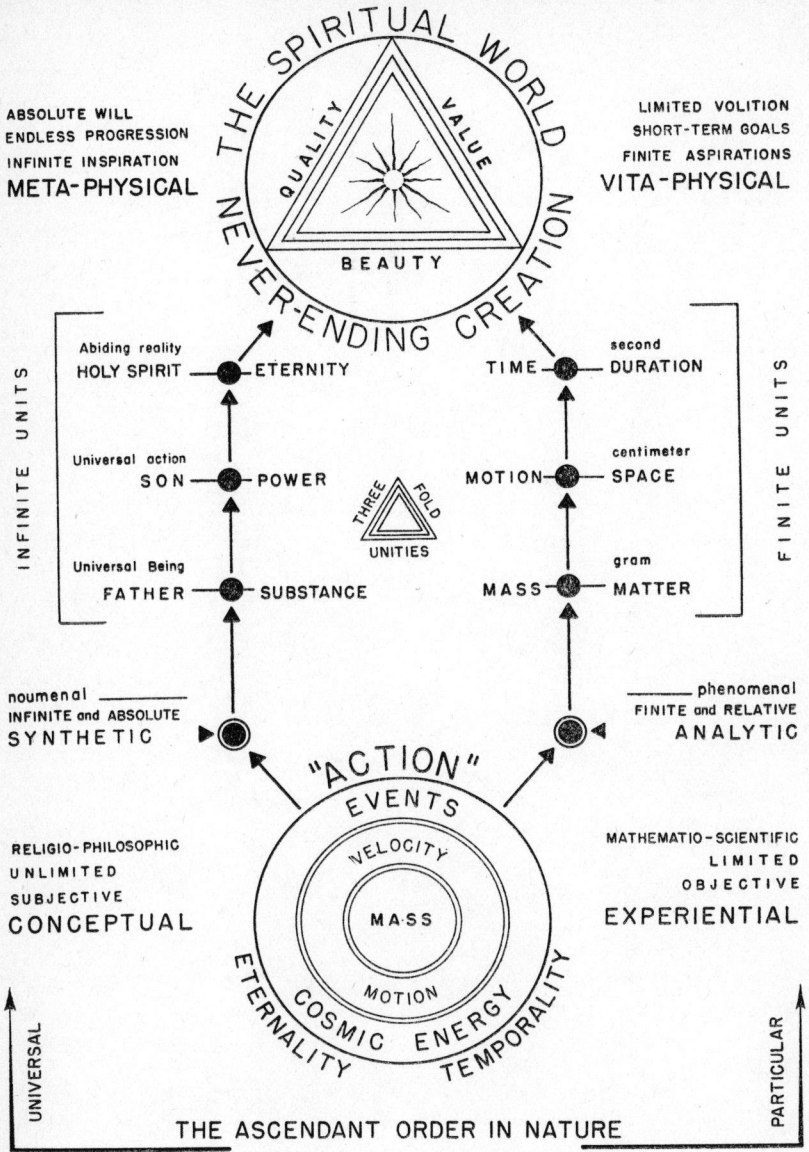

Diagram of General Philosophy.

## INDEX

Action, 55; defined, 229; see also Energy.
Administration, 102–103; defined, 235; basis of all business, 153; by owners, 126 ff; of a community, 141 ff; of public capital, 149; by non-owners, 143; as the social function of ownership, 124, 143; sales the ultimate object of, 159; see also Ownership, Public Administration.
Adulthood Necessary to Creativity, 24.
Advance, Social, 214; freedom essential to, 15; the business basis of, 113.
Age Groups; productivity versus reproductivity in, 42–43; effects of changes in average life-span on, 42–43, 36–38.
Ageing of the Population, 42.
Agricultural Communities, 86; see also Village Communities.
Alfred, Age of, 76, 80, 94.
Altar, 58, 203; defined, 242; function of, 54; see also Citadel, Market and Altar.
Alternative to Political Revenue and Administration, 93–94; see also Land Administration, Public Administration.
Altruism, 26; see also Motivation.
America, North: see North America.
"American Plan," 183.
Anglo-Saxon England, 80, 91, 94–95.
Anglo-Saxon Social Organization; based on ownership of land, 76; destroyed by Norman power, 76; flowering under Alfred, 76–77; proprietary public authority, 76–77; basic community pattern, 79.
Anglo-Saxons, 161.
Animal Life; supine status of, 24; highest destiny of, 25; limitations of, 116; versus plant life, 207; conditions of, 208.
Anti-Social Acts, 59; defined, 232; proper restraint of, 51.
Apartment Housing, 183.
Arts, 116; function of the, 218.

Association of Community Authorities, 85, 96.
Atlantic World, Wars of the, 67.
Authority, Contractual, 73; see also Ownership.
——, Political: see Political Government, Public Administration.

Barbarians, 75.
Barter, 105; limitations of, 46.
Basic Social Pattern, 71 ff; biological parallel, 79.
Bay Tree, The, 106.
Beauty, 216 ff; inspiration of, 20, 63–64, 197, 216 ff, 219; how manifested in man, 218; paen to, 223.
Biological Bonds: see Familial Organization.
Birth Rate: see Reproductivity.
Business; as administration of property, 153, 159; the basis of social advance 8, 113; see also Administration, Free Enterprise, Industry.
Business Administration, 141 ff.
Business, The Public; how administered, 148.

Capital, 159; defined, 127–128, 236; as an economic factor, 176–177; public, 112, 153; public versus private administration of, 182 ff; break-down of national-income to labor, capital and land, 180 ff.
—— Goods, Flow of, 124.
—— Value Defined, 242.
Cell; least biological unit, 207.
Century of Lengthening Life, 41 ff.
Change: see Environment, Energy; also see under Qualitative, 230.
"Child of God," 216, 217, 218.
Church fostered freedom, 92.
Citadel, 57; historic origins of the, 62; functions of the, 54, 62, 242; see also Citadel, Market and Altar.

Citadel, Market and Altar, 54, 55 ff, 203, 204, 242; imperfect differentiation of, 60–61, 202; interfunctioning among, 59; continuing evolution of, 59; see under *Society,* 231; see also separate headings.

Cities, Coastal, 93; law merchant, 106.

Civilization, 141; defined, 243; advance of, 139; distinguishing factors in, 104; based on contractual administration of property, 139.

Classical Traditions of Rulership, 79, 80, 90–92.

Climate and Conquest; influence of climate and terrain, 65 ff, 74.

Collectivism in Nature, 193.

Collectivist *Ideal;* tendency towards, 184; inherent in the capitalist system, 187.

Commendation, 62.

Common Law; property as a social convention, 98; instruments of exchange under law merchant, 106; see also under *Law,* 233.

Communism, Land, 123.

Community; first essential to, 50; out-of-doors, 142 ff, 179; hotel as a, 82, 141 ff; organization and operation, 141 ff; basic free pattern, 79; services by community owners, 98 ff; historic failures, 213; see also Land Administration, Public Administration, Village Community.

—— Business; how administered, 148; potentiality of, 214; see also Land Administration.

—— Capital; community properties as, 174; organization and management of, 141; see Public Capital.

—— Economics, The Basis of, 141 ff.

—— Services: see Public Services.

Competition; operation of, 117; as a measuring instrument, 117; regional, under proprietary public administration, 135; definition and discussion of, 239.

Conflict; essential to sovereignty and among pre-societal groups, 72.

Conquest; related to climate and terrain, 66.

Consanguinity, contract supervenes upon, 87; see also Familial Organization.

Contract; defined, 239; authority to make, 73; not a physical process, 159; peaceful distribution by, 175; see also Ownership, Contractual Relationship.

Contractual Process Distributes the Land, 72.

—— Relationship, 8, 23, 98; emergence of the, 76; origin in village community, 87; importance of, 119; medieval growth of, 92; 19th-Century expansion of, 44; application in public affairs, 52; transcendent nature of, 88; societal development through extension of the, 104 ff; see also Coöperation.

Coöperation; freedom in, 26 ff; effect of climate on, 65; universal principle, 83; see also Symbiosis, Contractual Relationship, Reciprocal Relationships.

Cosmic Energy: see Energy.

Cosmos; man as microcosm, 200; society related to the, 114, 195, 203.

Counterfeit Money, 106.

Creation, Society the Crown of, 205 ff.

Creative Change, 15 ff, 193 ff; see also Qualitative.

—— Synthesis, 206 ff; see also Synthesis.

Creativity; in a population dependent on proportion of adult years, 31–33; self-creative potential of man, 195.

Credit, 105–106; definition and discussion of, 240; as a time dimension in exchange, 46.

Culture; see under *Society,* 231–232.

Custom: see Familial Organization, Common Law.

Cycle; of an individual, of a population, 14; see also Duration, Life-Span.

Darwinian Survival, 67.

Death, Nature of, 29; see also Life.

Deflation: see Depression.

Demand Necessary to Value, 148.

Democracy, 98; defined, 233; political versus economic, 44; through popular proprietorship, 136.

—— of the Market, 44 ff, 175; mechanism of, 45.

Depression, 100–101, 163, 221.

INDEX 251

Differentiation; of function, of ownership, of institutions, 25; of structures in society, 58 ff; see also Society, Specialization.
Discoveries; in the natural world, 7, 216; motivation to, 216.
Distribution; as a change of relationship among men with respect to the thing distributed, 104–105; services of, 116; social versus political, 175.
Division of Labor; as affecting land ownership, 128–129, 154; see also Specialization.
Drawing Room, habits and manners of the, 192.
Duration; defined, 230; see also Life, Life-Span.
Durational Power of Society, 55–56.
Dyne; see under *Energy*, 229.

Economics; defined, 141, 235; basis of community economics, 141 ff.
Eddington on "Man-Years," 11.
Efficiency; measurement of, 115; see also Specialization.
—— Ratings Based on Time, 17.
Emergent Evolution, 206 ff.
Empire; consolidations of, 66; oceanic, 67; see also Political Government.
Empiricism in Social Practice, 60, 78, 106–107.
Energy; defined, 229; units of, 229; source of, 9, 16; manifestations of, 9, 114, 116, 193; periodicity of, 55; threefold nature of, 55, 229; composition of, 16–17, 55; internal change of proportions as qualitative, 16–17; measurements of, 114; conservation of, 114–115; transformations of, 114–115; durational element in, 19; creative potential in, 19; qualitative versus quantitative, 19; metaphysical aspects of, 19.
—— Concept of Population, 9 ff.
——, Cosmic, 9; nature of, 193; evolution of, 71; conservation of, 29; transformations of, 29; and human life, 21–22; man as microcosm, 200; society a manifestation of, 114.
—— of Exchange, 47 ff, 114 ff.

——, Human; social-ization of, 115; frustration of, 221; cannot be blotted out, 47–48, 221; sublimation of, 47–48, 221.
——, Mechanical, 115; forms of, flow of, qualitative differences in, 12.
——, Population, 9 ff, 30 ff; contrasting modes of flow, 12–13; transformations of, 13; continuity of, 14–15; qualitative changes in, 16 ff, 23; generations as energy waves, 21–23; conservation of, 28–29; creative transformation of, 30 ff; see also Population.
——, Societal, 14, 111–112, 114–118, 221.
Entropy; defined, 230.
Environment, 188–189; source of all life-forms, 49; extremes of, 65–66; familial organization predatory on, 86, 216–217; change desired in, 17; modification of, 195; dominion over, 18, 23–25, 49.
Erg; see under *Energy*, 229.
Esthetic Motivation: see Motivation.
Esthetics; see under Society, 231–232; see also Beauty.
Eternality; defined, 229; freedom the technique of, 26 ff; see also Duration.
Evil; negative nature of, 7, 217; nature of death, 29.
Evolution, 70, 206 ff; of the societal life-form, 209; the order of societal, 84 ff; cosmic, 71.
Exchange, 141, 213; defined, 240; time dimension in, 46; limitations of barter, 46, 105; function of money and credits in, 105; creation by, 47 ff; not a physical process, 48; a social process, 99; rationality of, 48; accountancy of, 117–118; retardation of, 118, ownership essential to, 48; essential to community functioning, 48–49; benefits of, 104, 106; effect on environment, 104; societal development through extension of the system of, 104 ff; value and exchange a system of social-ized energy flow, 114 ff; the energy of, 47 ff, 114 ff.
—— System, 106, 175; operation of the, 98; universality of the, 115; services contributed to the, 177; see also Ex-

change, Market, Contractual Relationship.
Experience Reflected in Language, 227.
Expropriation; evils of, 52; see also Public Revenue, Taxation.

Familial Organization, 84, 85 ff, 115; nature of, 71–72; dependent on conscious awareness, 72; predatory on environment, 86, 216–217; see also Village Community.
Federation, Political, 66; see also Political Government.
Fees Defined, 240–241.
Fertile Crescent, 89, 90.
Feudalism, Voluntary and Servile, 75, 84, 88, 90–92, 126.
Force; legitimate practice of, 51, 59, 232.
Free Enterprise; why so called, 77, 188; performing public services, 136, 214; potentials of, 187; defections from, 188; miracle of the modern age, 188.
Free Will; the exercise of choice, 53; gift of society, 193–197; see also Will.
Freedom; the key to abundance and long life, 23, 26 ff; in organization, 26 ff; nature of, 45; property the instrument of, 50 ff; essential to progress, 53; of choice, 53; potencies of, 69; in fertile flat lands, 74; in wooded mountain lands, 90; individual, 92; path to, 112; in North America, 173; gift of society, 193–197.
Freeholders, 62; reduced to serfs or slaves, 74.
Frequency, 15, 55.
Functioning Antecedent to Pathology, 7, 29; see also Growth.

Galileo, 200.
Generations; as energy waves, 22–23; overlapping of, 30; see also Population, Energy.
George, Henry, 122.
Germanic Institutions, 91.
Gifts of Nature; distribution of, 178; see also Land, Property in Land.
Golden Horn, 90.
Golden Rule Relationship, 189; see also Contractual Relationship.

Government; definition and general discussion of, 232–233; see also Political Government, Land Administration, Public Administration.
Great Society, The, 210.
Ground Rent; defined, 241; recompense for service, 74, 149, 178, 222; historic perversion of, 92; as public revenues in Saxon England, 94; the rise and fall of, 100; taxation as a charge against, 151, 156, 165–170; measure of net public services, 130–131, 132; index of public values, 146; springs from administration of the public capital, 149; fixed by the market, 221–222; nature of, 158, 221–222; see under Land, 237; see also Rent, Property in Land, Public Administration, Public Revenue.
Growth, 7; the nature of, 29; see also Life.
Guilds, 92.

Headship, 86.
Heaven's First Law, 71.
Heptarchy, 95.
History, Written; largely a negative account, 104.
Holmes, Justice Oliver Wendell, 2.
Hostility among Alien Groups, 86.
Hotel; model of free community, 82, 141 ff.
House of Life, The, 214.
House of Man Divided against Itself, 66.
Human Nature; improvement of, 23, 192; see also Man, Individuals.

Ideals, 19, 227; socialist, 184, 187.
Immortality, 40; measure of, 18; see also Life, Life-Span.
Income Value Defined, 242.
Income, Real, 176.
Individualism; historic emergence of, 76, 92.
Individuals; freedom of, 92; complexity of life under primitive conditions, 154; benefits of society to, 23, 32, 53, 189, 212, 213; constituent elements of, 57, 194, 201; units of societal organization, 194; statistical integration of, 4, 197; fate of in organization, 193 ff; changing role in society, 154; unique-

INDEX 253

ness of, 197; free will of, 7, 8, 53, 98, 193-197; habits and manners of, 192; self-realization of, 197, 243; future liberation of, 214-215; see also Man.

Industry; taxation of, 156, 165; liberation of, 168 ff; see also Business, Production.

Infancy; years of non-productivity, 24; infant versus adult life-years, 33.

Inflation; derangement of the system of exchange, 163.

Inspiration of Beauty, 20, 63-64, 197, 216 ff, 219; see also Beauty.

Installment Buying, 183.

Intellect; nature of, 201; the spiritual office of, 218, 219; see also *Rationality*, 230.

Interest, Defined, 241.

Investment; foreign, 41; in private versus public enterprise under proprietary public administration, 182 ff.

Japan, 76, 94.

Kingly Power, The, 161.

Kinship: see Familial Organization.

Kropotkin, Prince Pëtr, 87.

Land; profits of business source of demand for land and its services, 157; distributed by contractual process, 72; advent of free trade in, 95; ownership versus use of, 124-126; anomaly of the owner-user of, 128-129; effect of government on use of, 126, 139; consolidation of titles to, 135-136; services supplied through highways, 160; liberation of users of, 168 ff; taxation on ownership of, 169-171; as an economic factor, 177; primitive versus social ownership of, 124; break-down of national income to labor, capital and land, 180 ff; definition and general discussion of, 236; see also Ground Rent, Property in Land, Land Administration, Land Owners, Land Value.

—— Administration; defined, 238; essentials of 153, 156; access to community advantages as the primary public service of, 50 ff, 160-161; relation to public administration, 107; its potential productive and administrative powers, 134 ff; specialization of function, 124-129, 154, 183; extension into the public field, 63, 121, 153 ff, 222; future of, 50, 138, 171; see also Public Administration, Public Services, Ground Rent, Ownership.

—— Communism, 123.

—— Owners, 160-161; officers of society, 221-222; purged of political authority, 95, 106; services performed by, 100; unenlightened, 136; identified with the public interest, 165-170; beneficial owners of public capital, 150; compared with building owners, 155; obligations of, 150, 160, 222; authority of, 167; inattentive to public services, 156, 161; need for organization, 95, 159, 162, 166; golden opportunity of, 172, 180.

—— Question, The, 122.

—— Taxation, 169-171.

—— Value, 105, 139; defined, 174; in 19th-Century America, 173; dependent on efficient public services, 147, 157-158; recompense for distribution, 100; effect of tax reduction on, 151; how affected by taxation on industry and business, 156, 165; dependent on demand, 158; reflex of all other values, 174; future of, 174; see also Ground Rent.

Language Reflects Experience, 227.

Law; definition and general discussion of, 233.

——, Heaven's First, 71.

—— Merchant, Instruments of Exchange under, 106.

Laws, Natural, 3, 233; discovery and application of, 7; see also Science.

Labor; defined, 235; as an economic factor, 176-177; break-down of national-income to labor, capital and land, 180 ff.

Legal Tender; see under *Credits*, 240.

Liberty and Property; infringement of, 120-121.

Life, 13; versus death, 7, 29, 217; nature of, 9, 217; source of, 22, 49; human aspiration toward, 11; of an individual, of a population, 14; sensed as fleeting,

17; daily increase of, 22; a century of lengthening, 41 ff; necessities abundant as light and air, 222; complexity of primitive, 154; rationality of, 219; self-transcendent, 210; the House of Life, 214; see also Life-Span.

Life-Span; of societal organization, 14; of organizations and of units functioning in them, 71, 194; conditions of lengthening, 15, 18–19, 23, 26 ff; re-productivity correlated with, 23–24, 28, 38; lengthened span also favors increase in numbers, 37; extremes of old age, 42–43; effects on population of a changing life-span, 36–38; changes in age-groups resulting from lengthening of, 42–43; shortening of the, 68; see also Energy, Population, Reproductivity.

Life-Years; defined, 230; unit of population energy, 4, 11 ff; as horsepower-hours, 13; comparison of equal quantities of, 31 ff; infant versus adult, 33; proportion available in a population for creative functioning, 36; actual decrease in, 37; creative release of, 63; see also Energy.

Literature of Revolt and "Reform," 245.
Lobby Interests, 167.

Maine, Sir Henry Sumner, 87.
Man; versus animal, 28, 116; dominion of, 18, 23–25, 49, 209; three-fold nature of, 55 ff, 194, 201; divided against himself, 66; aspiration toward life, 11; as microcosm, 200; rational mind of, 201; adaptability of, 28, 208 ff; creative powers of, 116, 195, 210; instinct for social organization, 211; Nature's pride in, 213; essential endowment of, 195, 215, 216 ff; spiritual power of, 27–28, 53–54, 195, 204, 218, 219; un-social-ized state, 216–217; see also Individuals.
—— in Society, 209; functions and powers, 25; creativity of, 28, 195.
Management; importance of, 143; see also Administration, Ownership.
"Man-Year" as a Unit of Measurement, 11.

Market, 203; defined, 242; democracy of the, 44 ff, 175; as a social institution, 45; exercise of freedom in the, 45; time dimension in the, 46; function of the, 54; symbol for coöperation by contract and exchange, 58; operation of the, 98, 105–106, 117, 175; fixes ground rent, 221–222; its influence on the *Citadel*, 202; see also, Citadel, Market and Altar.
Mass, Defined, 229.
——, Motion and Time, 55, 60, 200, 229.
Mathematics in Nature, 200.
Measurement; science dependent upon, 3; competition as an instrument of, 117; *man-year* as a unit of, 11; of energy, 114; of population, 9 ff; of net public services, 130–132, 146; see also Units.
Merchandising; as distribution, 129–130; performed only by owners, 129–130; the essential equity of, 129–130.
Metabolism, Social, 48, 58, 114, 116, 118.
Metaphysical Aspects of Energy, 19.
Metaphysics Related to the Physical World, 19–20.
Method, Quantitative, 7.
Mexico, 76, 94.
Mill, John Stuart, 122.
Money; nature of, 46; counterfeit, 106; see under *Credits*, 240.
—— and Credits, Symbols for Measurement in Exchange, 105.
Monopoly; see under *Competition*, 239–240.
Morality; public versus private, 219–220; systems of, 227.
Mortality, 29, 86.
Motion, 55; defined, 229.
Motivation, Esthetic, 64, 111, 216 ff.
——, Profit, 69, 112–113.
——, Altruistic, 26, 113, 192.
——, Selfish, 26.
Mystical Sovereignty, 91.

National Income; a hypothetical distribution under proprietary public administration, 175 ff; break-down to labor, capital and land, 180 ff; growth of, 188; significance of, 189.

INDEX

Nationalistic States, 75–76; see also Political Government.
Natural Laws: see Laws, Natural.
Natural Sciences: see Science.
Nature; emergence of new orders in, 70; distribution of the gifts of, 178; the Great Collectivist, 193; organization of reflected in man, 200; method of organization, 206 ff; in relation to man, 210; her pride in man, 213.
———, Human, 23, 192; see also Man, Individuals.
Necessities of Life, abundant as light and air, 222.
Nineteenth Century, 41; democracy of the, 44; land question in the, 122; abundance of food in America in the, 183.
Nomadism; transition to village communities, 77.
Normality, 88.
Norman Conquest, 76, 95; see under Land Administration, 238.
——— Kings, The, 161.
North America; democracy in, 44; rise of land values in, 173; abundance of food in, 183.

Order; nature of, 71; see also Organization.
Organic Pattern, Persistence of, 71.
——— Society: see Society as a Life-Form.
Organization; in Nature, 206 ff; defined, 85; always numerical, 85; need for among land owners, 159; fate of individuals in, 193 ff; life-span of organizations and of units functioning in them, 71, 194; minimum limits of, 200; see also Coöperation, Society.
Outlaw, 50.
Owner-Administration, 126 ff; see Proprietary Administration.
Ownership, 62, 98 ff; essential to contract and exchange, 48, 73; importance of, 78–79, 99; inclusive of others, 73, 99, 123–124; the means of social-izing property, 98; specialization of, 124–129, 154–155, 183; defined, 234.

Pathology; the derivative nature of, 7, 29; of the societal life-form, 69.

Patriarchy, 74, 86–87.
Pax Romana, 67.
Periodicity of Energy, 15, 55.
Photosynthesis, 22.
Physics, the social order related to, 198.
Pirates, 93, 106.
Plant versus Animal Life, 207.
Political Government; term defined, 232–233; origins and development of, 66, 74, 85, 88–90, 93, 126; universal acceptance of, 80; attempted limitations on, 63; classical traditions of, 91; popular forms of, 93; aggrandizement of, 66–67, 75–76, 91, 93, 173; conflict essential to, 72; effect on use of land, 126, 139; impinging on national income, 177; necessity of taxation under, 52, 146, 164; moral considerations of, 219–220; domination by, 220, 221; transformation of, 62 ff, 102, 172, 222; see also Taxation, Public Administration and other categories under Public.
Politics versus Proprietorship, 158–159.
Population; defined, 231; measurement of, 9 ff; as energy waves, 14–15, 21–23, 30 ff; effect on environment, 21; qualitative change in, 16 ff, 18, 22, 23, 30 ff; increase of, 22; creative potential dependent on proportion of adult years, 31–33; age-groups in, 36–38; effects of changing life-span on composition of a, 36–38; ageing of the, 42; if moved to a new land, 173; see also Energy, Life-Span.
Power, Creative, 18, 216.
Predial, 90.
Pressure Groups, 167.
Price, Defined, 241
Private Enterprise; conversion to public under proprietary public administration, 182 ff; see also Free Enterprise.
Private Property: see Ownership.
——— in Land; explained, 122 ff; see also Property in Land.
Production; a physical process, 99; see also Industry.
——— and Exchange, factors in, 176–177.
Productivity versus Reproductivity, 21, 27.

Profit, 159; real-estate administration for, 153 ff; nature of, 241.
—— Motive: see Motivation.
Progress, Social, 214; freedom essential to, 53; the business basis of social advance, 113.
Property, 98 ff; defined, 234; as a social convention, 98; inclusive of others, 73, 99, 123–124; seizure of, 120–121, 161; specialization of, 124–129, 154–155, 183; see also Ownership, Property in Land.
—— the Instrument of Freedom, 50 ff.
—— in Land; explained, 122 ff; function of, 50, 63, 124, 126–127, 129, 131, 134, 160–161, 164, 166, 169; foundation of free society, 99; functionally anticipated in village moot, 87; historic emergence out of politics and its non-political nature, 73, 95, 101, 120, 238; historic origin of prejudice against, 101; public discussion of, 122, 137–138; importance of, 99, 102, 134; relation to public administration, 107; extension of functions, 63, 120–121; future of, 50, 95–96, 102, 202; see also Land, Ground Rent, Public Administration.
—— a New Relationship, alternative to slavery, 98.
——, Public: see Public Capital.
—— Title, 99; see also Ownership.
Proprietary Administration; in private affairs, 52; see also Ownership, Public Administration.
Proprietorship versus Politics, 158–159.
Psychology as an Extension of Physiology, 6.
Public Administration, 141 ff; need of sound principles in, 82; evolution of, 84 ff; proper to land owners, 126–127, 152; proprietary versus political, 158–159.
——, Political, 196; maintained by force, 52; Classical precedent of, 80; nature of, 129–131, 137, 167; no property of its own, 179; *quasi* public agencies, 186; modern tendency toward, 101; growing alternative to, 93 ff, 102–103; see also Political Government and other categories under *Public*.
——, Proprietary, 52, 134–136, 174; nature of, 129–131, 158–159, 222; examples of, 94; emergence out of nomadism and village communities, 78, 85, 87; historic lapse of, 74, 75, 92; three categories of services under, 178; the means of democracy, 136, a hypothetical distribution of national income under, 175 ff; regional competition under, 135; public versus private administration of capital under, 182 ff; natural limitations on, 185–187; proprietary community-service authorities, 85, 95–96; potentialities of, 96, 102–103; as artistry, 135; see also Land Administration, Property in Land and other categories under *Public*.
Public Affairs, need of sound principles in, 82.
Public Benefits; canceled by the political mode of supplying them, 68 ff, 130–131, 166; distribution of, 131; when not merchandised, are special privileges and create no value, 132–133, 137, 165; manufacture of, 136; in exchange for value received, 139, 164; supplied through highways, 160; access to through land owners, 160–161; see also Public Services, Public Administration, Public Works.
Public Capital, 112, 178; defined, 238; source of, 171; community properties as, 174; beneficial ownership of, 145, 150; administration of, 134–136, 141, 153 ff, 171, 174; administration proper to land owners, 129–131, 152; how raised and administered politically, 130; see under *Land,* 237; see also Public Administration.
Public Debt, 52.
Public Enterprises; financing of, 135; extension of, 182 ff.
Public Interest Identified with the Proprietary Interest, 129, 160.
Public Property: see Public Capital.
Public Revenue, 133–134; in Saxon England, 94; normal, 126; politically

raised and administered, 52, 93, 130; growing alternative to political administration of, 93–94, 102–103; see under *Land,* 237; see also Public Administration, Taxation.
Public Servants; recompense of, 133; properly a service class now unsupervised and irresponsible, 130, 148, 161–162; under proprietary administration, 214; see also Public Administration.
Public Services, 140, 220; defined, 221; as the function of land ownership, 131; measurement of, 130–131, 132, 146; performed by free enterprise, 136, 214; administration of real property as, 153 ff; necessity of, 166; without servitude, 82, 141 ff, 174; impracticability of duplicating certain facilities, 186; see also Public Benefits, Public Administration.
Public Utility Corporations, 186.
Public Works; popularity and nature of, 68; the tragedy of, 68 ff; inequitable burden of, 164; see also Public Benefits, Public Services.

Qualitative; defined, 230; differences in energy, 12; as creative, 19; change, 15 ff, 193 ff, 230; comparisons of equal quantities of life-years, 36; see also Energy.
—— Changes in Population Energy, 16 ff.
Quanta of *Action;* fundamental units of nature, 193; qualitative differences among, 199; see under *Energy,* 229.
Quantitative, 7; defined, 230.
Quiet Possession, 77, 87.

Race Suicide and Race Deterioration, 41–42.
Rationality; of the societal process, 73, 107; of the life-ward processes, 219; defined, 230; see also Intellect.
Real; as abiding, 64.
Real Estate: see Land Administration, Property in Land, Public Administration.
—— Administration for Profit, 153 ff.
Reality, 60, 200, 217; defined, 229.
Reason; nature of, 201; spiritual office of, 218, 219; see also Rationality, Intellect.
Reciprocal Relationships; in society, 15, 211, 216; freedom in, 26 ff; universal principle, 79, 83; effect of climate on, 65; see also Symbiosis, Contractual Relationship, Organization.
Recreations and Arts, 116, 218.
Reedemers of Mankind, 219.
Reform, 245.
Religion; the real office of, 217, 219; in the practice of the arts, 218.
Rent; defined, 241; see also Ground Rent.
Rental Basis, General Trend Towards, 154–155, 183.
Reproductivity, 86; acceleration of, 21; correlated with life-expectancy, 23–24, 28, 38; desirability of high birth rate, 27, 28; inverse to productivity, 27–28, 38–39; of youth versus productivity of age, 37–38; differential birth-rate, 38; related to sense of insecurity, 28, 43, 69, 210 ff; see also Life-Span, Population.
—— Inverse to Productivity, 27–28, 38–39; apparent exception to the general rule, 39.
Revolution, 245.
Rome, 90, 161; traditions of, 91.
Rugged Lands, 90.

Salaries Defined, 240.
Sales as the Ultimate Object of Administration, 159.
Salvation from Evil, 217.
Scherman, Harry, 52.
Science, 245; nature and methods of, 3, 111; employment of units in, 3; dependent upon measurement, 3; specific fields of, 6, 205; related to the metaphysical world, 19–20; applications of, 69–70; predictive power of, 111; the trinity of, 60, 200; interdependence of the sciences, 203; the spiritual office of, 19, 219.
—— and the Social Order, 70.
—— of Society: see Socionomy.
Security of Possession, by what means possible, 131.
Senior Citizens, 42.
Serfs; freeholders reduced to, 74.

Servant of All, The, 216.
Service; defined, 231; general term for social-ized energy, 118; of others versus self service, 177.
Services of Distribution, 116.
Shopping Centers, 183.
Slavery; in antiquity, 65–66, 74, 84, 89–90; in Saxon England, 95; taxation as a form of, 66; tax- versus slave-based sovereignties, 89.
Smith, Adam, 129.
Social, defined, 232.
—— Planning, 104.
"Social Will," 7, 8, 98, 196.
Socialist *Ideal;* tendency towards the, 184; inherent in the capitalist system, 187.
Social-ization; defined, 73, 99, 235; of property by means of ownership, 98; of human energy, 49, 115; of government, 62 ff, 102, 172, 222.
Social-ized Energy, 114 ff; *service* the general term for, 118; see also Energy.
Societal; defined, 232.
—— Life-Form: see Society as a Life-Form.
Society; defined, 231; functions of, 7, 104, 137, 212, 213, 231; durational power of, 55–56; changing role of individual in, 154; benefits to its members, 23, 32, 53, 189, 212, 213; structural differentiation of, 53 ff, 58 ff, 79, 137, 201 ff, 231; freedom the gift of, 193–197; disorganizing factors, 51, 59, 232; nature of pre-societal organization, 71–72, 84 ff, 216–217; distinguished from pre-societal organization, 15, 48, 72, 115, 154, 211; origins and development of, 76, 84 ff, 209; empiricism in social growth, 60, 78, 106–107; modern development of, 113, 123–124; the impending transformation, 8, 59, 104 ff, 107, 214; rationality of, 73, 107; its spiritual quality, 53–54, 195, 204; relation to the cosmic whole, 114, 195, 203; the crown of creation, 205 ff; see also, Society as a Life-Form, Individuals, Man, Energy.

—— as a Life-Form, 23, 27–28, 47–49, 53, 79, 104, 114, 116, 118, 137, 209, 214; organization and functions, 7, 53, 55 ff, 57, 104; world-wide, 38–39; metabolism of, 48, 58, 114, 116, 118; immaturity of, 220; pathology of, 69; permanence of, 56; qualitative transcendence, 56, 104; see also Society.
Socionomy, 4, 5, 107; defined, 231; delimitation of its field, 6 ff; employment of terms in, 228; application of, 7, 8, 15, 19, 60, 69–70, 107, 111, 119; see also Science, Energy, Population.
Sovereignty, 66; conflict essential to, 72; tax- versus slave-based, 89; mystical, 91; see also Political Government, Public Administration, Taxation.
Special Interests, 167.
Special Privileges, 132–133, 137, 165.
Specialization of Property and Ownership, 124–125, 128–129, 154–155, 183.
Speculation, Benefits of, 46.
Speculative Value, 105, 147; defined, 242.
Spencer, Herbert, 122.
Spirit; things of the, 64; of man, 216; appeal of the, 219.
Spiritual Gifts, tangible forms of, 216.
Spiritual Power of Man, 27–28, 53–54, 195, 204, 218, 219.
Spiritual World, 195; related to the material, 19–20.
Stand-by Services in the Distribution of Land or Any Property, 100.
Statistical Integration, 4, 197.
Structure; defined, 230; living versus non-living, 9; see also Organization.
Sublimation of Human Energies, 47–48, 221.
Sun, Energy from the, 16.
Sunlight, Source of all Organic Compounds, 22.
Survival of the Fittest, 25; applied to sovereignties, 67; among pre-societal groups, 72.
Symbiosis, 47; disjunctive, 38–39; plant and animal, 207; social, 217; see also Reciprocal Relationships.
Synthesis; in the social world, 7; physical

with metaphysical, 19-20; in science, 111; creative, 206 ff.

Taxation, 93; necessity under political public authority, 52, 146, 164; forms of, 52; in Saxon England, 80; related to slavery, 66, 89; cumulative evil of, 168; present extent of, 161; a charge against rent, 151, 156, 165-170; effect on community services, 130, 166; growing alternative to, 93 ff, 102-103; see also Public Revenue.

Tax Relief, 134; a public service, 150-151; dependent on land owners, 170; effect of general, 173; see also Land Administration, Public Administration, Public Revenue, Taxation.

Tenants as purchasers of services, 155-156.

Teutonic Tribes, 91.

Theology, 60, 200.

Threefold Nature; of energy, 55, 229; of man, 55 ff, 194, 201; of society, 54, 55 ff, 59-61, 201-204, 231, 242; see also Trinity.

Time; human sense of, 17; efficiency ratings based on, 17; credit as a time dimension in exchange, 46; as the rhythm of change, 48; mass, motion and time, 55, 60, 200, 229; see also Duration.

Titles; merger of, 135-136; see also Ownership.

Totalitarianism; 20th-Century trend towards, 101; see also Political Government, Public Administration, Taxation.

Trade-in Allowances, 183.

Tragedy of Public Works, 68 ff.

Transformation: see Energy; see Environment; see also under *Qualitative*, 230.

Tribes: see Familial Organization.

Trinity; of science, 60, 200; of theology, 60, 200; see also Threefold Nature, Energy, Society.

Twentieth Century; wars of the, 67; totalitarian trend of the, 101.

Units; of energy, 229; of measurement 3; in nature prerequisite to organization, 71; of societal organization, 194; of population, 9-11; of value employed in exchange, 117-118.

Utopian Dream, towards the, 175 ff.

Value, 102; defined, 242; speculative, 105, 147, 242; not intrinsic but social, 105; dependent on income and demand, 147-148; and exchange, a system of social-ized energy flow, 114 ff; see also Land Value, Ground Rent, Rent.

—— Tokens, Established by the Market, 105-106.

—— Units, Employment of in Exchange, 117-118.

Values and Ideals, 19.

Village Communities, 84, 86-88, 89; intermediate between nomadism and society, 77-78; allocation of lands in, 87; lack of effective defense, 87; lapse of, 74, 88-89; see also Familial Organization.

Village Moot, 87.

Voting, Proprietary, 136; see also Democracy.

Wages Defined, 240.

Wars of the Twentieth Century, 67.

Wealth; defined, 235; misconceptions about, 123-124; other than capital, 128.

Will; individual and social, 7, 8, 98, 196; see also Free Will.

—— to Live, 11; see also under *Qualitative*, 230.

Wilson, Woodrow, on Germanic Institutions, 91.

Words, 227-228.

Youth versus Age; reproductive versus productive power, 37-38.

Printed in Aldine Bembo type by
the Printing-Office of the Yale University Press
Designed by John O. C. McCrillis